COLORADO
HUT TO HUT

A Guide to Skiing, Hiking & Biking Colorado's Backcountry

Second Edition

Winter sunset over the Gore Range, from Janet's Cabin.

TEXT AND PHOTOGRAPHY BY
BRIAN LITZ

WESTCLIFFE PUBLISHERS

www.westcliffepublishers.com

ACKNOWLEDGMENTS

During the past few years, many people have contributed ideas, information, time, words of encouragement, technical expertise — even their precious bodies (as skiing companion and as models) — to help bring this project to fruition. Whether your help was over the phone, in my office, or on the trail, it has been deeply appreciated! I would like to thank (in no particular order) the following people: John Fielder, Dianne Howie, Mary Jo Lawrence, Suzanne Venino, Amy Duenkel, Jeff Cobb, Ken Morr, Pat Fortino, Beth Smith, Kirk Watson, Gordon Banks, Keith Comfort and the Mountain Sports folks, Cindy and Curt Carpenter, Vern and Linda Purdy, David Schweppe, Peter Looram, David Hiser, Doug Johnson, Bruce Ward, Mike Turrin, Joe Ryan, Yvonne "Bootsie" Brodzinski, Dr. John Warner, Leigh Girvin-Yule, Kurt Lankford, Josh Weinstein, Mark Kelley, Christopher George, Jerry Gray, Bernice Notenboom, Craig Steele, Dan Schaefer, Carrie Thompson, Lisa Paesani, Knox Williams, Melissa Bronson, Gary Gass, Doug MacLennan, Patrick Scannell, Hank Bivington, Ray Kitzen, Heidi Walker, Jean and Mary Pavillard, Colin Gray, Dale Atkins, Judy Hampton, Scott Messina, David "Cully" Cullbreth, and Kim Reed.

Additionally, I would like to thank the following people and equipment manufacturers for supporting me in this project — the gear was invaluable: Tom Meyers (Cascade Designs), Cheri Emerson (Gregory Mountain Products), Mark Bridges (Kazama Skis), Steve Hardesty (Kenko/Asolo/Tua), Jim Woodmency (Life-Link), Jeff Martin and Norma Hansen (Lowe Alpine), Michelle Mundt (Mountain Safety Research), William Stoehr (Trails Illustrated), Mary Zilmer (Trek Bicycles), Ken Keeley and Mark Wariakois (Voilé). Thanks again!

— B.L.

International Standard Book Number: 0-929969-85-5
Library of Congress Catalogue Card Number: 91-66710
Copyright Brian Litz, 1992; revised 1995. All rights reserved.
Editor: Suzanne Venino   Layout: Amy Duenkel
Printed in Korea by Palace Press International
Published by Westcliffe Publishers, Inc.
P.O. Box 1261, Englewood, CO 80150

10th Mountain Division Hut Association and Alfred A. Braun Memorial Hut System maps courtesy of the hut systems and Curt Carpenter. Page 6-7 map copyright Brian Litz and Gordon Banks/Moenkopi Digital Formations. All other maps by Brian Litz.

Westcliffe Publishers and Brian Litz are grateful to Eastman Kodak Professional Imaging for the generous contribution of film used for many of the photographs in this guidebook.

FOREWORD

Five years ago I decided to take up backcountry skiing. I wasn't happy with the winter scenic photography I was producing from the roadside, and I knew that cross-country skiing by day would not reveal the remote early morning and late evening images that I wanted.

To capture more secluded photographs of nature in winter I had skied out of bounds from downhill ski areas for years, but I knew that eventually they'd put me in jail for violating Colorado state law, which prohibits such activity.

I didn't want to make the investment in time to learn how to telemark ski, a nifty step up from cross-country technique that employs much sturdier skis, boots, and bindings. However, carrying 30 pounds of medium-format camera gear precluded anything less stable.

Then someone told me about alpine touring, or randonnée, equipment — skis, boots, and bindings much like downhill equipment — except that I could release my heels to ski up and across mountains in the nordic fashion and lock down the heels to descend in the same parallel style I used at downhill ski areas.

It was then that I also learned about the extensive and quickly expanding world of backcountry huts intended primarily for nordic skiers. The huts and randonnée skiing opened the door to the niveous world for a night — or even a week — in the wilderness without the rigors and inconvenience of living in a snow cave!

Under the expert guidance of Brian Litz, I rapidly became comfortable with life in the winter outback, especially when I could retreat to a warm, cozy cabin after a long day on the snow trail. In fact, without these huts, I would not have been able to produce most of the Colorado winter images in my files.

Much of my best photography is accomplished when sunlight is saturated with color, at both ends of the day. And though all of the huts are in remarkably scenic locations, I often like to ski up to the high ridges around the huts to take pictures. This requires an hour or more of skiing uphill, which is slow work in fresh snow and usually means I must leave or return to the hut in the dark. If it weren't for the hut as a base of operations, I would not have the energy or desire to make good photographs — for it is usually well below zero at night at 12,000 feet!

The Colorado hut systems are a rare treasure, for me to make my living, and for others as a way to enjoy what I've found to be the most tranquil of all seasons — a time when hardly a creature stirs and one can quietly contemplate the value of our natural environment.

I hope Brian's guidance and outstanding photographs will inspire you to discover for yourself the beauty of Colorado's backcountry.

— John Fielder
Englewood, Colorado

John Fielder surveys Blaine Basin and Mount Sneffels, outside the Ridgway Hut, San Juan Hut System.

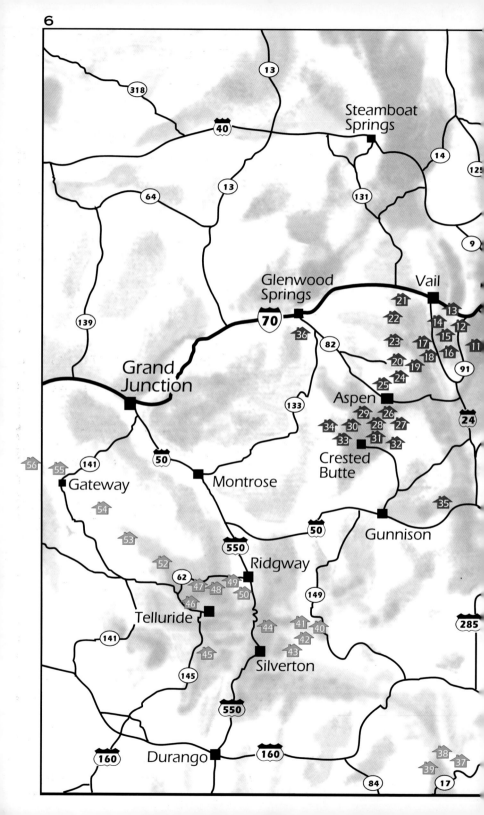

COLORADO
HUT TO HUT

Fort Collins

Boulder

Dillon

Denver

Colorado Springs

Pueblo

Walsenberg

Alamosa

Symbol	Description
	Trail
70	Interstate Highway
	Paved Road
	Secondary Paved Road
-----	Dirt Road
	Wilderness Area
— · —	Continental Divide
	Mountain or Ridge
	Lake
9	Hut
40	US Highway
14	State Highway
CR 105	County Road
FR 400	Forest Route
	City or Town
	Ski Resort
	Airport

THE HUT SYSTEMS

13 **Northern Huts**

27 Central Huts

42 Southern Huts

N

0   25   50   75
miles

© 1995 Brian Litz & Moenkopi Digital Formations

TABLE OF CONTENTS

CENTRAL HUTS continued

PREFACE

Alpine peaks, expansive grasslands, sandstone mesas, and swiftly flowing rivers… Colorado is a land of incomparable beauty, a rugged environment where lovers of the natural world can retreat for a few days or a few weeks to escape the bounds of everyday life.

Throughout the seasons there is a wealth of wilderness recreation in the Colorado Rockies. Fly-fishing and kayaking, mountain biking and rock climbing, hiking and horseback riding draw outdoor enthusiasts here from the first spring thaw until the last, waning days of autumn. In winter there is snowshoeing, ice climbing, cross-country and downhill skiing.

Some people are content to simply ride a chair lift up a mountain and ski down groomed slopes at the edge of the backcountry. Others are not. I am one of those people.

I remember my first winter camping trip in 1976. My friend Brock Richardson and I watched as my father's car slowly pulled away from the Glacier Gorge parking lot in Rocky Mountain National Park. Two fourteen-year-old boys, we already considered ourselves hardened mountaineers with many seasons of "peak bagging" and downhill skiing under our belts. However, backcountry in the winter was a new world to us, one we were determined to explore. We received a blustery salutation from the ever-present winds as we hiked into the snow-covered mountains.

Our first night passed relatively uneventfully as we pitched our tent on a bed of frosty snow and burrowed into roomy down sleeping bags. The second night we slept in an abandoned snow cave, sequestered from the incessant winds and snug in our cozy home. At dawn, the feeling of well-being quickly dissipated when we awoke to find our doorway drifted over. During the night a blizzard had sealed us into a darkened world of ice and snow. We tunneled toward freedom and headed for home wearing frozen parkas and frozen smiles. I have never forgotten that early expedition, and I have never lost my love of the alpine world.

Today, adventurers can take advantage of an incredible range of resources to facilitate their travels to the high country. Colorado, in fact, boasts the largest and the most diverse selection of backcountry cabins, huts, and yurts in the lower 48 states. This eclectic collection of shelters provides any individual willing to strap on skis, lace up hiking boots, or mount a bike the opportunity to enjoy this mountain paradise. The Colorado huts are waiting for you…hurry!   — BRIAN LITZ

This book is dedicated to my mother, Jean Marie Litz, Mother's Day, 1992

Skiing below Castle Peak, near the Goodwin-Greene Hut,
Alfred A. Braun Memorial Hut System

INTRODUCTION

In recent years there has been a tremendous increase in the number of visitors to the backcountry huts of Colorado. In fact, at times it is hard to believe just how popular the "hut" experience has become and how quickly overnight visitations have increased. During the 1991–92 season, when I was working on the first edition of *Colorado Hut to Hut,* there were roughly 11,000 visitors to the 10th Mountain Division huts. Just two seasons later, the huts booked through the 10th Mountain Division reservation system counted nearly 30,000 visitors.

Other hut systems are also seeing steady increases in numbers of visitors. This, the second edition of *Colorado Hut to Hut,* covers ten new huts, and there is talk of building even more. It appears as if "hut mania" has hit the high country!

Huts are permanent and/or semi-permanent backcountry shelters that can be rented on an overnight basis. They include renovated mining buildings, abandoned Forest Service shelters, log cabins, simple wood structures, and canvas, tentlike yurts. Some are tiny and almost primitive, others are modern, fully equipped, stone-and-wood cabins with architecture worthy of a magazine spread. Backcountry huts allow skiers, hikers, and mountain bikers to escape to the natural world, emphasizing a sense of adventure and placing a premium on a shared wilderness experience with good friends.

What are the ramifications of this explosive growth of huts on Colorado's wilderness and on the backcountry experience? In managed numbers huts minimize the impact that overnight visitors have upon the often delicate plants and soils of the high country, while encouraging people to spend longer periods of time in the wilderness. Consequently this allows people to truly immerse themselves in the rhythms and the beauty of nature. Wilderness is as much a state of mind as a place.

Why is hut-to-hut travel becoming so popular? One reason, I believe, is that many alpine skiers have become bored with an increasingly packaged, groomed, and catered "product." Also, there are more and more people moving to the Rocky Mountain region from other areas of the country. Another factor is that outdoor recreation gear has been greatly improved in recent years. Today's equipment is lighter and performs extremely well, allowing outdoor enthusiasts of all abilities to enjoy the backcountry. And finally, it's just doggone fun!

Backcountry — the landscape beyond the plowed roads and groomed slopes — beckons to a wide variety people with the challenge of unknown terrain, the thrill of virgin snow, panoramic vistas, colorful sunsets, and the chance to relax in the warmth of an inviting, cozy cabin overlooking the heart of the Rockies.

HOW TO USE THIS GUIDE

Writing a guidebook presents the author with a quandary: provide directions as detailed as "go 100 feet and turn left at the 15th aspen tree"? Or, provide only the basic data? Some guidebooks give so much information and conversation that the user becomes frustrated merely trying to assemble the relevant facts; other guidebooks are so terse that the users end up wondering why they purchased the book in the first place.

With regard to this guidebook, my vision was to create a field guide, as well as a backcountry "wish book." It is designed both to provide general information and advice for aspiring hut-to-hut travelers and to inspire the seasoned ski-mountaineer who may be looking for new and unknown challenges. The beginner can read through the "On the Trail" section of this introduction and follow the detailed trail descriptions, while the expert can simply scan the trail summaries to get a quick overall "feel" for a tour or an untried hut system.

Colorado Hut to Hut not only features routes and hut system information, but also includes sections that highlight equipment recommendations and hut etiquette, as well as avalanche information and some of the more common problems encountered on hut-to-hut expeditions. It also contains several appendixes with important phone numbers, including emergency and reservation numbers. The bibliography (Appendix G) provides suggestions for further readings on a range of topics important to hut-to-hut skiers and bikers.

This book is certainly not the only source of information that should accompany adventurers into the wilderness, nor is it a substitute for experience. Every skier heading into the backcountry needs to be pro-active in obtaining the necessary experience and education to ensure an enjoyable and safe adventure in the Colorado Rockies. Skiers, hikers, and bikers are strongly encouraged to carry a selection of maps, including United States Geological Survey's 7.5-minute topographic maps ("topos"), *Trails Illustrated* maps, as well as maps produced by the various hut systems. In addition, such books as *The ABCs of Avalanche Safety, Snow Sense,* and *The Pocket Doctor* are invaluable resources for mountain expeditions. These books fit easily into a pack, provide informative evening reading, and cover important topics too complex to be detailed fully in this guidebook. To get the most out of this book, please take the time to read the following brief summary of its overall organization.

First, *Colorado Hut to Hut* divides the Centennial State's backcountry shelters into three main regions: Northern Huts, Central Huts, and Southern Huts. Each regional heading begins with a brief overview of the hut systems located in that part of the state, giving a bit of local history, the type of skiing found in the area, and also general descriptions of hut amenities.

Individual huts and tours are then described in detail, once again highlighting each hut's history and special features. Each tour description has two parts. The first part is a capsule summary of the most important tour information, including level of difficulty, estimated travel time, mileage, elevation gain and loss, as well as pertinent map sources. The second portion is a detailed narrative of the route. A route is described in detail only once. That is, if a tour that runs from Uncle Bud's Hut to Skinner Hut is described under the Uncle Bud's Hut section, it will not be described again in reverse under the Skinner Hut entry.

Hut tours are separated into two categories: trails that travel from a trailhead to a hut and tours that travel between huts — "hut-to-hut." As a general pattern, the hut systems and the trails that link huts within a system are described from north to south and/or from east to west. (Please note however, that this rule does not hold true for the San Juan Hut System: The San Juan ski huts are described from southwest to northeast; the San Juan bike huts from southeast to northwest.)

Many hut entries also include "recommended day tours," which briefly describe day excursions from the hut. Annotated USGS 7.5-minute topo maps show routes to and surrounding each hut. These maps are for general reference only; you should purchase your own topo maps for route finding.

Doug Seyb stokes the fire at the Fowler/Hilliard Hut,
10th Mountain Division Huts.

DIFFICULTY

Each tour is assigned a rating of overall difficulty. These ratings are subjective, but they do follow generally accepted criteria.

Novice routes present few difficulties, require less complex navigation, and feature minimal elevation gain. The novice rating does not include people who have never skied cross-country; it is assumed that novice hut skiers have been on skis before. A novice-level skier ideally should have completed at least five to ten backcountry day trips and have a basic mastery of double poling and snowplowing. Because novice skiers are generally still gaining wilderness savvy in areas such as navigation and avalanche awareness, it is recommended that these skiers participate in guided trips or in group trips with more experienced skiers.

Intermediate routes are the most common type of tour in this book and most closely define the term "classic tour." Intermediate-level skiers usually have been skiing for at least several seasons and have participated in five or more hut trips. Their wilderness experience and their fitness levels are solid, and they are able ski to and from huts with ease. They also enjoy off-trail skiing, although they may not have completely mastered the telemark turn. Carrying heavy, overnight backpacks is also not new to these skiers.

Advanced skiers have generally been backcountry and hut skiing for many seasons, have skied and traveled in a wide variety of weather conditions, and can telemark down steep, timbered slopes and through diverse types of snow. They also have a full understanding of avalanches and rescue procedure. Most important, advanced skiers will never tell you where the best powder is!

ICONS

Included in each tour description is an icon of a cross-country skier, a bicycle, or hikers. These icons indicate whether the trail to the hut is available for skiing, biking, or hiking. Huts with all three icons are open year round. Some huts are only open in winter (due to permit restrictions), so only a skier will be shown. Because bicycles are prohibited in wilderness areas, routes that pass through wildernesses are closed to mountain bikers. The San Juan Hut System linking Telluride to Moab, Utah, is listed for biking only, because of the great distances covered (sometimes 30 miles a day).

TIME

The travel times listed are general guesstimates of how long the "average" group will take to complete a route. They include time for a lunch break and several snack/water breaks. While stronger parties can easily make quick work of most trails, slower groups — those who are new to backcountry skiing or those who are breaking trail in powder snow — might consider using a figure of one mile per hour in estimating tour lengths, plus one hour per 1,000 feet of elevation gain.

DISTANCE

Distances listed are one-way mileages measured from trailheads to huts or from hut-to-hut. (Mileages to trailheads, as detailed in the text portion of the tour, may differ slightly due to variance in car odometers.)

ELEVATIONS

Three elevations are given in the capsule information for each tour. The first elevation is for the point where the trail begins, whether that is a trailhead or a hut. The second elevation is for the destination hut. The final pair of elevations is for the gain (+) and loss (-) that are accumulated over the length of a trail. (These figures should be reversed if you are traveling in the opposite direction.) In trail descriptions, an elevation that corresponds to a USGS 7.5-minute topo map reference is referred to as an Elevation Point.

AVALANCHE NOTE

In this guidebook, I use the avalanche hazard rating system created by Richard and Betsy Armstrong that I have used in previous skiing guides. What is extremely useful about this system is that it gives an overall feel for the terrain. This is important because daily or seasonal avalanche hazards may change, but terrain does not.

Snow conditions can change rapidly; the decision to ski or not ski a potential avalanche route is entirely yours. Remember that most people are caught in small slides that occur in unlikely or unobvious avalanche terrain, such as in a creek drainage or in the middle of a forest. Play it safe and always assume that you will be traveling in avalanche conditions.

The four categories of avalanche terrain used in this guidebook are:
1. *None.* Normally safe under all conditions.
2. *Some avalanche terrain encountered; easily avoided.* Still safe in all conditions when skiers remain on standard trails. However, there is some dangerous terrain in the general vicinity that should be easy to spot and avoid.
3. *Route crosses avalanche runout zones; can be dangerous during high-hazard periods.* This trail's normal route lies below a known avalanche path. Skiers will not likely serve as a trigger, although they could be caught in a spontaneous slide.
4. *Route crosses avalanche slopes; prone to skier-triggered avalanches during high-hazard periods.* This route travels directly across a known hazard and skiers can easily set off a slide, given the right combination of ingredients and/or conditions.

Note: If the Colorado Avalanche Information Center says the avalanche hazard is high, avoid trails with ratings of three or four as listed above. (See Appendix E for the phone number for avalanche information.)

MAPS

Colorado Hut to Hut lists relevant USGS 7.5-minute topographic maps, national forest maps, *Trails Illustrated* maps, and specialty maps for each tour, and also references for maps included in this book.

USGS topo maps are the mainstay for mountaineers and skiers, providing the greatest detail of elevations, contours, and natural features. National forest maps are large-scale maps that are almost useless for navigation; however, they do provide road and trailhead information, as well as an overview of the area. *Trails Illustrated* maps are very useful resources for backcountry travelers — especially mountain bikers — because they cover the equivalent of eight USGS topo maps. These maps are up to date and virtually indestructible. *Trails Illustrated* maps are listed only if they are available. Specialty maps include any maps produced by a hut association, such as the 10th Mountain Division Hut Association. These maps are revised often and are very popular.

Maps included in this book are referenced by page number at the end of the map listings. These maps are for basic orientation only; use the maps recommended in the capsule information for route navigation. Keep in mind that a map's degree of usefulness is directly related to its date of publication. Old maps will not have the most current information on roads, trails, etc. Remember to check the publication date of any map.

Note: A 1:160,000-scale "topo atlas" published by DeLorme Mapping is available for Colorado. This is one of the single most useful sources of information for anyone traveling the backroads of the state and is highly recommended. See Appendix H for map sources.

ON THE TRAIL

BEFORE YOU GO

As someone (perhaps a backcountry skier) once said, "Education teaches us the rules. Experience teaches the exceptions." The mountains can be a very dangerous and unpredictable place for the unknowing and ill-prepared — as well as for the highly skilled and seasoned backcountry traveler. Skiers, hikers, and mountain bikers all must understand that even the "easiest" trail can be very challenging, that weather patterns can and do change quickly and dramatically, that equipment fails. Those headed into even the most readily accessible huts must accept responsibility for their own and their companions' safety and well-being. Self-sufficiency is a must.

For individuals who are interested in learning more about hut-to-hut travel, courses are offered by major sports equipment retailers, guide services, universities, and recreational clubs, as well as many city and county recreation departments. These classes range from "layering clothes for cold weather" and "basic mountain bike repair and maintenance" to weekend avalanche seminars. These evening and weekend sessions can be excellent sources of basic as well as more advanced backcountry information.

Successful and safe expeditions do not just happen — they are the result of organization and planning. Use the following outline to aid in organizing your hut-to-hut adventure:

1. Use *Colorado Hut to Hut* to choose trips that match your group's wants, needs, and skill level. Talk to the hut systems' personnel to help plan a trip appropriate to your group's experience and fitness level. They can also help you decide whether your group needs a guide. (See Appendix A for hut system addresses and phone numbers.)

2. Call the hut system to reserve the hut(s) you want. Remember that weekends, holidays, and full moons are usually reserved first. Be prepared to pay for the trip in full when you make your reservations.

3. Designate a leader for your group. The leader could be the individual responsible for disseminating information and seeing that all risk waivers (if required) are returned to the proper hut system.

4. Purchase any necessary trail and road maps.

5. Plan meals and snacks. Purchase food and repackage to reduce bulk.

6. Inspect equipment (zippers, pack straps, etc.) and take it for a dry run. Purchase flashlight and avalanche transceiver batteries, ski waxes, skin glue, etc. Restock first-aid and repair kits. Make sure all binding screws are tight and that binding cables (if any) are in good repair. Organize group gear. Rent any gear necessary. Test transceivers.

7. Practice packing your pack. Make sure essential and often-used items (sunglasses, goggles, sunscreen, maps, headlamps, compass, snacks, knives) are in a handy location.

8. Plan car shuttles. (Call the hut system if you need assistance in planning car shuttles; they may be able to recommend shuttle services.)

9. Before you leave for the trailhead, be sure to call the Colorado Avalanche Information Center (CAIC), the U.S. Weather Service, and the Colorado Department of Transportation (see Appendix B) to check avalanche, weather, and road conditions.

10. Provide a responsible party back home with trip itinerary, expected time of return, where you plan to park, and hut system phone numbers.

11. Establish an emergency plan and assess the group's first-aid knowledge.

12. Finally, DO NOT forget hut lock combinations and/or keys. Play it safe and have several individuals carry these. Keep a flashlight handy in case you arrive at the hut after dark.

A special note on equipment: Modern equipment is so well made and sophisticated that many people have become complacent concerning the proper maintenance and routine inspection of their gear. Take the time to check your equipment thoroughly. Look for loose screws and loose cables on bindings, worn laces on boots, bent poles, broken zippers, loose brakes on bikes, etc. Make sure that you have all of your gear (see checklist in Appendix F). Carry a repair kit and know how to use it. The time to learn how to repair gear is before you leave home — not in the middle of a blizzard at midnight.

GENERAL TRAIL CONSIDERATIONS

When traveling in the backcountry, be sure that your group arrives at the trailhead early; traveling hut-to-hut requires an equally early start. Try to build extra time into your schedule just in case problems arise. The three rules of backcountry travel are: "Stay together, stay together, and — of course — stay together." Think what could happen if someone in the back of the group breaks a binding or needs a blister kit while the leader speeds away in a Zenlike trance. Any member of your group could end up lost — or dead — if he or she makes a wrong turn in a winter whiteout. Consider using a buddy system to ensure that each member of your group is accounted for.

Each group should carry emergency equipment consisting of rudimentary camping gear, such as a stove, a pot, and a tarp, so that members can construct an emergency shelter if necessary. Also carry high-energy snack food and quick trailside meals (such as soups), as well as first-aid kits, flashlights, and avalanche gear. Be sure to test your transceivers as a group each and every day, and discuss emergency procedures before your group heads into the backcountry

Finally, each member of the group should carry maps and a compass. Many skiers and mountain bikers have become too dependent on guidebooks, but map reading, navigation, and compass skills are abilities that all backcountry travelers should acquire and practice. It is essential to keep maps and compasses handy and refer to them often, especially when confronted with a trail intersection, confusing routes, and/or foul weather. Get in the habit of matching real-world landmarks to features on the map and watching out for trail markers — both obvious and not so obvious.

Backcountry trail markers exist in a variety of forms: blue diamonds for nordic ski trails, orange diamonds for snowmobile routes, old tree blazes, as well as others. On the trails covered in this book you may encounter any or all of these markers — or none.

HYPOTHERMIA, FROSTBITE, AND THE SUN

Hypothermia and frostbite are the two most common cold weather injuries afflicting skiers and winter mountaineers. Both are preventable — and reversible — if caught in their earliest stages.

Hypothermia is a general cooling of the body's core temperature. It takes only a minor change in this core temperature to produce noticeable effects such as feeling chilled or cold, impairment of muscle coordination (especially of the hands), apathy, confusion, and/or shivering. Try to stay dry and warm, drink warm fluids, snack regularly, and check each other during the course of the day.

Frostbite is a localized freezing of soft tissue due to exposure to temperatures at or below freezing. Keep all body parts protected from the wind and cold, and keep them dry! Watch for skin that turns whitish and loses sensation (frost nip and mild frostbite).

Both frostbite and hypothermia can be easily avoided by staying dry, warm, and rested and by limiting your skin's exposure to the cold air and bitter winds. Carry and wear a variety of clothes, "layering" them so that you can quickly regulate your body's temperature and humidity by shedding or adding layers, especially a wind-protection layer. Your skin and eyes need "clothing," too. Pack plenty of sun block, at least SPF 20 to 30, as well as lip protection. Consider bringing moisturizing lotion or aloe to soothe skin. Purchase high-quality sunglasses that screen out the most dangerous ultraviolet radiation and carry an extra pair in the first-aid kit. On mountain bike trips, bring light-colored clothes, such as thin tights and long-sleeved T-shirts that you can wear during the day to shield your skin from the sun.

ALTITUDE

Unless you have been routinely exercising at higher elevations, you will probably feel the effects of altitude. Colorado's huts lie roughly between 8,500 and 12,000 feet in elevation. Because there is less oxygen at these high elevations, your body will consequently be forced to work harder during physical exertion. It is not unlikely that you may experience the effects of altitude sickness, with symptoms such as shortness of breath, dizziness, headaches, lack of appetite, or nausea.

Slow acclimation is the best way to minimize and eventually eliminate the effects of altitude. It takes about three weeks of continual exposure to a given altitude to become fully acclimatized. Fortunately, the human body adapts quickly, and you can easily lessen the effects of altitude by building a little time in to your trip and starting out slowly. If you are visiting the mountains from a lower elevation, say 6,000 feet or below, plan a day or two at the beginning of your trip to stay at a mountain town before hitting the trailhead. Additionally, choose an itinerary that allows your group to gain elevation gradually; hut system personnel can help you plan an appropriate trip. Also, stay several nights at one hut so you can further acclimatize. Remember that a hut trip is not a race — take your time and enjoy it.

Be sure to consult a physician if you have any questions concerning your health and your ability to function at high altitude.

NUTRITION AND HYDRATION

Dehydration is one of the single biggest factors contributing to Acute Mountain Sickness (AMS) and High-Altitude Pulmonary Edema (HAPE), as well as headaches, nausea, restless sleep, and a feeling of malaise. Colorado's dry climate and high elevations cause human bodies to work harder. It is almost impossible to drink too much water. Plan on at least three to four quarts per person per day!

Rather than waiting and watching for signs of dehydration, prevent it! Make sure you drink plenty of fluids each morning when you get up, at meals, and throughout the day. Drink tea or water after a hard day of skiing, biking, or hiking. Begin dinner with a light soup and keep a bottle of water next to your bed. Consider carrying two water bottles or one water bottle and a thermos. Fill one container with plain water and a second with a soup, cider, or a fruit-flavored, electrolyte-replacement beverage.

Because hut skiing allows you to travel with less camping gear, there is no excuse for not bringing enough food to eat. Cook good, nutritious meals with plenty of carbohydrates. Soups are excellent for times when your appetite is suppressed. Have snacks handy on the trail and snack routinely. Taking a steady supply of fuel and liquid into the body throughout the day will work wonders at warding off exhaustion.

Frank Penniciaro and Pamela Crane stop for a water break.

WEATHER

Colorado weather is predictable in that it is always unpredictable. The weather is generally sunny and clear. Winter storms sometimes descend out of Canada, dropping temperatures far below zero for extended periods, but these storms usually moderate rapidly. In winter, the midday temperatures in the high country normally remain in the +15 to +30 degree (F) range, with nighttime temperatures dropping to 0 to -10 degrees. When storms move in, they seldom stay for more than a few days.

Early-season skiing (late November through early January) can range from excellent to nonexistent. During this time of year, it is often possible to travel hut-to-hut on packed trails, though day skiing is often limited due to shallow snow cover that leaves rocks and logs exposed. Late in the season, as snowstorms become more frequent and the snow has a higher moisture content, conditions start improving. "Good" off-trail skiing usually begins in January, when the snowpack starts to settle and skiers are able to float well above any obstacles, like rocks and tree stumps. The more southern huts tend to get a deeper snowpack earlier and often have great skiing as early as December.

As spring approaches, the days become longer and warmer, although winterlike storms are still very real threats in the high country. This is when storms with heavier, moisture-laden snow move through the mountains and the deepest snowpack accumulates. Many skiers — both nordic and downhill — feel February to April is the best time to ski, especially at higher elevations.

In the summer, the high country belongs to hikers and mountain bikers. Colorado summers are beautiful, with warm to hot days and cool nights. Probably the greatest dangers to people using huts during the summer are dehydration and lightning. Summer thunderstorms build with extreme rapidity and can easily strand groups on exposed mountain peaks, high passes, or in the middle of treeless parks. These storms, which usually hit in the afternoons, often move off as quickly as they arrive. Watch the skies, including the sky behind you.

Storms should not be treated lightly. If you are caught in a storm during summer or in winter (yes, there are occasional lightning storms even in winter and spring), immediately leave high points such as ridges, passes, or peaks; move away from lone objects such as boulders, trees, or bicycles; sit on the ground, not in caves or gullies (because of ground currents); and wait until the storm passes.

Many Coloradans feel that autumn is the finest season in the Rockies. The weather is stable, with crisp daytime temperatures and chilly nights. Normal temperatures range from the 60s and 70s during the day and the high 30s to 40s at night. This is probably the best time of year for mountain biking and hiking. Fall can also see turbulent weather, as rainstorms move across the mountains, dusting the highest peaks with snow. Keep an eye out for rainbows.

AVALANCHES

Perhaps the most spectacular, most widespread, and least understood threat to the winter backcountry traveler is an avalanche. By its most basic definition, an avalanche is a large mass of snow that moves downhill under the force of gravity. Avalanche activity reflects a very complex process that belies its apparent simplicity.

More and more people are dying in avalanches because more and more people are skiing, snowshoeing, snowboarding and snowmobiling. People new to backcountry skiing should consider a guided trip their first time out. The purpose of this discussion is to give you a rudimentary understanding of just what an avalanche is, how to avoid one, and what to do if you must cross an avalanche slope.

The best way to prepare yourself to travel safely in the Rockies is to first read *Snow Sense* and *The ABC's of Avalanche Safety* (see Appendix G). Carry these with you. For further information, read *The Avalanche Book* and

Avalanche Safety for Climbers and Skiers. Enroll in an avalanche course and spend some time really digging into the snowpack. Or check out some of the new videos that have hit the market in recent years, such as "Avalanche Awareness: A Question of Balance and Winning the Avalanche Game."

Avalanches come in two basic varieties. The first is the loose-snow or point-release avalanche. Point-release avalanches usually begin at a specific point and flow downhill in a structureless mass, forming an inverted V. The second kind is the slab avalanche, which begins when a large, cohesive section of snow starts sliding at one time, leaving a well-defined fracture line. Slab avalanches are the more dangerous of the two types of slides because they involve huge amounts of hard, often wind-packed snow. Slab avalanches kill the most people and cause the most property destruction.

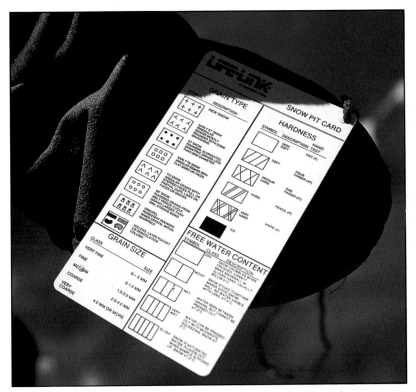

Life-Link card for assessing snow type and avalanche hazards.

A slab avalanche is initiated when something serves as a trigger to upset the snowpack, which may have very little internal strength. Likely triggers are the wind, weather, temperature, and, of course, people. Think of the snowpack as a cake — a cake may be made up of a single, stable layer or it may have several layers. Now think of what will happen when that cake is tilted at an angle. Often these layers are held together in a delicate equilibrium and may stay in this precarious state for days or weeks. Then along comes a potent snowstorm, a warm spell, a wild animal, or a skier to disrupt that delicate balance.

Backcountry travelers should consider three factors when assessing a slope's potential for sliding: terrain, weather, and snowpack. When thinking about the terrain, remember that most avalanches occur on north- and east-facing slopes with angles between 25 and 55 degrees. The vast majority of avalanches occur on slopes with angles between 30 and 45 degrees. Avoid snow cornices that overhang ridges away from the prevailing winds. Keep in mind however, that wet-snow avalanches can occur on slopes of even 10 degrees, especially on south-facing slopes during spring. Remember to check the ground cover; the more rocks and trees there are to anchor the snow, the better.

Weather factors include rapid changes in conditions, such as wind, air temperature, and snowfall. Any of these factors can create a change in the structure and equilibrium of the snowpack, causing a slide. Remember that most avalanches occur immediately after a storm as the new snow slides off the old surface. Be especially watchful during periods when there are constant winds over 15 miles per hour. Also watch for storms that dump more than one inch per hour or a total accumulation of six inches or more. An increase in the air temperature can also strongly affect the internal integrity of the snowpack.

The third factor, snowpack, is a little more difficult to observe, since it requires digging into the snow and having some training in assessing just what you're looking at when you do. A Life-Link card is extremely useful for assessing snow type.

Once in the backcountry, the most important thing that skiers can do to avoid tragedy is to make simple, informed observations. These include taking note of any slides or movements of snow, noticing any old slide paths, paying close attention to any settling of the snowpack (particularly after you ski across it), listening for the "whumpfing" sounds that occur when air is being forced out from under the snowpack, and looking for any cracks in the snow.

Try to avoid avalanche slopes by staying in the forest or skiing along the crest of a ridge. If you must cross a known or suspected avalanche slope, first remove all ski leashes and pole straps and loosen or undo pack straps and waist belts. Cross the slope one skier at a time and observe the others in your group as they cross. Every member of your group should be wearing a transceiver; make sure that your transceiver is turned on and set to transmit on the same frequency as everyone else in your group. The new standard worldwide frequency is 457 kHz. The old 2.275 kHz transceivers that have been the standard in the United States are now being phased out.

If you do get caught in a slide, attempt to "swim" in the snow, shedding any gear. When you sense the slide coming to a stop, place your hands in front of your face to create an air pocket. Remain calm and wait for rescuers to reach you. Individuals not caught in the slide should begin rescue operations immediately.

Before you leave on a hut trip, be sure to call the Colorado Avalanche Information Center to get the most recent snow conditions and avalanche activity report (see Appendix E).

Hut Etiquette

Hut life can be joyous, or it can be hellish. Often huts are large enough to hold up to twenty people, and more than one group may be booked at the same time. The quality of the hut experience depends on the groups sharing a hut treating each other with respect and courtesy. If sharing a hut with strangers does not appeal to you, be sure to reserve the hut exclusively for your own group. Here are a few rules to keep in mind — whether you are sharing a hut with another party or have it to yourselves. These courtesies extend to groups that may be arriving after your group departs.

When you arrive:

1. Leave skis and poles outside.
2. Clean snow from boots and clothes outside.
3. Read any hut instructions and post reservation confirmation lists.
4. Build a fire, shoveling out old ashes if necessary, and begin to melt water. Chop lots of wood.
5. Turn on electricity and propane.
6. Be tidy. Do not drop clothing and equipment all over the communal living area.
7. Be polite and quiet, especially in the evenings.
8. Wash dishes promptly and thoroughly.
9. Leave your dog at home with a multi-day steak bone. "Just say no to yellow snow."

Before you leave:

1. Make sure fires are out.
2. Be sure windows and doors are shut and locked.
3. Turn off propane and photovoltaic electric system.
4. Shut outhouse doors.
5. Pour out water to prevent freezing.
6. Sweep.
7. Pack out trash and extra food.
8. Bring any tools, axes, etc., inside and stow them in their proper places.
9. Chop more wood, especially kindling.

Carrie Thompson, avalanche shovel in her backpack, skis below Clark Peak near Ruby Jewel Yurt.

NORTHERN HUTS

NORTHERN HUTS

Northern Colorado offers a wealth of diverse skiing within relatively short distances of major population areas and mountain resorts. From the Never Summer Nordic Yurts of the Medicine Bow Mountains to the Guinn Mountain Hut just south of the Indian Peaks Wilderness, nordic skiers of all skill levels will enjoy fine trail skiing, excellent telemark terrain, and the beauty of Colorado's ruggedly glaciated peaks.

The backcountry shelters covered in this section emphasize readily accessible ski terrain. All of the huts have relatively short approach routes and most require only modest skiing ability. In addition to overnight destinations, they also make ideal base camps for extended day tours and backcountry powder skiing.

Craig Snowden telemarks through the trees.

True hut-to-hut skiing, mountain biking, and hiking are available in northern Colorado only at the Never Summer Nordic Yurts. Privately owned and operated, these tentlike structures are the modern descendants of the transportable animal-skin tents used by Mongolian nomads. Today yurts are generally made of rubberized canvases and nylons. What makes these yurts so special is their cozy "cabiny" feel, complete with wood-burning stoves. All of the Never Summer Nordic Yurts can be reached with tours of two miles or less. Connecting them into a multi-day trip is also easy.

Colorado State Forest has closed one of these huts, the Lake Agnes Cabin, because of its deteriorating condition. However, a new structure called the Nokhu Cabin will be built just north of the old Lake Agnes Cabin site during the fall of 1999. The brief 1.5-mile approach to the cabin makes it one of the shortest advanced-skill tours covered in this guide.

Well to the south of the Never Summer Nordic Yurts, hidden away in Colorado's Front Range, are the cabins owned and operated by the Colorado Mountain Club (CMC), the state's largest outdoor recreation club. The Brainard Lake Cabin and Guinn Mountain Hut have been favorite haunts for Front Range skiers for decades. The CMC huts are located near areas of superb nordic skiing with classic backcountry trails. They are popular destinations for introductory overnight trips and jumping-off points for longer cross-country excursions, such as skiing over Rollins Pass. The First Creek Cabin and Gwen Andrews Hut are closed indefinitely while the US Forest Service conducts site evaluations.

Also included in this first section is an independently operated hut. The Tennessee Mountain Cabin lies within the Eldora Nordic Center, west of Boulder and Nederland. This is an easy hut to reach, and there are a number of routes to the cabin via the nordic area's groomed trails.

North Rawah
Peak

NEVER SUMMER
NORDIC YURTS &
LAKE AGNES CABIN

N

0   1   2
miles

South Rawah
Peak

Kelly
Lake

Rawah
Wilderness
Area

Medicine Bow Mountains

**NORTH FORK
CANADIAN
YURT**

3

Winter
Closure

Clark Peak

Jewel Lake

2

**RUBY
JEWEL
YURT**

Chambers
Lake

14

**DANCING
MOOSE
YURT**

4

Colorado State
Forest

to Walden

North Michigan
Resevoir

1

**GRASS CREEK
YURT**

Diamond
Peak

Zimmerman
Lake

Gould
Mountain

Cameron Pass

Gould

14

North Park

**LAKE AGNES
CABIN**

5

Nokhu
Crags

Lake Agnes

Mount
Richthofen

See map key on pages 7

© Brian Litz 1995

NEVER SUMMER NORDIC YURTS
& LAKE AGNES CABIN

The Never Summer Nordic Yurts are located within the Colorado State Forest, which is operated as a state park. Situated on the eastern edge of North Park, the yurts are hemmed in by the valley's flat expanse on the west and by the ridgelike ramparts of the Medicine Bow Mountains and the Rawah Wilderness Area to the east. Remote and beautiful, this environment is ideal for moderate ski touring, mountain biking, and hiking.

All of the yurts are reached by routes that follow obvious trails and roads. Although this area has been logged over the years, the terrain is still pristine and the old logging roads provide easy access to the yurts. Whether you are a beginner or a more experienced skier or biker, you can easily spend several days exploring the areas around these remote shelters. Telemarkers will find many acres of skiable terrain to satisfy their appetites for challenging backcountry skiing.

North Park is home to a herd of moose. These animals, once indigenous to the area but later eradicated through hunting, were re-introduced here in 1978. These incredible creatures roam free and are an added attraction to the other abundant wildlife species in the Medicine Bow Mountains.

Because the Never Summer Nordic Yurts are in the Colorado State Forest, a valid day/overnight state parks pass is required. Passes are available from a self-service dispenser near the entrance during the winter and also at the entrance booth during the summer. The daily fee is about $3.00.

The yurts are circular, white canvas tents atop wooden substructures. Each yurt sleeps four to six people on bunks and mattresses, except for the new Dancing Moose Yurt, which sleeps eight to twelve. The yurts are fully stocked with pots and pans, utensils, propane stoves and lanterns, wood-burning stoves, and electric lights. With the wood stove stoked, occupants stay warm even on the coldest winter night.

Tours to the yurts are normally self-guided, but guided trips can also be arranged through the Never Summer Nordic Yurt system. The yurts can be booked exclusively by a single group on a nightly basis. Rates vary according to the season and night of the week. Friday, Saturday, and Sunday nights are more expensive, as is Christmas week. Reservations should be made in advance; last-minute reservations are accepted if there is space available. Make reservations through Never Summer Nordic Yurts (see Appendix A).

To reach the yurts, take CO 14 to the entrance of the Colorado State Forest, 19 miles east of the town of Walden or roughly two miles west of Gould. (From the Fort Collins area, the entrance is approximately 72 miles west of the intersection of CO 14 and US 287.) The turnoff into the state forest is marked by a large KOA campground sign.

The road from the park entrance to the trailheads for Never Summer Nordic Yurts is narrow, winding, traveled by heavy vehicles, and often snow covered. Drive carefully! For specific trailhead parking directions, refer to individual hut listings.

A blue diamond marks the trail as John Fielder skis the high country.

1   GRASS CREEK YURT

The Grass Creek Yurt is the southernmost of the three yurts in this system and is located less than one mile from the trailhead — an example of just how readily accessible backcountry shelters can be. Once at the shelter, skiers can continue up Grass Creek via the road for a day tour or climb Gould Mountain for immediate to advanced off-trail telemarking.

Grass Creek Yurt, which sleeps six, is the perfect introduction to overnight winter camping for individuals and families. Make reservations through the Colorado Division of Parks and Outdoor Recreation (see Appendix A).

TOUR 1A   NORTH MICHIGAN TRAILHEAD

Difficulty:	Novice
Time:	1 to 2 hours
Distance:	0.8 mile
Elevations:	Trailhead 8,940', Yurt 9,040', +140'/-40'
Avalanche Note:	None
Maps:	USGS 7.5': Clark Peak, 1977; Gould, 1955
	National Forest: Routt
	Colorado State Forest
	Trails Illustrated: Map #103 (Winter Park/
	Central City/Rollins Pass)
	See map pages 30 and 38-39

To reach the trailhead, proceed through the entrance for the Colorado State Forest (for directions to entrance, see page 31) and follow the road to North Michigan Reservoir. Drive to the far end of the reservoir near the 3-mile road marker. On the left is a small parking area that is plowed in winter. After parking, cross the road (carefully!) and drop off the roadbed and down across the North Fork of the Michigan River.

Ski east up toward the forest on the east side of Michigan Creek, gaining roughly 80 to 100 feet in elevation before traversing along the east side of Grass Creek. Traverse Grass Creek and intercept the Grass Creek Road. Cross the road and the creek and continue south away from the creek along the east edge of the forest, gaining very little altitude. Grass Creek Yurt is located near the edge of the trees 0.3 mile from the creek.

RECOMMENDED DAY TOUR 1: Return to the road on the north side of Grass Creek. Turn south and tour along the road through this gentle valley, heading upstream parallel to Grass Creek. You will find nice, moderate trail skiing here. Total distance is roughly 1.5 miles, one way.
RECOMMENDED DAY TOUR 2: Gould Mountain has acres of hidden telemark glades and slopes. For an intermediate run, ascend to Elevation Point 9,700' (south of the yurt) and ski down Lary's Run. This run drops east/northeast from the small saddle immediately south of Elevation Point 9,700' and takes you back down to the road.

TOUR 1B   GRASS CREEK YURT TO RUBY JEWEL YURT

Difficulty:	Novice/Intermediate
Time:	3 to 5 hours
Distance:	4 miles
Elevations:	GC Yurt 9,040', RJ Yurt 9,640', +740'/-100'
Avalanche Note:	Some avalanche terrain encountered; easily avoided
Maps:	USGS 7.5': Clark Peak, 1977; Gould, 1955
	National Forest: Routt
	Colorado State Forest
	Trails Illustrated: Map #114 (Walden/Gould)
	See map pages 30 and 38-39

To travel from the Grass Creek Yurt to the Ruby Jewel Yurt, leave the Grass Creek Yurt and retrace your tracks to the point immediately southeast of the North Fork of the Michigan River. Instead of returning to the parking area, turn east and traverse along a slope south of the Michigan River through the forest, following a trail marked by blue ski diamonds.

After just over 0.5 mile, you will reach a trail that drops to the north across the North Fork of the Michigan River. Cross a road and climb onto a second road. Remain on this second road until you cross a small creek, then turn to the right. Leave the road, turn north and climb the open slope adjacent to the creek, passing two buildings. Ascend a small saddle behind Elevation Point 9,180'. Follow the trail down and to the west before climbing up to the Jewel Lake Road. Follow the signs to the Ruby Jewel Yurt.

Note: The summer mountain bike route returns to the North Michigan Reservoir Trailhead, heads north along the road, then follows the Ruby Jewel trail to the yurt. Total length is 5.8 miles, with an elevation loss of 140 feet and roughly 500 feet of gain.

2   RUBY JEWEL YURT

The Ruby Jewel Yurt is at the highest in elevation of any of the three Never Summer Nordic Yurts. It is also the most remote and offers the greatest variety of backcountry challenges. East of the yurt is Jewel Lake, a tiny alpine tarn cradled in a glacial cirque below the west face of Clark Peak. Skiing, biking, or hiking to the lake makes a very scenic intermediate day trip from the yurt.

Recommended telemark excursions include skiing to Jewel Lake, climbing the ridge south of the yurt to the 10,804-foot level, and skiing on and around Margi's Knoll, the ridge that juts to the southwest of Jewel Lake. Margi's Knoll is more suited for strong intermediate-to-advanced skiers. The yurt sleeps six. Make reservations through the Colorado Department of Parks and Outdoor Recreation (see Appendix A).

TOUR 2A   JEWEL LAKE TRAILHEAD

Difficulty:	Novice/Intermediate
Time:	2 to 4 hours
Distance:	2 miles
Elevation:	Trailhead 9,146', Yurt 9,640', +494'
Avalanche Note:	None
Maps:	USGS 7.5': Clark Peak, 1977; Gould, 1955
	National Forest: Routt
	Colorado State Forest
	Trails Illustrated: Map #114 (Walden/Gould)
	See map pages 30 and 38-39

To reach the trailhead, drive from the Colorado State Forest entrance (see directions, page 31) past North Michigan Reservoir to a small parking area on the right. Plowed in winter, this parking area is on the east side of a small hairpin curve and is marked with a Jewel Lake/Ruby Jewel Yurt sign near the 5-mile road marker.

From the parking area, ski to the southeast and immediately intercept the snow-covered, four-wheel-drive road that leads to the yurt. Begin climbing as you follow the gentle contour to the northeast. Once on the road, navigation is no problem as you follow the road toward the high peaks. The steepest section is near a noticeable switchback in the road as you climb onto a forested ridge. This switchback is near Elevations Point 9,590'.

Be aware of two turnoffs: one heads south toward the Grass Creek Yurt and a second turns north and leads to the North Fork Canadian Yurt. The first turnoff is only 0.7 mile from the trailhead; the second is reached after ascending through the aforementioned switchback and is marked by a sign that reads "Ruby Jewel Yurt/North Fork Canadian Yurt." Having skied several hundred yards past the marked turnoff to the NFC Yurt, watch for a small sign on the south marking the turnoff to the Ruby Jewel Yurt, which is 75 feet from the trail in a small clearing.

Should you decide to tour the area, there are many secondary logging roads that do not appear on the maps. While these logging roads make fine tours, pay attentions to where you're going so you don't get lost.

RECOMMENDED DAY TOURS: From the yurt, ski east on an obvious roadbed through the forest to a small clearing where the trail begins to contour sharply to the southeast. This site is known as the Saw Dust Pile and marks the end of the novice skiing terrain.

The trail splits into three separate roads at the south edge of the clearing. The first two forks on the right do not appear on the maps. The first road switchbacks up to Elevation Point 10,804'. The middle road ascends into the valley on the north side of Elevation Point 10,804' (known locally as Lynx Gulch) and is an intermediate tour.

Jewel Lake (11,260 feet), at the top of the left fork, is the best day trip in the area. Climb the road up to the summer vehicle closure. Ski up the valley along the path of least resistance, remaining close to the creek. As you leave the forest, be sure to remain near the creek, avoiding the avalanche slopes on the north side of the valley. The tour is 5 miles round trip, with 1,620 feet of elevation gain.

TOUR 2B   RUBY JEWEL YURT TO NORTH FORK CANADIAN YURT

Difficulty:	Intermediate
Time:	3 to 6 hours
Distance:	4.3 miles
Elevations:	RJ Yurt 9,640', NFC Yurt 8,770', -870'
Avalanche Note:	None
Maps:	USGS 7.5': Clark Peak, 1977; Gould, 1955
	National Forest: Routt
	Colorado State Forest
	Trails Illustrated: Map #114 (Walden/Gould)
	See map pages 30 and 38-39

Skiing between the Ruby Jewel Yurt and the North Fork Canadian Yurt can be either a fast descent or a steady climb. The trail connecting the yurts drops consistently from 9,640 feet at the Ruby Jewel Yurt to the North Fork Canadian Yurt at 8,770 feet. The recommended direction of travel is from south to north, making for a fun run down through the forest on a wide, twisting trail. The trail is marked with blue diamonds and is easy to follow. Should you opt for the north-to-south trip, you will have a steady climb.

The south end of the trail begins 0.6 mile west of the Ruby Jewel Yurt at an obvious, marked fork in the trail and descends immediately. A second fork in the trail is quickly reached (this is a new logging road not yet on the topo map). Follow the right fork down through a fast turn across the South Fork of the Canadian River. A very short climb takes you out of this drainage as the descent continues. Eventually, the trail breaks out into a meadow lined with evergreen and aspen trees. Cross the meadow, exiting west through thin stands of trees into a second meadow.

Next you will arrive at a marked turnoff. Here the ski trail leaves the well-traveled (shared by snowmobilers) route and heads north into stands of aspen. At Elevation Point 8,800' is another meadow, which you enter from the south. Ski through the center of the meadow, heading north. The north end of the meadow is bordered by the North Fork of the Canadian River. Blue trail diamonds lead down to and across the river, through a short stretch of willows, and up across the open, south-facing bank to the yurt.

Stars streak the sky above Ruby Jewel Yurt.

Never Summer Nordic Yurts & Lake Agnes Cabin

Scale 1:24,000   Contour Interval 40 Feet

0   1/2   1

SCALE IN MILES

MN 12°

Hut

Trailhead •

Wilderness — — — —

Trails, including US Forest Service trails may or may
not be marked. USFS trails and roads are not maintained and their exact location may vary. This map is not a
substitute for good route-finding skills. This map is an
aid to help locate routes. These are suggested routes
only. Hazards exist in the backcountry, including
avalanches. Common sense and good judgement can
reduce but not eliminate these hazards.

© 1995 Brian Litz

RAWAH WILDERNESS

North Fork Canadian Trailhead
8,580'

3 A

North Fork Canadian Yurt
8,770'

2 B

0.62 miles to Ruby Jewel Yurt
1.40 miles to Jewel Lake Trailhead
3.72 miles to North Fork Canadian Yurt

2 A

Ruby Jewel Yurt
9,640'

0.70 miles to Jewel Lake Trailhead
1.30 miles to Ruby-Jewel Lake
2.70 miles to Grass Creek Yurt

Jewel Lake Trailhead
9,146'

1 B

4 A

Dancing Moose Trailhead
9,080'

Bancing Moose Yurt
9,120'

North Michigan Trailhead
8,940'

1 A

1.22 miles to North Fork Canadian Yurt
3.12 miles to Ruby Jewel Yurt

Grass Creek Yurt

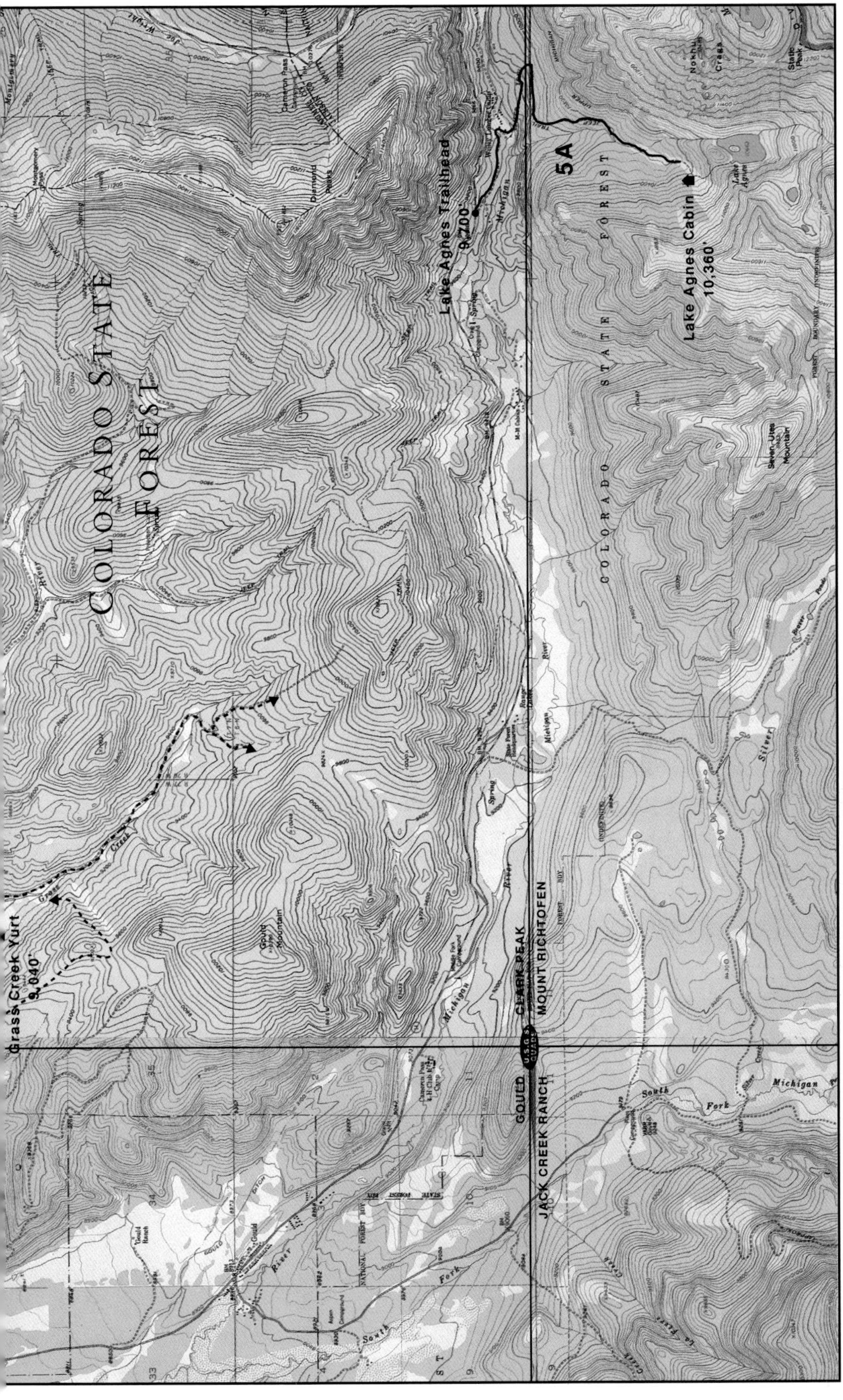

COLORADO STATE FOREST

Lake Agnes Trailhead
9,200'

5A

COLORADO STATE FOREST

Lake Agnes Cabin
10,360'

Grass Creek Yurt
9,040'

CLARK PEAK
MOUNT RICHTOFEN

GOULD

JACK CREEK RANCH

South Fork

Michigan

3   NORTH FORK CANADIAN YURT

The North Fork Canadian Yurt is on an open slope above the North Fork of the Canadian River — really more of a creek than a river. The south-facing yurt, which sleeps six, has great views of the peaks to the east. The skiing to and around the yurt is very gentle and well suited for beginning backcountry skiers.

When the state forest road is plowed to its end, the tour is less than a mile from the parking area. The road is normally plowed, but call the state forest or the yurt system to confirm this. Add 5 miles to the mileage if the road is not plowed. Make reservations through the Colorado Division of Parks and Outdoor Recreation (see Appendix A).

TOUR 3A   NORTH FORK CANADIAN TRAILHEAD

Difficulty:	Novice
Time:	I to 2 hours
Distance:	I mile
Elevations:	Trailhead 8,680', Yurt 8,770', +170'/-80'
Avalanche Note:	None
Maps:	USGS 7.5': Clark Peak, 1977; Gould, 1955
	National Forest: Routt
	Colorado State Forest
	Trails Illustrated: Map #114 (Walden/Gould)
	See map pages 30 and 38-39

From the Colorado State Forest entrance (see directions, page 31), pass the reservoir, proceed to the end of the plowed road and park. Go through a gate and follow a road east down and across to the north side of the North Fork Canadian River.

This initial stretch of trail follows the road to Kelly Lake and Clear Lake. Once across the creek, the road climbs a short hill through a small S curve. On the east side, heading southeast across the open slopes roughly 80 feet above the creek, is the marked trail to the yurt. Follow the land's contours southeast on a traverse above the creek for several hundred yards to the yurt. Watch for moose! They like to feed on willow bushes in the creek bed.

RECOMMENDED DAY TOURS: Fine backcountry touring may be found by exploring Mossman Pole Patch Creek and also by heading north and east from the yurt up to Elevation Point 9,200'. Follow the ditch north uphill to the Kelly Lake Trail as far as your group feels comfortable skiing.

Lisa Paesani at the North Fork Canadian Yurt.

4   DANCING MOOSE YURT

The Dancing Moose Yurt is the newest structure in the Never Summer Nordic Yurt system. It is not really a "backcountry yurt" but rather a large, near-roadside structure that works well as a base camp for day tours, as a place to spend the night before launching a hut-to-hut trip to the other yurts, or as a great destination for anyone wanting to experience hut/yurt life without undertaking a major expedition. It only takes about a 10- to 20-minute ski to reach it. Additionally, with a capacity of eight to twelve people, it is the largest yurt covered by this guide, making it a great spot for families or large parties (as in people, not festivities). And finally it is fully wheelchair accessible during the summer and autumn months. Make reservations through Never Summer Nordic Yurts (see Appendix A).

Kelly Stone and Barbie Schmidt on the way to
Dancing Moose Yurt.

TOUR 4A   DANCING MOOSE TRAILHEAD

Difficulty:	Novice
Time:	Half hour
Distance:	0.1 mile
Elevation:	Trailhead 9,080', Yurt 9,120', +140'
Avalanche Note:	None
Maps:	USGS 7.5': Clark Peak, 1977; Gould, 1955
	National Forest: Routt
	Colorado State Forest
	Trails Illustrated: Map #114 (Walden/Gould)
	See map pages 30 and 38-39

To reach the trailhead, drive from the Colorado State Forest entrance (for directions, see page 31) past North Michigan Reservoir and the Grass Creek Yurt Trailhead. Near the 4.3 mile mark there is a small, narrow, plowed parking area on the east side of the road. This area is on the north end of a large clearing. To the west, the clearing spans the creek. The yurt is just visible from the road and sits to the west in a finger of the clearing that reaches up into the forest. The route itself is straightforward and self-evident.

Skiers ascend toward a peak, carefully avoiding the overhanging snow cornice to the left.

5   LAKE AGNES CABIN

NOTE: Colorado State Forest has closed the Lake Agnes Cabin because of its deteriorating condition. Thankfully the new Nokhu Cabin, slated for construction during the 1999 fall season, will replace it. Nokhu Cabin will be located just north of the former Lake Agnes Cabin, along the access road. Contact Never Summer Nordic Yurts for current information (see Appendix A). If you have confirmed with Never Summer Nordic Yurts that Nokhu Cabin is open and are planning a trip there, please note that some of the following information may have changed.

TOUR 5A   LAKE AGNES TRAILHEAD

Difficulty:	Advanced
Time:	3 to 5 hours
Distance:	2.6 miles
Elevations:	Trailhead 9,700', Hut 10,360', +660'
Avalanche Note:	Some avalanche terrain encountered; easily avoided
Maps:	USGS 7.5': Clark Peak, 1977; Mount Richthofen, 1977
	National Forest: Routt
	Colorado State Forest
	See map pages 30 and 38-39

The trailhead for the cabin is 2.5 miles west of Cameron Pass. The parking area is on CO 14, approximately 20 miles east of Walden or 59 miles west from the intersection of CO 14 and US 287 (north of Fort Collins).

On the south side of CO 14 is a small parking area. In winter the road is closed by a gate; ski past the gate and proceed down the access road 0.5 mile to the entrance to the state forest. Turn right onto a summer four-wheel-drive trail marked for Lake Agnes.

Cross the creek, ascend through a hairpin curve, at a fork in the road, take the right fork (west). Contour to the southwest and ascend into the Lake Agnes Creek drainage. Follow the road upward approximately 0.6 mile to the cabin, which sits on the south edge of a meadow.

The area is in the Colorado State Forest, and a valid daily or annual state park pass is required on all vehicles. The passes may be purchased at a self-service station at the forest entrance or at the office near the turnoff to the Never Summer Nordic Yurts (for directions, see page 31).

COLORADO MOUNTAIN CLUB
& INDEPENDENT HUTS

The Front Range of Colorado provides Denver metro area adventurers with a variety of huts within a one- to two-hour drive. For many decades, in fact, mountaineers and skiers have enjoyed several shelters operated by the various chapters of the Colorado Mountain Club, as well as several privately-owned cabins and lodges.

Perhaps the best-known Front Range hut is the Brainard Lake Cabin in the Indian Peaks Wilderness. The trailhead to this popular spot is just off the Peak to Peak Highway, north of the town of Ward. To use the Brainard Lake Cabin, one member of your group must be a member of CMC.

West of the historical mining community of Nederland are two huts perched high above the Eldora nordic and downhill ski areas. The Guinn Mountain Hut and the Tennessee Mountain Cabin are favorite destinations for Boulder-area skiers and hikers and are open year round. These two huts work well for shorter trips and as base camps for a diverse selection of day ski, mountain bike, and hiking trips. They share a common trailhead at the base of the Eldora Ski Area near the nordic center office. The Guinn Mountain Hut is operated and maintained by the Boulder chapter of the Colorado Mountain Club, while the Tennessee Mountain cabin is operated by the Eldora Nordic Center.

Between Interstate 70 and the resort town of Winter Park, on US 40, is the infamous Berthoud Pass. This sinuous roadway climbs up and over the Continental Divide through some of the finest nordic mountain skiing terrain in northern Colorado. Since the early part of the century Berthoud Pass and its environs have provided generations of Colorado skiers with their first backcountry, tree-skiing experience and deep-powder face plants.

First Creek Cabin and the Gwen Andrews Hut are closed indefinitely while the US Forest Service conducts site evaluations. Contact the Hot Sulphur Springs Ranger District of the Arapaho National Forest for current information (see Appendix C).

6   BRAINARD LAKE CABIN

Built in 1928, the Brainard Lake Cabin is well hidden in the trees and is surrounded by some of the most diverse nordic touring terrain to be found in the Denver-Boulder vicinity. While there are several recommended tours to the cabin, the entire area is laced with superlative day skiing. Whether you enjoy energetic treks along sinuous trails, climbing to alpine lakes, or ski-mountaineering, there are ample opportunities for skiers of every persuasion.

West of the cabin is the Indian Peaks Wilderness Area, considered by many to be one of the most spectacular wilderness areas close to a major population center. The glacially carved valleys that lead from the cabin to the high peaks hold boundless acres of incredible telemark skiing terrain. Peaks such as Mount Audubon are excellent goals for winter or spring mountaineering.

The cabin, which is open for year-round use, sleeps eight to ten people comfortably and has two levels. The rustic and cozy main floor is the cooking and socializing area, and the second level is for sleeping. Heat is provided by a fireplace and a wood-burning cookstove. Water can be obtained by melting snow, or from the creek flowing across the road to the west (you will often need to break through the ice). Creek water should be boiled or treated before using.

Backcountry skiers should be prepared for all weather conditions when venturing into alpine terrain.

Stocked with plenty of cookware, utensils, and reading materials, the Brainard Lake Cabin ranks as one of the best nordic huts in the state for all levels of skiers. Weekends may be very crowded, though, as the cabin also serves as a warming hut for day skiers — for a small fee. The cabin is owned and operated by the Boulder chapter of the Colorado Mountain Club and is rented on a nightly basis for a very reasonable fee. However, at least one person in your group must be an active member of CMC. Skiers will find many maps in the cabin marking day tours in the area. CMC also produces a map highlighting the nordic trails in the area. For membership information and reservations, call the club at the number listed in Appendix A.

TOUR 6A   RED ROCK LAKE TRAILHEAD

Difficulty:	Novice
Time:	2 to 3 hours
Distance:	2.1 miles
Elevations:	Trailhead 10,080', Hut 10,400', +380'/-100'
Avalanche Note:	None
Maps:	USGS 7.5': Ward, 1978
	National Forest: Roosevelt
	Trails Illustrated: Map #102 (Indian Peaks/ Gold Hill)
	See map pages 51 and 53

Gentle, straightforward, and very scenic, the Brainard Lake Road is the simplest approach to the cabin. Nearly anyone who can strap on a pair of skis should be able to manage this trail. The tour follows a wide road that is distinct and nearly devoid of elevation gain. The Brainard Lake Road is one of the most scenic of the introductory-level tours in this book. Throughout the tour, skiers enjoy vistas of the central Indian Peaks.

To reach the trailhead, drive on CO 72, the Peak to Peak Highway, to the turnoff to the Brainard Lake Recreation Area (FR 102). The turn is immediately north of the town of Ward and just south of the Millsite Inn (great bluegrass music on Saturday nights!).

Occasionally, this turn is somewhat obscured by large snowbanks, so drive slowly and keep an eye open for signs. Once on the curvy road, drive west 2.6 miles to the winter public road closure. There is ample parking here, except on weekends when day skiers are present.

After donning skis, leave the west end of the parking area, pass a metal barricade and continue along the road as it contours northwest up and around a hill. Once past this incline, the trail gently rolls west and is easy to follow. The road eventually reaches the east end of the open meadowlands that surround the lake. Aim for the north side of the lake and cross the bridge and dam at the outlet stream. Contour around the north edge of the lake in the trees.

On the northwest corner of the lake (in the forest) is a turnoff to the Long Lake and Mitchell Lake trailheads. Take this turn and follow this new road as it bends sharply to the north. Pass a left turn to the Long Lake parking area and then pass a "Parking in designated areas only" sign. Finally, as you reach the southeast edge of a clearing, you'll arrive at a sign marking the trail to the cabin and the CMC Waldrop Trail. The Brainard Lake Cabin is directly east of the sign in the trees. Remember to follow the primary road and avoid any turnoffs to other ski trails, summer campsites, and secondary roads.

RECOMMENDED DAY TOUR 1: From Brainard Lake Cabin you can ski to either Mitchell or Blue lakes (skiing to Mitchell Lake is for intermediate-level skiers; Blue Lake is for strong intermediate to advanced skiers). From the road near the cabin, continue north around a large curve to the west, up to a large meadow/parking area. On the west edge of this clearing, near two small wooden structures, is the trailhead to Mitchell and Blue lakes.

Enter the forest and climb west into this spectacular valley. The trail traverses up and across the main creek via a small bridge, then along the south side of the stream to Mitchell Lake. Beyond Mitchell Lake, the trail gets steeper and the terrain more alpine as the trees begin to thin out. Treeline is near Blue Lake as the trail ascends along the north side of the creek. This trail is less traveled than the section below Mitchell Lake, and route finding to Blue Lake is slightly more difficult.

RECOMMENDED DAY TOUR 2: Easy touring describes the trail to Long Lake. From the cabin, head south and take the turnoff to the Long Lake Trailhead parking area, proceeding past the trail marker into the forest. Ski for roughly 0.25 mile until you reach the clearing that surrounds the lake.

The trail continues along the north edge of the lake. At the far northwest edge of the lake, skiers may return along the same path or tour around the south shore via the Jean Lunning Trail, which will bring you back to the outlet at the east edge and a rendezvous with the main Long Lake Trail.

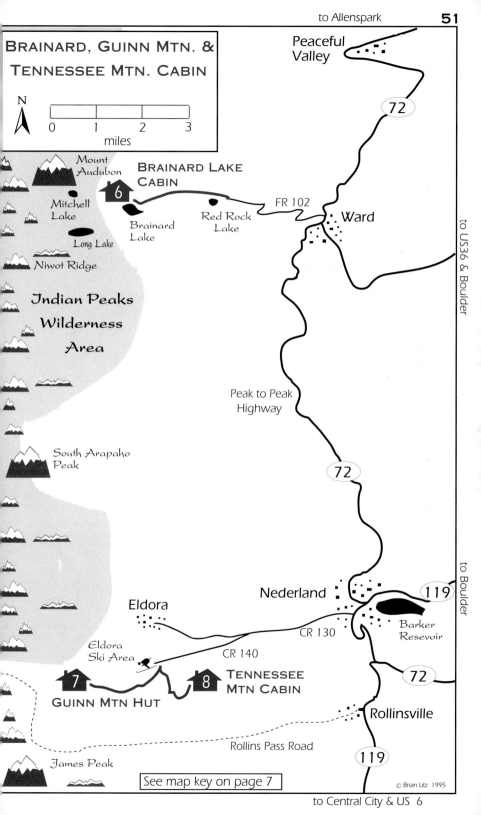

BRAINARD, GUINN MTN. &
TENNESSEE MTN. CABIN

N

0   1   2   3
miles

Peaceful
Valley

72

Mount
Audubon

BRAINARD LAKE
CABIN

6

Mitchell
Lake

Brainard
Lake

Red Rock
Lake

FR 102

Ward

Long Lake

Niwot Ridge

Indian Peaks
Wilderness
Area

Peak to Peak
Highway

72

South Arapaho
Peak

Nederland

119

Eldora

CR 130

Barker
Resevoir

Eldora
Ski Area

CR 140

7

8

TENNESSEE
MTN CABIN

72

GUINN MTN HUT

Rollinsville

James Peak

Rollins Pass Road

119

See map key on page 7

© Brian Litz 1995

to US36 & Boulder

to Boulder

TOUR 6B   NORTH & SOUTH TRAILS

Difficulty:	Intermediate	🚶 🚲 👫
Time:	2 to 4 hours (each tour)	
Distance:	2.6 miles (each tour)	
Elevations:	Trailhead 10,080', Hut 10,400',	
	+420'(NT), +110'/-360' (ST)	
Avalanche Note:	None	
Maps:	USGS 7.5': Ward, 1978	
	National Forest: Roosevelt	
	Trails Illustrated: Map #102 (Indian Peaks/	
	Gold Hill)	
	See map pages 51 and 53	

Slightly more demanding routes to the cabin are found on the CMC North and South Trails. Rules on the proper direction of travel have changed: The North Trail (the Waldrop Trail) is now the recommended route to the cabin, and the South Trail is designated for return trips to the parking lot. Both of these trails are slightly more advanced than the Brainard Lake Road but are still quite manageable for most skiers.

To reach the North Trail, ski west from the Red Rock Lake parking area and past the barricade. As you begin to round the corner on the road's initial climb, you will reach a large trail sign marking the turnoff to the North Trail. Drop off the road and head north into the forest.

From here, the trail contours around to the west and then parallels the main road on the north. Lying below the road elevation, the trail traverses west, above South Saint Vrain Creek. Eventually begin a gradual descent to the creek.

Cross the creek and climb northwest to an intersection with the South Saint Vrain Trail. Turn west/southwest, traverse down and around a steep curve that crosses South Saint Vrain Creek for a second time. This well-marked trail climbs steadily to the southwest through thick evergreen forests until it reaches a clearing near the Mitchell Lake Road and the Brainard Lake Cabin. The easiest way to find the cabin is to ski to the road and head south to the sign marking the turnoff to the cabin.

To return to the parking area, leave the cabin and return to the Mitchell Lake Road. Turn south, pass the turnoff to the Long Lake Trailhead and continue to the main Brainard Lake Road. Ski along the road around the west edge of the lake. As the road begins to contour to the east around the south edge of the lake, turn off into the trees near a willowy meadow. Enter the forest, passing some old, free-standing chimneys and the turnoff to the Little Raven Trail.

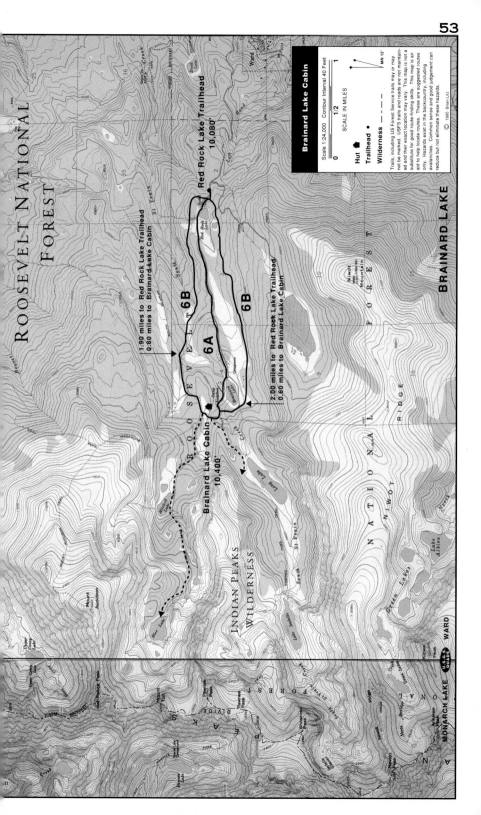

ROOSEVELT NATIONAL FOREST

INDIAN PEAKS WILDERNESS

BRAINARD LAKE

WARD

MONARCH LAKE

Brainard Lake Cabin

Scale 1:24,000   Contour Interval 40 Feet

SCALE IN MILES

Hut

Trailhead •

Wilderness — — — —

Trails, including US Forest Service trails may or may not be marked. USFS trails and roads are not maintained and their exact location may vary. This map is not a substitute for good route-finding skills. This map is an aid to help locate routes. These are suggested routes only. Hazards exist in the backcountry, including avalanches. Common sense and good judgement can reduce but not eliminate these hazards.

© 1995 Brian Litz

MN 12°

Red Rock Lake Trailhead 10,080'

1.90 miles to Red Rock Lake Trailhead
0.80 miles to Brainard Lake Cabin

2.00 miles to Red Rock Lake Trailhead
0.60 miles to Brainard Lake Cabin

Brainard Lake Cabin 10,400'

6A

6B

6B

The South Trail traverses along the south edge of the lake in the forest and is well marked and well traveled. It is less strenuous and technical than the North Trail but slightly harder than the Brainard Lake Road. A short descent occurs just before reaching the parking area. This drop is steep; take off your skis and walk if necessary! Skiers ascending a trail have the right of way, so watch for skiers climbing up this hill — and for those who have crashed and are sticking out of the snow alongside the trail!

7   GUINN MOUNTAIN HUT

Between the Eldora Ski Area and Rollins Pass is 11,200-foot Guinn Mountain. Perched just below and to the east of the summit is the diminutive Guinn Mountain Hut. Built in the early 1970s, it is the brainchild of Boulder residents Ingevar and Jofrid Sodal, who wanted to build a cabin similar to the cross-country huts found in their native Scandinavia. This hut is also known as the Arestua Hut; *arestua* means shelter in Norwegian.

Protected from Front Range winds, and with a commanding view of the Great Plains, this hut has been a favorite overnight refuge for skiers for many years. The trail to the hut is steep and strenuous, but the sight of the twinkling lights far below, out on the plains, makes the journey worth the effort. The skiing around the summit of Guinn Mountain is limited and often windblown. However, an ascent to the very top provides skiers with practically a 360-degree view of the Front Range peaks. The Guinn Mountain Hut also is the place to spend the night for groups planning to cross the Continental Divide to Winter Park via Rollins Pass.

Guinn Mountain has enough sleeping space for seven people. A wood-burning stove, wood, pots and pans are provided, but you will want to bring a small backpacking stove for meal preparation. Pressurized camp stoves are allowed in the cabin. Be careful!

Gail Keefe at Guinn Mountain Hut.

This hut is open year round on a first-come, first-served basis. There is no fee, but a donation is appreciated, since the cabin is maintained by volunteers, and all donated monies go directly for upkeep.

Access across the Eldora Ski Area is a courtesy of the resort. If the ski area is closed, do not park in their parking areas, or your car may get locked in. Parking is also available just in front of the gate.

TOUR 7A   ELDORA NORDIC CENTER TRAILHEAD

Difficulty:	Advanced	🚶 🚲 🚶🚶
Time:	5 to 7 hours	
Distance:	4.5 miles	
Elevations:	Trailhead 9,360', Hut 11,120', +1,991'/-180'	
Avalanche Note:	None	
Maps:	USGS 7.5': Nederland, 1972; East Portal, 1958	
	National Forest: Roosevelt	
	Trails Illustrated: Map #103 (Winter Park/	
	Central City/Rollins Pass)	
	See map pages 51 and 58	

To reach the trailhead, drive on CO 119 southwest from the mountain town of Nederland to the well-marked turnoff (north) to CR 130 and the Eldora Ski Area. After 1.5 miles, take the left fork onto CR 140, ascending the south wall of the valley. Park in the first parking lot to the left. The trail begins near the building that serves as the nordic ski area office.

From the building, the route ascends the easternmost ski run of the downhill area via a signed public right of way. Stay well east of the ski lift (watching for downhill skiers and nordic area touring trails) and follow the signs into the forest just above the top of the ski lift. From here, the trail crosses a rolling, forested ridge before the final wild and exciting descending traverse to Jenny Creek (avoid a left fork that leads to private property). Jenny Creek is on the south side of Guinn Mountain and is, in itself, a fine tour.

Ski west up Jenny Creek for 0.25 mile until you reach a trail intersection. Turn to the northwest and start climbing. From this point, the route climbs almost constantly to the Guinn Mountain Hut. After another 0.5 mile, turn west, then northwest at another trail marker. Continue over moderate terrain until you reach a cabin ruin at the top of a treeless meadow.

Follow the trail west past the ruin to the top of the small gully and re-enter the forest. From here the trail turns sinuous and less steep through the forest. Watch for trail markers above the ruin; they are sometimes difficult to see. Near the top of the mountain, you will enter a meadow. Begin searching the south edge of the clearing for the hut against a stand of evergreen trees.

The two greatest challenges of this tour are the location of the trail into the woods just past the ruin and actually locating the hut once you enter the small meadow. Pay attention at these spots and you shouldn't have any trouble. During the summer, the trail past the ruin is a faint animal trail and may be hard to follow; some orienteering skills may be required.

Dave Mention gets a glacial facial.

Guinn Mountain Hut & Tennessee Mountain Cabin

Scale 1:24,000   Contour Interval 40 Feet

SCALE IN MILES

0   1/2   1

Hut

Trailhead •

Wilderness – – – – –

MN 12°

Trails, including US Forest Service trails may or may not be marked. USFS trails and roads are not maintained and their exact location may vary. This map is not a substitute for good route-finding skills. This map is an aid to help locate routes. These are suggested routes only. Hazards exist in the backcountry, including avalanches. Common sense and good judgement can reduce but not eliminate these hazards.

© 1995 Brian Litz

ROOSEVELT NATIONAL FOREST

Tennessee Mountain Cabin
9,860'

Eldora Nordic Center Trailhead
9,360'

LAKE ELDORA SKI AREA

NATIONAL   FOREST

8A

7A

BM 2.10 miles to Eldora Nordic Center Trailhead
BM 2.40 miles to Guinn Mountain Hut

Guinn Mountain Hut
11,120'

NATIONAL

ROOSEVELT

LAKE ELDORA

NEDERLAND

EAST PORTAL   U.S.G.S.

8   TENNESSEE MOUNTAIN CABIN

Tennessee Mountain Cabin is an independently owned hut located on the south flank of Tennessee Mountain near the Eldora Ski Area. This cozy shelter is reached by following the groomed nordic area trails. Because of this, skiers may opt for lighter touring equipment. Amenities include sleeping space for up to 10 people, a wood-burning stove for heat, lantern, cookware, and utensils. Your group should bring backpacking stoves for cooking.

The normal routes to the cabin are somewhat strenuous. Since these are maintained trails, route finding is not a problem and skiers rarely need to break trail. While day tours from the hut are limited mainly to the nordic area's trails, the large capacity of the hut, combined with its close proximity to the Denver-Boulder metro area and straightforward approach, make this hut a nice choice for large groups looking for a destination that does not require a long drive.

A valid nordic area pass is required to use this cabin and the network of nordic area trails on the mountain. The passes are complimentary for cabin users and can be picked up at the Eldora Nordic Center. This hut is open for year-round use. Reservations are made through Eldora Nordic Center (see Appendix A).

TOUR 8A   ELDORA NORDIC CENTER TRAILHEAD

Difficulty:	Intermediate
Time:	2 to 3 hours
Distance:	2 miles
Elevations:	Trailhead 9,360', Hut 9,860', +500'
Avalanche Note:	None
Maps:	USGS 7.5': Nederland, 1972
	National Forest: Roosevelt
	Trails Illustrated: Map #103 (Winter Park/
	Central City/Rollins Pass)
	See map pages 51 and 58

To reach the trailhead, drive on CO 119 southwest from the mountain town of Nederland to the well-marked turnoff (north) on CR 130 to the Eldora Ski Area. After 1.5 miles, veer left onto CR 140 ascending the steep south wall of the valley. Park in the first parking lot to the left. The trail begins near the nordic ski area office Remember to stop at the office to obtain any required trail passes and to pick up a nordic area map.

The most direct route starts at the office and heads east on a trail named Dixie. Next, follow the Mill Iron Trail to Buck Eye Basin Loop, then onto Rising Sun, which climbs directly to a saddle southwest of Tennessee Mountain. At an intersection with the Tennessee Mountain Trail, turn east and follow the Tennessee Mountain Trail up to the cabin.

Note: For summer use, follow the trail marked "17th Avenue" to either Twin Twisted or Phoebe B, then connect with Rising Sun (near Siding and Sawmill) and follow that route up onto the Tennessee Mountain Trail.

RECOMMENDED DAY TOUR: The short tour to the top of Tennessee Mountain makes for a quick and scenic day trip that offers views of the Indian Peaks Wilderness.

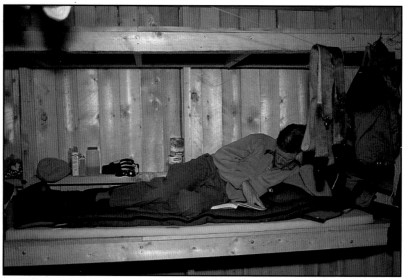

Culley Culbreth relaxes in a typical hut bunk.

9   FIRST CREEK CABIN

NOTE: The First Creek Cabin is closed while the US Forest Service conducts a site evaluation to assess whether the hut is in safe, habitable condition, whether it merits formal designation as a historical location, or whether it should be replaced by a new hut, if any. Contact the Hot Sulphur Springs Ranger District of the Arapaho National Forest for current information (see Appendix C).

A log structure, First Creek Cabin was an excellent destination for short trips when skiers were interested in getting away with minimal logistical complications. The trail is short, steep, often is not broken, and will require some route finding as you climb the slopes below the cabin.

This cabin is less than one mile from US 40, yet can be difficult to find. The valley where the cabin is located is small and the west end of the valley is precipitous, with several avalanche slopes. Backcountry skiing is limited to short tours around and west of the cabin along several benches.

TOUR 9A   FIRST CREEK TRAILHEAD

Difficulty:	Intermediate
Time:	1 to 2 hours
Distance:	0.7 mile
Elevations:	Trailhead 10,442', Hut 10,920', +478'
Avalanche Note:	Route crosses avalanche slopes; prone to skier-triggered avalanches during high-hazard periods
Maps:	USGS 7.5': Berthoud Pass, 1957
	National Forest: Arapaho
	Trails Illustrated: Map #103 (Winter Park/ Central City/Rollins Pass)
	See map pages 62 and 65

To reach the trailhead, take US 40 to Berthoud Pass, which is between the town of Empire (near I-70) and Winter Park. The parking area and the trailhead lie just over 4 miles down the Winter Park (north) side of the pass at the third obvious drainage. The first two drainages are Current Creek and Second Creek, respectively, which are also very popular touring areas. Park on the west side of the road in a plowed turnout.

The cabin is almost due north of the parking area up the hillside. Leave the trailhead and ski into the trees along the creek. The trail climbs to the hut in a giant **S** by first heading west up the creek, curving up and around to the east, then back to the north, and finally west to the cabin. The route covers very few miles, but you must pay attention to the map and the terrain.

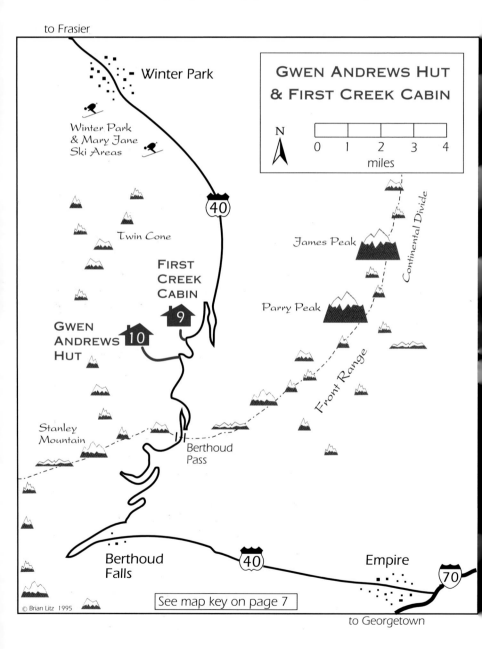

to Frasier

Winter Park

Winter Park & Mary Jane Ski Areas

GWEN ANDREWS HUT & FIRST CREEK CABIN

N

0   1   2   3   4
miles

Twin Cone

40

James Peak

Continental Divide

FIRST CREEK CABIN

Parry Peak

GWEN ANDREWS HUT

10

9

Stanley Mountain

Front Range

Berthoud Pass

Berthoud Falls

40

Empire

70

© Brian Litz 1995

See map key on page 7

to Georgetown

10   GWEN ANDREWS HUT

NOTE: The Gwen Andrews Hut is closed while the US Forest Service conducts a site evaluation to assess whether the hut is in safe, habitable condition, whether it merits formal designation as a historical location, or whether it should be replaced by a new hut, if any. Contact the Hot Sulphur Springs Ranger District of the Arapaho National Forest for current information (see Appendix C).

Formerly a Forest Service cabin, the quaint Gwen Andrews Hut is also known as the Second Creek Hut. It is one of the most popular backcountry nordic skiing areas in the state and with good reason: It is close to the Denver metro area, the terrain is ideally suited for touring and telemark skiing, and the snow is generally superb. The A-frame cabin has provided Colorado skiers with shelter on many cold stormy nights. The tour to this cabin is short and scenic.

The Gwen Andrews Hut is surrounded by many acres of small bowls and glades, excellent terrain for skiers of all abilities. Skiers could cruise to the hut for the night or use it for a day lunch spot. Winter Park Ski Resort is easily reached from the hut, and combining a night at the hut with a tour to the base of the ski area added up to a classic Colorado backcountry adventure.

TOUR 10A   SECOND CREEK TRAILHEAD

Difficulty:	Intermediate
Time:	2 to 3 hours
Distance:	1.1 miles
Elevations:	Trailhead 10,580', Hut 11,340', +760'
Avalanche Note:	Route crosses avalanche runout zones; can be dangerous during high-hazard periods
Maps:	USGS 7.5': Berthoud Pass, 1957
	National Forest: Arapaho
	Trails Illustrated: Map #103 (Winter Park/ Central City/Rollins Pass)
	See map pages 62 and 65

To reach the trailhead, take US 40 to Berthoud Pass, which is between the town of Empire (near I-70) and Winter Park. The parking area and the trailhead lie just under 3 miles down the Winter Park (north) side of the pass, at the second obvious drainage. The first drainage is Current Creek, another very popular touring area. Park on the west side of the road in a large, plowed turnout.

The most popular and safest route through this short valley departs the trailhead and ascends along the north side of the creek. The forest here is broken and navigation is fairly straightforward.

Ski west in and out of small clumps of trees for several hundred yards, departing from the main creek en route. Climb slightly to the northwest as the terrain opens up even more. The steepest section of the tour, a treeless slope, is reached near the halfway point. The easiest route up this steep slope climbs the north, or right-hand, side. As the grade becomes more gentle, traverse around the south end of a small ridge with rocky outcrops. Some skiers climb directly to the cabin via a small ridge immediately to the north of the small outcrops. However, most skiers contour around the south edge of the ridge.

Enter the flat basin below the huge, avalanche-prone mountain to the west. The route turns up the ridge or gully several hundred feet north. The Gwen Andrews Hut is hidden in a stand of evergreen trees and can be difficult to see until you ski right up to it.

When skiing to the hut, stay away from the avalanche slopes off the eastern aspect of Elevation Point 12,092'! This is a very dangerous area, and prudent skiers will stay well away from both the slopes and the avalanche runout zones at the base of the slopes.

RECOMMENDED DAY TOUR: For an intermediate-level tour from the cabin, climb directly west up to the Nystrom Trail. Treeline is easily reached as you follow upper First Creek to the alpine ridge to the west. The bowls in this area offer superb intermediate telemark skiing. Stay off the steeper, avalanche-prone slopes on the south edge of the drainage.

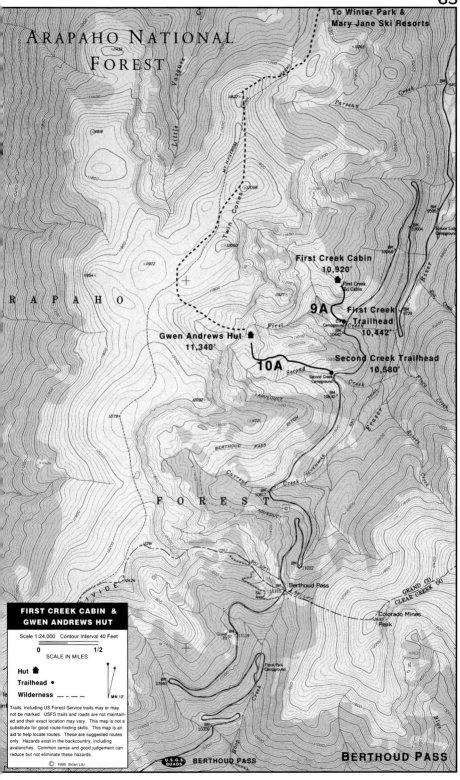

Craig Snowden telemarking north of the Peter Estin Hut, 10th Mountain Division Hut System

CENTRAL HUTS

CENTRAL HUTS

The central Colorado Rockies contain spectacular and diverse topography, claiming many of state's highest and most famous peaks. The Mount of the Holy Cross, Mount Massive, Mount Elbert, Castle Peak, the Maroon Bells, and Pyramid Peak are a few of the 14,000-foot peaks found here. Thick, boreal spruce forests and aspen groves have overgrown glacially scoured valleys. Mirrorlike alpine lakes speckle the landscape. From the igneous and metamorphic rocks of the Gore and Sawatch ranges to the violet-hued sedimentary cliffs of the Elk Mountains, the state's complex geologic past is vividly apparent to visitors.

The central mountains are the focus of Colorado hut-to-hut travel, offering skiers and mountain bikers the greatest variety of huts, trails, peaks, and backcountry glades in the state. Four hut systems are covered in this chapter, beginning with the Summit Huts Association, the new kid on the "super" hut-system block. Conceived in the mid-1980s, the Summit Huts Association has benefited from careful planning and the dedicated commitment of staff and volunteers, ensuring that — when competed — this will undoubtedly be one of the finest hut-to-hut systems in the Rockies.

The inaugural hut, Janet's Cabin, is one of the most majestic huts in the state. This thoughtfully crafted cabin has made a visible and enduring statement on the future of hut-to-hut adventure in Colorado. A second hut, Francie's Cabin, became operational in January 1995. It is located southwest of Breckenridge near treeline, below the northeast face of Crystal Peak.

Southwest of Vail Pass is perhaps the most famous hut system in existence. Named in honor of the soldiers of the 10th Mountain Division, the 10th Mountain Division Hut Association system is by far Colorado's largest and most sophisticated hut system, providing access to a staggering selection of backcountry challenges. Skiers and mountain bikers could spend several years' worth of vacations exploring the trails and old roads that lace the mountains between Aspen, Vail, and Leadville, let alone explore all of the hidden bowls and windblown peaks accessible from the huts. Most the 10th Mountain Division huts share a similar architecture — being at once rustic, roomy, and fully equipped for large numbers of skiers.

The Elk Mountains form a linear partition between swank Aspen and rural Crested Butte. The towering peaks and avalanche-prone valleys of this range discourage winter travel; nevertheless, the Elk Mountains are home of the first true backcountry hut system in Colorado created specifically for skiers and snowshoers. Consisting of six high-country huts, the Alfred A. Braun Memorial Hut System is a favorite among experienced skiers, providing access to some of the best alpine skiing in Colorado.

On the Crested Butte side of the Elk Mountains, the Friends Hut, Gothic Cabin, the Elkton Cabins, and the Cement Creek Yurt are available to all skiers, especially those less experienced in off-trail skiing and winter wilderness travel.

Two independent huts are covered in this section. The Lost Wonder Hut is a renovated mining cabin below Mount Aetna, near Monarch Pass. The Sunlight Backcountry Cabin is also a historic cabin. Less than a mile west from the Sunlight Mountain Resort ski area near Glenwood Springs, this shelter is a great destination for novice skiers and anyone who wants to experience the backcountry without a major commitment of time.

Mount Massive, at 14,421' the state's second highest peak, from *Uncle Bud's Hut*, 10th Mountain Division Hut System.

SUMMIT HUTS ASSOCIATION

Historically, Summit County was the mountain homeland of the Ute Indians, the dominant tribe in the Colorado Rockies. During the warm summer months, small bands of Utes lived in the high mountain valleys, hunting game and gathering plants, such as the wild yampa root. In winter they descended to lower elevations to take advantage of more temperate climates. Diverse wildlife provided an abundant source of meat for the Utes, though on occasion they ventured onto the plains to hunt buffalo.

The Ute way of life began to change as European explorers swept through North America in search of mythical cities of gold. Spanish explorers arrived in the American Southwest during the 1500s and 1600s, coming into contact with Native Americans with increasing frequency. However, it was not until the 1800s, with the discovery of gold and silver in the Colorado high country, that the Ute lifestyle changed dramatically. A rush of humanity in search of wealth soon drove out the indigenous peoples.

Precious metals were first discovered in Summit County in the early 1800s. From that moment on, the county would never be the same. Tents, mining shacks, and every other conceivable kind of shelter appeared in the high valleys as prospectors chipped away at mountains in eager pursuit of the mother lode. Along with the miners came assay offices, hardware stores, brothels, saloons, churches, and rail lines. The population swelled as mining towns sprang up in valleys and basins throughout the Colorado Rockies.

Surviving the notorious boom-and-bust cycles inherently associated with mining, Summit County has remained one of Colorado's most profitable mountain areas. Today, Summit County's scenic beauty draws explorers seeking the natural treasures of the great outdoors.

The Summit Huts Association is based in Breckenridge, the southernmost town in Summit County. One of Colorado's busiest resort communities, Breckenridge offers year-round recreation ranging from nordic and alpine skiing to mountain biking and fly-fishing, as well as sailing and kayaking on Lake Dillon.

With the growing popularity of hut-to-hut skiing, especially the success of the 10th Mountain Division Hut Association, skiers in Summit County decided that a hut system connecting the eastern and western parts of the county would be appropriate and popular. When the system is completed, backcountry skiers will be able to tour from the Keystone area to the Copper Mountain area near Vail Pass, spending each night in a warm, comfortable cabin. From Copper Mountain, skiers then will be able to connect with the 10th Mountain Division hut system and ski continuously hut-to-hut all the way to Aspen, across the heart of the Colorado Rockies.

The first hut completed in this system was Janet's Cabin, which immediately became one of Colorado's most frequented nordic lodges. Francie's Cabin, the closest hut to Breckenridge, opened in January of 1995. Future plans for this hut system include nine more cabins scattered throughout Summit County.

Carrie Thompson and Dan Schaefer at Janet's Cabin, Summit Huts.

11 FRANCIE'S CABIN

Francie's Cabin, the second structure to be constructed in the Summit Huts Association system, opened in January 1995. This lovely and roomy log shelter sits at treeline in the Crystal Creek drainage. Stunning alpine peaks and colorful sunrises lie just beyond the warmth of the crackling wood stove. Francie's cabin is a memorial to Francis Lockwood Bailey, a Breckenridge resident who died in a plane crash.

The hut's design is similar to Janet's Cabin, with a winter sleeping capacity of 20 people and a summer capacity of 14. During the winter the cabin is accessible via a classic and moderate cross-country trail, although the last mile does climb quite steeply.

Once at the cabin skiers are within a hundred yards of true alpine terrain and its attendant hazards, i.e., avalanches. Consequently, touring around the hut is limited and is only recommended for experienced groups of skiers who have the proper equipment and necessary knowledge for traveling in avalanche country. So exercise caution.

Francie's Cabin is open during the summer for bikers and hikers and is accessible to people with disabilities, although the approach road is rough and requires a high-clearance, four-wheel-drive vehicle. The route to Wheeler Flats Trailhead (Tour 11B) is also rough and is really only appro-

Francie's Cabin opened in 1995.

priate for summer hikers; it is not recommended for biking or skiing. Also note that the location of Francie's Cabin does not lend itself to true hut-to-hut travel. Make reservations through the 10th Mountain Division Hut Association (see Appendix A).

TOUR 11A   BURRO TRAIL TRAILHEAD

Difficulty:	Intermediate	
Time:	3 to 5 hours	
Distance:	4 miles	
Elevations:	Trailhead 9,680', Hut 11,360', +1,680'	
Avalanche Terrain:	None	
Maps:	USGS 7.5': Breckenridge, 1988	
	National Forest: Arapaho	
	Trails Illustrated: Map #109 (Breckenridge/ Tennessee Pass)	
	Summit Huts Association Map: Francie's Cabin	
	See map pages 74 and 77	

The trailhead, summer or winter, for the Burro Trail is at the base of Breckenridge Ski Area's Peak 9, located on the south side of the Beaver Run Resort near the southwestern edge of town. Keep in mind that there is no "official" designated parking for Francie's Cabin, and because there is no overnight parking allowed at the E lot (the closest parking area) in winter, parking instructions are different for winter and summer.

To reach the drop-off spot for the trail (winter or summer), drive to the southern end of Main Street in Breckenridge and turn right at a stop light, onto Park Street. Head west and turn left onto Village Road, which leads directly to the Beaver Run Resort. Continue uphill until you reach the ski area and a large parking lot to the south of the Beaver Run complex. Enter this lot and cross to the south side. You can park here in the summer.

In the winter you must park in one of the lower town lots and ride a shuttle bus back up to the trailhead. Drop off your gear near the trailhead, following the directions above, and leaving someone to watch over it, then drive back down Village Road to Park Street. Turn left onto Park Street and proceed north, past Ski Hill Road and the Miner's parking lot on the right, and park in the Tailings parking lot. Now you need to catch the Beaver Run shuttle bus back to the trailhead.

If downhill skiers are not yet parking at the Tailings and no shuttle buses are servicing this lot, then walk south to the Miner's lot bus stop. If the Miner's lot is not open yet, walk south to the intersection of Park Street and Ski Hill Road. From the bus stop on Ski Hill Road, in front of the FirstBank, take either the Breckenridge Town Trolley or the ski area bus back up to the Beaver Run Resort and the trailhead. This is all a test; if you can negotiate these parking procedures then skiing to the hut will be no problem! Note: Be sure to leave the parking permit that is part of your reservation packet in the window of your vehicle; make copies of the permit for all of the cars in your group.

When you are ready to hit the trail, leave the parking area and head south, past the maze for the Beaver Run quad chair, to the ski school area. Watch out for skiers coming downhill! Near the creek and the ski school yurt there is a Forest Service sign marking the trailhead. Launch onto the trail, which is marked by blue diamonds, cross the creek and begin skiing south along the eastern edge of the creek. The trail runs along this side of the creek for 0.7 mile. Be sure to avoid a left fork that goes uphill to a plowed road and huge homes. Instead, take the right fork and ski past a small, yellow sign.

Continue on the trail, gradually ascending through forest for 1.2 miles until the trail veers west. The trail climbs a small hill and intercepts an old

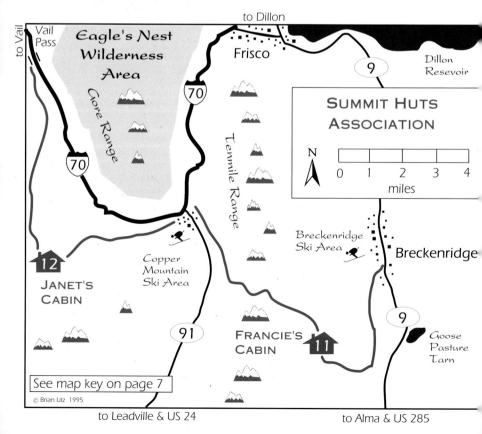

jeep trail. Turn left (south) onto this trail, which is marked by a diamond with a small black arrow. Follow this obvious, marked trail south on a very gradual ascending traverse for 2.4 miles until you reach another trail intersection. Three trails lead off from this intersection: a trail marked by blue diamonds leads southwest to Spruce Creek Road; downhill to the east is a steep trail; and uphill to the west is the continuation of the trail to the hut. It is unmarked and steep. (The route back to Breckenridge is marked by a Burro Trail sign.)

Shift into low gear (you may want skins for the rest of the climb) and begin the final climb to the hut, about 1 mile. The trail contours and climbs west into the Crystal Creek drainage, where it intercepts the aqueduct road on the south, marked by a "No Snowmobilers" sign. Continue on the trail past a "Motorized Restriction" sign, break through a final stand of trees, and enter a clearing near treeline. There are two posts with brown trail diamonds just beyond the edge of the trees. From this spot Francie's Cabin is a long stone's throw away. Turn to the north and climb up through the clearing, over a hill crest, and ski to the hut.

TOUR 11B   WHEELER FLATS TRAILHEAD

Difficulty:	Advanced	🚶🚶
Time:	5 to 8 hours	
Distance:	6.5 miles	
Elevations:	Trailhead 10,580', Hut 11,360', +1,300'/-200'	
Avalanche Note:	Not recommended as a winter route	
Maps:	USGS 7.5': Copper Mountain, 1987;	
	Vail Pass,1987	
	National Forest: Arapaho	
	Trails Illustrated: Map #108 (Vail/Frisco/Dillon);	
	Map #109 (Breckenridge/Tennessee Pass)	
	10th Mountain: Resolution Mountain	
	See map pages 74 and 77	

The Wheeler Trail crosses the Tenmile Range through a pass between Peak Eight and Peak Nine. At 12,390 feet, far above Breckenridge and Copper Mountain, this passage can be very taxing. It is recommended as a summer-use-only route, due to the high avalanche hazard at the pass. Get an early start, for this trail is exposed to the vagaries of mountain weather.

This tour begins near the intersection of I-70 and CO 91 at Copper Mountain (immediately south of I-70). Turn east off CO 91 onto the frontage road. Then veer north, proceeding 0.4 mile to an obvious parking area. Leave the parking area, pass the Forest Service sign, and begin the Wheeler Trail by crossing Tenmile Creek via a footbridge. After the bridge, turn east and follow the trail south along a gas-line road until you begin climbing the Wheeler Trail/Colorado Trail. (Be sure not to follow the Colorado Trail northeast to Frisco.)

This is an easy route following a well-traveled summer trail. Be sure to continue on a southeast course over the Tenmile Range. From the top of the pass the trail descends steeply off the eastern side and continues southeast on a traverse across the slopes of Peak Nine and Peak Ten. Once in the Crystal Creek drainage, the trail intercepts the Crystal Trail, then the Crystal Creek four-wheel-drive road. Follow this road to Francie's Cabin.

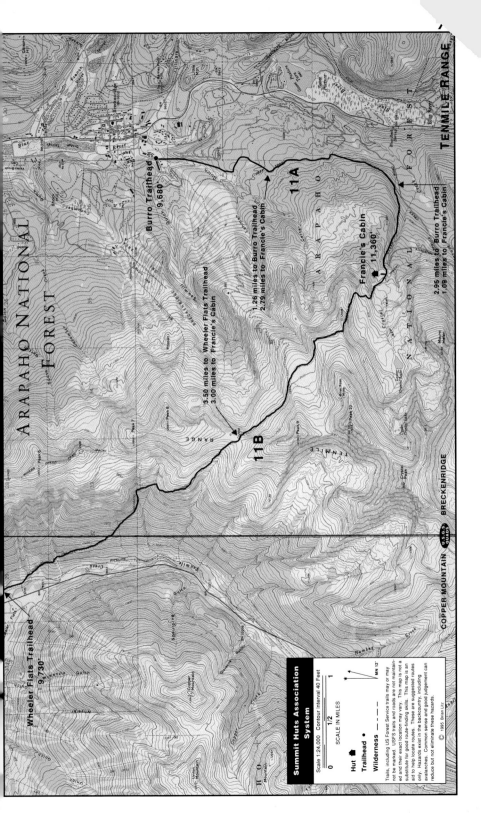

ARAPAHO NATIONAL FOREST

TENMILE RANGE

ARAPAHO NATIONAL FOREST

Burro Trailhead 9,680

11A

Francie's Cabin 11,360'

1.26 miles to Burro Trailhead
2.79 miles to Francie's Cabin

3.50 miles to Wheeler Flats Trailhead
3.00 miles to Francie's Cabin

11B

TENMILE RANGE

2.96 miles to Burro Trailhead
1.09 miles to Francie's Cabin

Wheeler Flats Trailhead 9,730

COPPER MOUNTAIN

BRECKENRIDGE

U.S.G.S. QUAD

Summit Huts Association System

Scale 1:24,000   Contour Interval 40 Feet

0   1/2   1

SCALE IN MILES

MN 12°

Hut
Trailhead •
Wilderness — — — —

© 1995 Brian Litz

Trails, including US Forest Service trails may or may not be marked. USFS trails and roads are not maintained and their exact location may vary. This map is not a substitute for good route-finding skills. This map is an aid to locate routes and scales. These are approximate routes only. Hazards exist in the back-country, including avalanches. Common sense and good judgement can reduce but not eliminate these hazards.

12   JANET'S CABIN

Janet's Cabin is a memorial to Janet Boyd Tyler, who was a colorful fixture on the Colorado ski scene for many decades. The cabin is at the head of Guller Creek, adjacent to the Colorado Trail. Built in 1990, Janet's Cabin is one of the most popular backcountry huts in Colorado and may be crowded on weekends. Much of its popularity is due to the fact that the trailhead is a very short drive from the center of Summit County, Vail, and the Denver metro area.

The relatively short and uncomplicated tour to the hut also contributes to the number of visitors, as skiers of all abilities can ski to Janet's Cabin. The hut's location allows intermediate and expert skiers access to the fine bowl skiing near Searle Pass and Sugarloaf Peak, an area used extensively for winter training by the U.S. Army's 10th Mountain Division ski troops during World War II.

This roomy structure is state-of-the-art and fully equipped to sleep 20 skiers. The main floor is huge and has couches and tables for several groups,

Dan Schaefer relaxes at Janet's Cabin, Summit County huts.

as well as plenty of cooking space. Also located on the main floor are composting toilets, a ski/boot room, and a large south-facing deck. (The cabin cannot be accessed via the south deck, however, so skiers need to enter the cabin from the north entrance.) There is a wood-burning stove for heat, electric lights, a gas cook stove, and cookware. Upstairs, there are several large bedrooms. This luxurious hut even has a sauna; the Nancy Dayton Memorial Sauna was airlifted into the cabin in October 1991.

Janet's Cabin is not open for day use. Nor is it open for summer use, due to wildlife habitat studies nearby. Make reservations through the 10th Mountain Division Hut Association (see Appendix A).

TOUR 12A   UNION CREEK TRAILHEAD

Difficulty:	Novice/Intermediate
Time:	3 to 5 hours
Distance:	4.6 miles
Elevations:	Trailhead 9,820', Hut 11,610', +1,970'/-180'
Avalanche Note:	None
Maps:	USGS 7.5': Copper Mountain, 1987
	National Forest: Arapaho
	Trails Illustrated: Map #108 (Vail/Frisco/Dillon);
	Map #109 (Breckenridge/Tennessee Pass)
	10th Mountain: Resolution Mountain
	See map pages 74 and 84-85

The Union Creek Trailhead is the most popular route to Janet's Cabin. The route runs up the center of a long, almost treeless valley where navigation is easy and skiers will rarely need to break trail. However, this route is a true backcountry trip to a high-altitude cabin; don't let the high-skier volume lull you into nonchalance. Be prepared and get an early start.

The most confusing part of the trip is finding the parking area, getting to the shuttle buses, and finding your way up and out of the Copper Mountain downhill ski area.

To reach the trailhead, drive to the Copper Mountain Resort. Turn west into the main entrance, then take a left into the first parking lot. Drive to the north end of the lot and look for the area with Janet's Cabin overnight parking signs. These parking spots are immediately north and east of the shuttle bus stop and transportation system building. Hop on a shuttle bus (buses run between 7 A.M. and 10 P.M.) and ride to the farthest stop west, which is at the nordic center and shuttle turnaround point. The route begins on the west side of the nordic center building.

Ascend the west edge of the ski area until you reach a public access trail that traverses into Guller Creek. This ascent can be accomplished by one of two methods. One option is to strap on your skins and climb a ski run named West Tenmile Trail (while dodging downhill skiers and keeping a sharp eye out for the nordic trail entrance). The second and more popular choice is to present your hut reservation slip (good for one complimentary ride) to either the ticket window or the lift operators and ride up the K or L lift to the top. From the top of the lift, backcountry skiers descend West Tenmile Trail for a few hundred feet to the access trail. The point of entry for the trail is marked with a blue diamond and a Forest Service sign. Finding this trail is tricky, since the entrance is in the forest on the west edge of the ski run just below the top of the lifts; most skiers usually drop down too far.

Follow the nordic trail into the woods on a steep drop, then along a traverse into the Guller Creek drainage. You will intersect the Colorado Trail/Guller Creek Trail at a point where the trail crosses Guller Creek. A sign reading "Vail Pass/Backcountry Uses in Winter" marks the intersection.

For the next 0.5 to 1 mile, the trail cruises up Guller Creek first on the northwest side of the creek, then crossing to the southeast side midway through a large meadow. As you approach the head of the valley, marked by steep, forested slopes, begin a traversing ascent along the forest's edge. Continue along the southeast edge of the valley until you enter a distinct treeless gully that climbs steeply south toward alpine peaks and bowls. Janet's Cabin, its roof visible to a sharp eye, is at the top of this gully on the right, hidden in a stand of trees.

TOUR 12B   VAIL PASS TRAILHEAD

Difficulty:	Advanced
Time:	4 to 7 hours
Distance:	5.7 miles
Elevations:	Trailhead 10,580', Hut 11,610', +1,300'/-200'
Avalanche Note:	Route crosses avalanche runout zones; can be dangerous during high-hazard periods
Maps:	USGS 7.5': Copper Mountain, 1987; Vail Pass, 1987
	National Forest: Arapaho
	Trails Illustrated: Map #108 (Vail/Frisco/Dillon); Map #109 (Breckenridge/Tennessee Pass)
	10th Mountain: Resolution Mountain
	See map pages 74, 84-85, and 88-89

Decidedly more difficult than the standard Guller Creek Trail to Janet's Cabin, this less-traveled route is very enjoyable and scenic. The trail is a rolling, high-altitude traverse that gives skiers a taste of treeline skiing, as well as more challenging route finding. Vail Pass also makes a nice trailhead for those wishing to ski to Janet's Cabin and exit via Guller Creek, which is part of the Janet's Cabin to Shrine Mountain Inn route (see Tour 12D)

To reach the trailhead, drive on I-70 to the Vail Pass exit (Exit 190), which is 15 miles east of the town of Vail, or 5 miles west of Copper Mountain. From the exit, proceed west to the overnight parking area above the rest stop building.

Begin the tour by walking down to the lowest part of the parking area. Ski south across West Tenmile Creek and begin a moderate traverse that contours south then southwest down into Wilder Gulch. Cross Wilder Creek and begin the longest ascent of the tour by skiing southwest up the blunt northeast ridge of Elevation Point 12,207'. This ridge forms the southeast boundary of Wilder Gulch.

After gaining roughly 700 feet of elevation, the ridge begins to narrow noticeably near a shoulder. From here, the route leaves the ridge and begins to climb through the forest, in generally the same direction, below the steep southeast side of the ridge.

Make a dogleg around a subtle shoulder directly below Elevation Point 12,207'. The route then traverses around the head of Stafford Creek. Cross over a low point on the westernmost part of the ridge (near treeline) that separates Guller Creek and Stafford Creek. Make the final gentle descent to Janet's Cabin. As you approach the cabin, continue to traverse directly toward the highest reaches of Guller Creek, just above treeline.

TOUR 12C   JANET'S CABIN TO FOWLER/HILLIARD HUT

Difficulty:	Advanced
Time:	4 to 6 hours
Distance:	5.5 miles
Elevations:	J Cabin, 11,610', F/H Hut, 11,500', +950'/-40'
Avalanche Note:	Route crosses avalanche slopes; prone to skier-triggered avalanches during high-hazard periods
Maps:	USGS 7.5': Copper Mountain, 1987; Pando, 1987
	National Forest: Arapaho, White River
	Trails Illustrated: Map #108 (Vail/Frisco/Dillon); Map #109 (Breckenridge/Tennessee Pass)
	10th Mountain: Resolution Mountain
	See map pages 84-85 and 88-89

Machine Gun Ridge runs north from Sugarloaf Peak. During World War II the 10th Mountain Division ski troops trained in this area by fortifying the ridge with a machine-gun pit and sniper positions. In winter they often lived in snow caves on the ridge. (For more information on the history of the 10th Mountain Division, see Appendix G).

Machine Gun Ridge is not an official 10th Mountain Division hut-to-hut trail, but it makes for a very direct route between Janet's Cabin and the Fowler/Hilliard Hut. Consider this route only when avalanche and weather conditions are stable. Strong beginner or intermediate skiers should be accompanied by skiers versed in untracked, backcountry skiing.

From Janet's Cabin, follow the Vail Pass/Janet's Cabin route (see Tour 12B) west for a little over 0.5 mile. Then strike off due west, aiming for the 12,140-foot low spot north of Sugarloaf Peak. Several dangerous slopes threaten the eastern aspect of this ridge; however, there are a series of small benches that access the pass. To find them, ski directly toward the low spot which forms a subtle, low-angle ramp up to the pass.

Once on the pass, follow the ridge north, over Elevation Point 12,293' and across a flat saddle, then begin climbing toward Elevation Point 12,370'. Contour west about 200 feet below the top of Elevation Point 12,370'. Begin a descending traverse to the road switchback below the south side of Ptarmigan Pass. Once on the road, descend west until you can turn onto the main Resolution Creek Road (FR 751). Begin climbing this road, contouring around the south face of Ptarmigan Hill. Follow the road for 2 miles to

JANET'S CABIN **83**

the forested pass east of the hut, where the road intersects with the Shrine Mountain Inn Trail from the north. From the wooded pass, follow a trail along the ridge to the southwest, past a gate and over a small knoll to the Fowler/Hilliard Hut.

TOUR 12D JANET'S CABIN TO SHRINE MOUNTAIN INN

Difficulty:	Advanced
Time:	5 to 8 hours
Distance:	8.4 miles
Elevations:	J Cabin 11,610', SM Inn, 11,209', +829/-1,320'
Avalanche Note:	Route crosses avalanche runout zones; can be dangerous during high-hazard periods
Maps:	USGS 7.5': Copper Mountain, 1987; Vail Pass, 1987
	National Forest: Arapaho
	Trails Illustrated: Map #108 (Vail/Frisco/Dillon); Map #109 (Breckenridge/Tennessee Pass)
	10th Mountain: Resolution Mountain
	See map pages 84-85 and 88-89

Skiing between these two huts makes for a long day; be sure to get an early start. The route combines Tour12B (Vail Pass Trailhead to Janet's Cabin) and Tour 13A (Vail Pass Trailhead to Shrine Mountain Inn). Refer to those tours for complete descriptions.

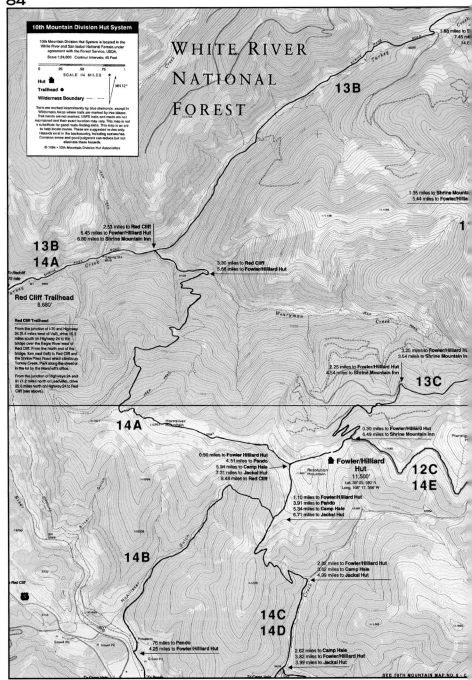

10th Mountain Division Hut System

10th Mountain Division Hut System is located in the White River and San Isabel National Forests under agreement with the Forest Service, USDA.

Scale 1:24,000   Contour Intervals: 40 Feet

0   .25   .50   .75   1
SCALE IN MILES

★ MN 12°

■ Hut
● Trailhead
Wilderness Boundary ———

Trails are marked intermittently by blue diamonds, except in Wilderness Areas where trails are marked by tree blazes. Trail heads are not marked. USFS trails and roads are not maintained and their exact location may vary. This map is not a substitute for good route-finding skills. This map is an aid to help locate routes. These are suggested routes only. Hazards exist in the backcountry, including avalanches. Common sense and good judgment can reduce but not eliminate these hazards.

© 1994 • 10th Mountain Division Hut Association

WHITE RIVER NATIONAL FOREST

13B

1.88 miles to S
7.45 mi
14E

1.35 miles to Shrine Mounta
5.44 miles to Fowler/Hilla

1

2.53 miles to **Red Cliff**
6.45 miles to **Fowler/Hilliard Hut**
6.80 miles to **Shrine Mountain Inn**

**13B
14A**

Gaging Sta

To Redcliff
.79 mile

3.30 miles to **Red Cliff**
5.68 miles to **Fowler/Hilliard Hut**

Red Cliff Trailhead
8,680'

Wearyman

Red Cliff Trailhead

From the junction of I-70 and Highway 24 (5.4 miles west of Vail), drive 10.3 miles south on Highway 24 to the bridge over the Eagle River west of Red Cliff. From the North end of the bridge, turn east (left) to Red Cliff and the Shrine Pass Road which climbs up Turkey Creek. Park along the street or in the lot by the Marshall's office.

From the junction of Highways 24 and 91 (1.2 miles north of Leadville), drive 22.6 miles north on Highway 24 to Red Cliff (see above).

3.25 miles to **Fowler/Hilliard Hut**
3.54 miles to **Shrine Mountain Inn**

2.25 miles to **Fowler/Hilliard Hut**
4.54 miles to **Shrine Mountain Inn**

13C

14A

Hornsilver Mountain

0.30 miles to **Fowler/Hilliard Hut**
6.49 miles to **Shrine Mountain Inn**

0.50 miles to **Fowler Hilliard Hut**
4.51 miles to **Pando**
5.94 miles to **Camp Hale**
7.31 miles to **Jackal Hut**
8.48 miles to **Red Cliff**

■ **Fowler/Hilliard Hut**
11,500'
Lat. 39° 29.580' N
Long. 106° 17.356' W

Resolution Mountain

**12C
14E**

1.10 miles to **Fowler/Hilliard Hut**
3.91 miles to **Pando**
5.34 miles to **Camp Hale**
6.71 miles to **Jackal Hut**

14B

2.82 miles to **Fowler/Hilliard Hut**
3.62 miles to **Camp Hale**
4.99 miles to **Jackal Hut**

Red Cliff

.76 miles to **Pando**
4.25 miles to **Fowler/Hilliard Hut**

**14C
14D**

2.62 miles to **Camp Hale**
3.82 miles to **Fowler/Hilliard Hut**
3.99 miles to **Jackal Hut**

Gravel Pit

To Camp Hale

SEE 10TH MOUNTAIN MAP NO. 6 • C

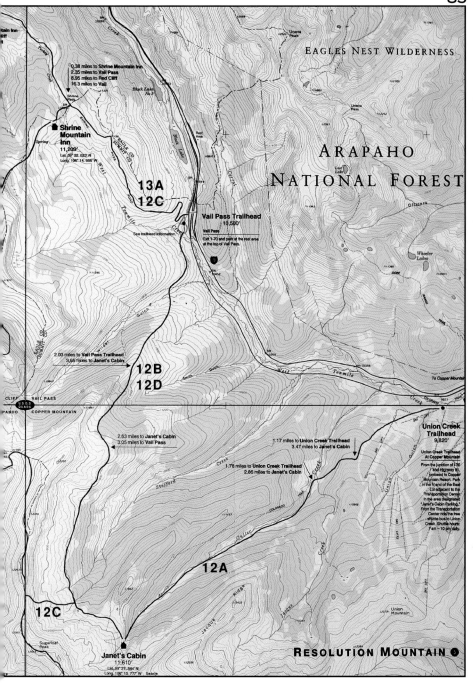

EAGLES NEST WILDERNESS

ARAPAHO
NATIONAL FOREST

0.38 miles to Shrine Mountain Inn
2.35 miles to Vail Pass
8.95 miles to Red Cliff
16.3 miles to Vail

Uneva
Peak

Uneva
Pass

🏠 **Shrine
Mountain
Inn**
11,209'
Lat. 39° 32.622 N
Long. 106° 14.966 W

Wheeler
Lakes

**13A
12C**

Vail Pass Trailhead
10,580'
Vail Pass
Exit I-70 and park at the rest area
at the top of Vail Pass.

See trailhead information.

To Copper Mountain

2.03 miles to Vail Pass Trailhead
3.65 miles to Janet's Cabin

**12B
12D**

CLIFF   VAIL PASS
PANDO   COPPER MOUNTAIN

2.63 miles to Janet's Cabin
3.05 miles to Vail Pass

1.17 miles to Union Creek Trailhead
3.47 miles to Janet's Cabin

1.78 miles to Union Creek Trailhead
2.86 miles to Janet's Cabin

**Union Creek
Trailhead**
9,820'

Union Creek Trailhead
At Copper Mountain

From the junction of I-70
and Highway 91,
proceed to Copper
Mountain Resort. Park
in the lot of the East
Lot adjacent to the
Transportation Center
in the area designated
"Janet's Cabin Parking."
From the Transportation
Center ride the free
shuttle bus to Union
Creek. Shuttle hours:
7 am – 10 pm daily.

Union
Mountain

12A

12C

Sugarloaf
Peak

Janet's Cabin
11,610'
Lat. 39° 27.844 N
Long. 106° 13.777 W   Searle

RESOLUTION MOUNTAIN ◉

10TH MOUNTAIN DIVISION HUT ASSOCIATION

The 10th Mountain Division huts have become synonymous with the finest that backcountry hut skiing has to offer. Situated between the mountain communities of Aspen, Vail, and Leadville, the 10th Mountain Division hut-to-hut system is the most extensive backcountry hut system in the United States, if not all of North America. In fact, the 10th Mountain Division huts are so well known that it is nearly impossible to open an outdoor travel/adventure magazine and not find a reference to this incredible system.

The hut system is named in honor of the soldiers of the U.S. Army's 10th Mountain Division, an elite ski corps commissioned during World War II for duty in the European Alps. For three winters, from 1942 until 1945, some 14,000 soldiers were based at Camp Hale, the division's training center north of Leadville. Wearing seven-foot-long skis, 90-pound packs, and camouflaged in winter whites, these "phantoms of the snow" ranged throughout the mountains on maneuvers in the Gore and Sawatch ranges. On windswept ridges in temperatures far below zero, they engaged in military exercises and mock warfare as they trained for combat against the Nazis.

When the war ended, a number of men returned to the mountains they had come to know so well, and many of these veterans were the moving forces behind the Colorado ski industry. Today little remains of Camp Hale, just the concrete foundations of old army barracks. But the memory and the spirit of the 10th Mountain Division soldiers live on. For those interested in more information on the history of the 10th Mountain Division, refer to *Ski the High Trail: World War II Ski Troopers in the High Colorado Rockies*, the memoirs of Private Harris Dusenbery (see Appendix G).

The first hut in this system was built in 1982. Today there are 20 huts (13 owned by the 10th Mountain Division Hut Association and seven more by private groups) and several hundred miles of trails providing a wide array of skiing, hiking, and mountain biking adventures for backcountry enthusiasts of every ability and temperament. The 10th Mountain Division Hut Association located the huts so that nearly all are accessible to intermediate-level skiers. Many hut routes are also within the abilities of experienced novice skiers, while a few are reached only via strenuous or technically demanding trails. While avalanche hazards do exist, the routes were planned to avoid the most threatening slopes.

The majority of the trails linking the 10th Mountain Division huts are classic cross-country tours through dense evergreen forests. The hut association envisioned a comprehensive series of trail markers (blue diamonds) along the most popular routes. However, it is impossible — and unnecessary — to staple markers to each and every tree. Indeed, the trails often pass through meadows and above treeline as well as through federally designated wilderness areas, where it is illegal to mark trails permanently.

Each individual participating in a trip to 10th Mountain Division huts must be prepared for serious backcountry travel, must understand basic route finding, map and compass reading, and must have at least a rudimentary knowledge of avalanche hazards and rescue protocol. Anticipating a warm shelter at the end of the trail, too many wilderness skiers travel imprudently and ill prepared. In the mountains an ounce of prevention and thoughtful planning is worth a pound of cure (and frozen extremities!). Several well-qualified guide services offer a variety of trips throughout the year. If you are new to the backcountry, consider hiring a guide for a satisfying and safe wilderness experience.

Each of the 10th Mountain Division huts is thoroughly equipped, including a wood-burning stove for heating, firewood, outhouse facilities, electric lights, propane cook stoves, and all the cookware you could ever hope to use. Huts generally accommodate 15 to 19 people. The most common floor plan divides the huts into ground-level living and cooking areas and upstairs sleeping quarters. The sleeping quarters come complete with mattresses and are generally separated into several bedrooms and an open, yet partitioned, community sleeping area.

Remember that this is a communal living experience, and you will most probably be sharing your hut with other skiers, hikers, or bikers. If your group is uncomfortable with this reality, consider getting a large group

Skiing to Aspen from McNamara Hut through Van Horn Park, with the Maroon Bells-Snowmass Wilderness in the distance.

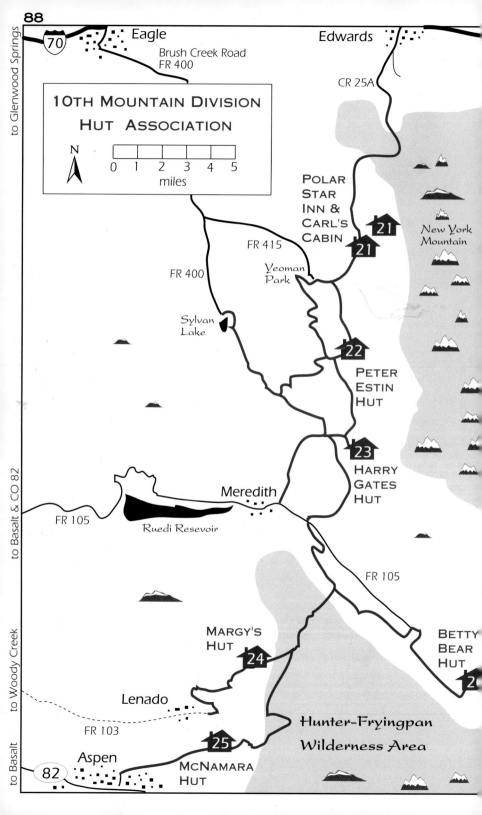

to Glenwood Springs

70

Eagle

Brush Creek Road
FR 400

Edwards

CR 25A

10TH MOUNTAIN DIVISION
HUT ASSOCIATION

N

0 1 2 3 4 5
miles

POLAR
STAR
INN &
CARL'S
CABIN

21

21

New York
Mountain

FR 415

FR 400

Yeoman
Park

Sylvan
Lake

22

PETER
ESTIN
HUT

23

HARRY
GATES
HUT

to Basalt & CO 82

Meredith

FR 105

Ruedi Resevoir

FR 105

MARGY'S
HUT

24

to Woody Creek

Lenado

FR 103

BETTY
BEAR
HUT

2

Hunter-Fryingpan

Wilderness Area

to Basalt

82

Aspen

25

McNAMARA
HUT

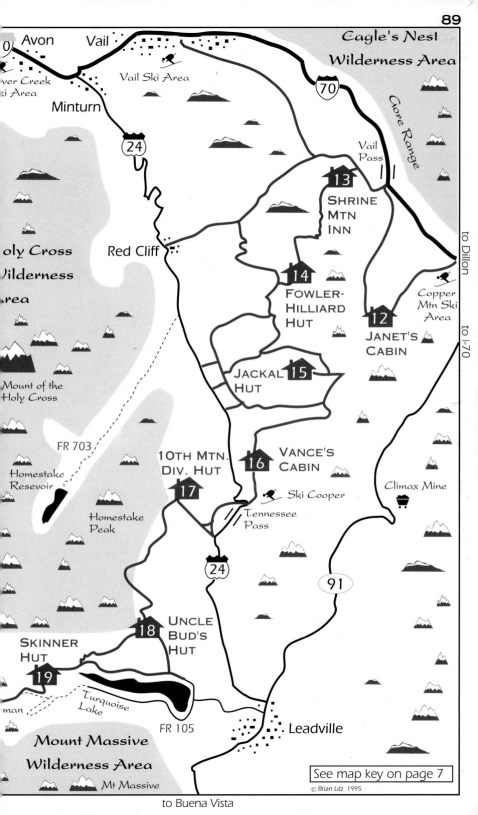

Avon   Vail

Eagle's Nest
Wilderness Area

ver Creek
ki Area

Vail Ski Area

Minturn

I-70

Gore Range

to Dillon

to I-70

Vail
Pass

24

13

SHRINE
MTN
INN

oly Cross
Wilderness
rea

Red Cliff

14

FOWLER-
HILLIARD
HUT

Copper
Mtn Ski
Area

12

JANET'S
CABIN

Mount of the
Holy Cross

15

JACKAL
HUT

FR 703

Homestake
Resevoir

10TH MTN.
DIV. HUT

16

VANCE'S
CABIN

Climax Mine

17

Homestake
Peak

Ski Cooper

Tennessee
Pass

24

91

18

UNCLE
BUD'S
HUT

SKINNER
HUT

19

man

Turquoise
Lake

FR 105

Leadville

Mount Massive

Wilderness Area

Mt Massive

See map key on page 7

© Brian Litz 1995

to Buena Vista

together to rent an entire hut or going to a different hut system with smaller huts. The 10th Mountain huts are open during the winter and summer months, but not during spring or late fall. The exception to this rule is McNamara Hut, which is closed during the summer.

A word on trailhead parking: Over the past few years there has been increasing vandalism to cars parked at the trailheads, especially the South Camp Hale Trailhead, Crane Park, Turquoise Lake, and the summer Skinner Hut Trailhead on the south side of Turquoise Lake. The Turquoise Lake parking area has now been moved two miles back down the to a location just east of the Arkansas River/Tennessee Creek and the Denver & Rio Grande Western Railroad tracks. This parking lot is more open, lighted, and is on the sheriff's patrol route. Nevertheless, do not leave valuables in your car and, if possible, do not leave expensive cars at the lots mentioned above.

And finally, in the past many skiers visiting the western 10th Mountain Division huts stayed at or took advantage of the shuttle services offered by the Diamond J Ranch. Recently the Diamond J was sold and became the Diamond Joy Retreat. It appears that they will not be working with the system's visitors. There is a bed-and-breakfast downriver, at Meredith, called the Double Diamond, and they are setting themselves up to fill the void left by the Diamond J.

For reservations call the 10th Mountain Division Hut Association and for information on the Double Diamond Bed & Breakfast refer to Appendix A.

13 SHRINE MOUNTAIN INN

The Shrine Mountain Inn, above Shrine Pass and a few miles west of Vail Pass, is a perfect overnight weekend getaway or base camp for day tours in the area. There are plenty of powdery glades, airy ridges, and backcountry roads to explore nearby. The rolling landscape features open meadows with thick stands of trees. Shrine Mountain Inn is a great choice for skiers of all abilities. The short, easy approach is accessible to anyone — skier, hiker, or biker — interested in visiting the inn.

The Shrine Mountain Inn is actually three individual structures. The main structure, Jay's Cabin, is a magnificent lodge that sleeps 12. Guests share two indoor bathrooms and a kitchen. A potbellied stove provides heat. There are electric lights, a sauna, and a large, south-facing porch with great views of the Gore and Tenmile ranges.

The second structure, Chuck's Cabin, features two separate units; each sleeps six and is equipped with a bath. Its separate upstairs and downstairs quarters can be reserved individually. The upstairs must be reserved entirely by one group, while the lower quarters can (and will) be filled by multiple groups if necessary by the 10th Mountain reservationists.

The third and newest structure is Walter's Cabin. It is similar to Chuck's Cabin and has the same reservation requirements as well. All three cabins are open year round. From July 4th through Labor Day the restaurant also serves lunch and dinner to day visitors. For reservations, call the 10th Mountain Division Hut Association (see Appendix A).

TOUR 13A   VAIL PASS TRAILHEAD

Difficulty:	Novice
Time:	2 to 4 hours
Distance:	2.7 miles
Elevations:	Trailhead 10,580', Hut 11,209', +629'/-20'
Avalanche Note:	None
Maps:	USGS 7.5': Vail Pass, 1987
	National Forest: Arapaho, White River
	Trails Illustrated: Map #108 (Vail/Frisco/Dillon)
	10th Mountain: Resolution Mountain
	See map pages 84-85 and 88-89

The Shrine Pass Road, which travels between Vail Pass and Red Cliff, has been a popular recreation area for decades. The name comes from views of the Mount of the Holy Cross as seen from several points along the way. At one time, there was interest in building a place of worship near the summit of the pass, but this never came to fruition. In summer the road is pleasant but often crowded. In winter the route is one of the most popular ski tours in the state. The road climbs 2.5 miles to Shrine Pass and then descends continuously into Red Cliff. If the road surface has been packed by snowmobilers, the trip can be very fast and very exciting.

The trail to the Shrine Mountain Inn simply follows the road from Vail Pass to the summit of Shrine Pass, then turns southwest into the woods, following a trail 0.3 mile to the inn. This route is one of the easiest, most beautiful hut tours in this book.

To reach the trailhead, drive on I-70 to the Vail Pass exit (Exit 190), which is 15 miles east of Vail, or 5 miles west of Copper Mountain. From the exit, proceed west to the overnight parking area above the rest stop building.

From the parking area, walk north along the road toward I-70. Where the road turns east to the on/off ramps, the Shrine Pass Road (CR 16) begins to the west. Ski past a Forest Service winter use/avalanche information sign and begin the ascent to the pass. Head west and north up a treeless switchback, then begin a long traverse west, then northwest, above West Tenmile Creek.

After 1.7 miles, the trail contours near the top of Black Lakes Ridge, crosses a saddlelike depression, then makes a very gradual descent across a meadow to Shrine Pass. (This is a subtle pass near a White River National

Shrine Mountain Inn, a backcountry lodge near Vail Pass.

Forest sign.) Turn onto a well-traveled road, heading southwest into the woods. The inn is 0.3 mile from Shrine Pass.

RECOMMENDED DAY TOUR 1: Black Lakes Ridge is the treeless ridge directly northeast of the Shrine Pass Road. Leave the inn and return to the road. Turning toward Vail Pass, ski southeast along the road for 0.7 mile, then onto the ridge. This gentle ridge is a perfect spot to cruise around. It is also possible for experienced skiers to drop off the east face into the Black Lakes drainage for some superb telemark skiing. From the ridge, ski south along a road back to the Vail Pass parking area, then return to the inn. The basic ridge tour is suitable for novices, while the descent of the east face is recommended for advanced skiers.

RECOMMENDED DAY TOUR 2: Between Shrine Pass and the Vail ski area is the famous Commando Run, one of the most difficult tours in the state. This tour drops northwest, down along the Shrine Pass Road, into Turkey Creek for 1.5 miles. Turn north onto the Timber Creek Road (marked) and traverse up along this road to the northwest, until the road splits on a wooded saddle. Contour west and southwest on the main (left) fork toward Lime Creek. After several hundred feet, begin a steep climb through the woods to the top of Elevation Point 11,611'. Once on top of the ridge, follow it west and then north, rolling along the crest until a long descent deposits you on Two Elk Pass, near the eastern boundary of the back bowls of the Vail downhill ski area.

Ascend north across the windswept south face of Red ("Siberia") Peak, then ski down its northeast ridge. Descend west into Mill Creek through unrivaled backcountry terrain and gain the Mill Creek Road. Follow the road to the Vail ski area and, finally, ski to the bottom of the downhill area via the trail of your choice.

This tour is 18.7 miles from Vail Pass to the bottom of the ski area. Gaining over 2,000 feet of elevation and losing over 5,000 feet, it is an advanced run that requires a shuttle car in Vail (fee parking). Note: Skiers taking this tour need an additional map, USGS 7.5-minute Vail East, as well as maps noted under Tour 13B.

TOUR 13B   RED CLIFF TRAILHEAD

Difficulty:	Intermediate	𝍅 ᚶ 𝍆
Time:	5 to 8 hours	
Distance:	9.3 miles	
Elevations:	Trailhead 8,680', Hut 11,209', +2,529'	
Avalanche Note:	Some avalanche terrain encountered; easily avoided	
Maps:	USGS 7.5': Red Cliff, 1978; Vail Pass, 1987	
	National Forest: Arapaho, White River	
	Trails Illustrated: Map #108 (Vail/Frisco/Dillon)	
	10th Mountain: Resolution Mountain	
	See map pages 84-85 and 88-89	

This route follows the western portion of the classic Shrine Pass route. From Shrine Pass, the road drops steadily to the town of Red Cliff. If you are descending into Red Cliff, be prepared for the ride of your life, especially if the road has recently been packed by snowmobilers. If you are skiing up to the inn from Red Cliff, be prepared for a long, taxing ascent.

To reach the trailhead from the north, take I-70 and exit at Minturn (Exit 171), which is 5.4 miles west of Vail. Proceed south on US 24, driving 10.3 miles to the bridge at Turkey Creek. Approaching from Leadville, drive north on US 24 from the intersection with CO 91 (just north of Leadville) for 22.6 miles to the Turkey Creek bridge. From the north end of this spectacular bridge, turn east and drive into Red Cliff. Look for the Shrine Pass Road (CR 16). Park along this road or in a parking lot near the marshal's office.

The Shrine Pass Road up Turkey Creek begins in a deep valley; the actual starting point varies depending on how far the road has been plowed. Initially, the road is on the south side of the creek. Soon the road crosses over the creek and continues climbing below south-facing slopes for 2.5 miles. Pass the turnoff and bridge to Wearyman Creek (the beginning of the Hornsilver Mountain route from Red Cliff to the Fowler/ Hilliard Hut, Tour 14A) and follow the road up and across Turkey Creek.

Ascend through thick forest for 1.9 miles, then cross back to the north side of the creek near some old cabin ruins. Continue up the valley for 2.8 miles until you pass the turnoff to the north for the Timber Creek Road. Climb through a steep, tight turn and eventually pass an outhouse on the right before entering a flat, treeless basin 7.3 miles from Red Cliff. Follow the road up the north side of the basin through a steep gully. Then contour to the south, following the less distinct creek up to 11,720-foot Shrine Pass.

You are near the pass when you can look to the southwest to the Tenmile Range. (An altimeter may help if the weather is inclement.) A Forest Service sign also marks the spot. From here, cross the southwest side of the clearing, enter the forest and follow the well-traveled trail to the inn.

TOUR 13C   SHRINE MOUNTAIN INN TO FOWLER/HILLIARD HUT

Difficulty:	Advanced	
Time:	5 to 8 hours	
Distance:	6.8 miles	
Elevations:	SM Inn 11,209', F/H Hut 11,500', +1,211'/-920'	
Avalanche Note:	Some avalanche terrain encountered; easily avoided	
Maps:	USGS 7.5': Pando, 1987; Red Cliff, 1978; Vail Pass, 1987	
	National Forest: Arapaho, White River	
	Trails Illustrated: Map #108 (Vail/Frisco/Dillon); Map #109 (Breckenridge/Tennessee Pass)	
	10th Mountain: Resolution Mountain	
	See map pages 84-85 and 88-89	

The standard inter-hut trail linking the Shrine Mountain Inn and the Fowler/Hilliard Hut is a scenic route that will test your fitness level and route-finding abilities. Overall, this challenging trail follows the most direct and common-sense route between the huts; however, it always seems to take longer than expected, so get an early start. The first half of the trail travels for 1.5 miles, high across the west side of the south ridge of Shrine Mountain near treeline. Consequently, it is exposed to foul weather and wind from the west. If the weather is severe, consider bypassing the high traverse of Shrine Mountain by skiing through Wilder Gulch by way of the Shrine Pass Road (CR 16).

The trail leaves the Shrine Mountain Inn and begins a 1.3-mile southwesterly climb onto the pass. A compass reading may be helpful here; the rock near the summit of the mountain is a handy orientation point. This ascent is facilitated by a scattering of blue diamond trail markers showing the route up through sparsely timbered slopes and tree stumps. Break out of the trees and ascend west onto 11,720-foot Shrine Pass just south of the summit of Shrine Mountain.

From the pass, turn south and begin a long, gently descending traverse across the west face of the south ridge of Shrine Mountain, just above treeline. Ski through small islands of trees, following the occasional trail marker. As you near the south end of the ridge, contour slightly to the southeast and begin descending steeper slopes into the forest. Continue south down toward the creek, following the path of least resistance through ever-steepening, forested slopes. Eventually, this descent ends in a small meadow near the head of Wearyman Creek.

The trail into the woods on the south side of the creek is probably the hardest section of this route to locate, so take a little time to find the proper point of entry. Ski west through the meadow until the creek leaves the meadow and begins to drop steeply. On the south side of the creek, you will find trail markers for the route to the Fowler/Hilliard Hut. (Avoid the summer road, which continues down the valley to Red Cliff; it heads west above the creek at this same spot.)

Enter the woods and begin a 200-foot descent to a tiny clearing (shown on the USGS topo map). Ski to the southwest until you gain a wide, gentle road. Follow the road for 2 miles on a seemingly interminable low-angled climb until you reach a series of switchbacks that head directly uphill to the southeast. Ascend through these to the 11,460-foot saddle east of the hut. Turn west and ski 0.3 mile over a small hill to the Fowler/Hilliard Hut.

If you ski from the Fowler/Hilliard Hut north to Shrine Mountain Inn, remember to climb uphill through the small meadow at the head of Wearyman Creek. Exit the clearing to the northeast to begin the ascent across the west side of the south ridge of Shrine Mountain.

14 FOWLER/HILLIARD HUT

The Fowler/Hilliard Hut is one of the most spectacular sites in the 10th Mountain Division system. From atop a ridge on the northeast side of Resolution Mountain, you can look south over terrain where ski soldiers of the 10th Mountain Division once trained. Experienced skiers especially love this hut because there are hundreds of acres of skiable terrain in every direction. The hut route is long and hard, but those who can manage the trip will be treated to as much skiing as their knees can handle.

The Fowler/Hilliard Hut sleeps 16 and is divided into a main-floor living and eating area and a second-story sleeping loft, which has several private and semi-private rooms. Hikers and mountain bikers should bear in mind that water may be difficult to obtain during the summer because water sources are some distance from the hut. Directions inside the hut will tell you where to find water, which should be treated or boiled before drinking.

John Fielder and Cully Culbreth, Fowler/Hilliard Hut.

This hut is wheelchair accessible, and in summer you can drive directly to it. Make reservations through the 10th Mountain Division Hut Association (see Appendix A).

TOUR 14A   RED CLIFF TRAILHEAD

Difficulty:	Intermediate
Time:	7 to 11 hours
Distance:	9 miles
Elevations:	Trailhead 8,680', Hut 11,500', +3,170'/-350'
Avalanche Note:	Some avalanche terrain encountered; easily avoided
Maps:	USGS 7.5': Pando, 1987; Red Cliff, 1978
	National Forest: White River
	Trails Illustrated: Map #108 (Vail/Frisco/Dillon); Map #109 (Breckenridge/Tennessee Pass)
	10th Mountain: Resolution Mountain
	See map pages 84-85 and 88-89

From Red Cliff, the Hornsilver Mountain route to the Fowler/Hilliard Hut is a long and steep prospect. The 5-mile climb from Wearyman Creek to Resolution Mountain is nothing more than an exercise in high-altitude aerobics — with a pack! Following marked roads and trails the entire way, you will not have to worry about intricate route finding. However, when you travel to the hut through Resolution Narrows, you do need to pay attention so that you don't end up skiing down into McAllister Gulch or onto any of the potential avalanche slopes on the north side of Resolution Mountain. Individuals headed to Red Cliff from the Fowler/Hilliard hut will find this the most expedient avenue of egress.

To reach the trailhead from the north, take I-70 to the Minturn exit (Exit 171), which is 5.4 miles west of Vail. Proceed south on US 24, driving 10.3 miles to a bridge across Turkey Creek. If you are approaching from the Leadville area, drive north on US 24 from the intersection with CO 91 (just north of Leadville) for 22.6 miles to the Turkey Creek bridge. From the north end of this spectacular bridge, turn east and drive down the narrow road into Red Cliff. Look for the Shrine Pass Road (CR 16). Park along this road or in a parking lot near the marshal's office.

The Shrine Pass Road up Turkey Creek begins in a deep valley; the actual starting point varies depending on how far the road has been plowed. Initially, the road is on the the south side of the creek. Soon it crosses the creek and continues climbing below the south-facing slopes for 2.5 miles until you reach the turnoff to Wearyman Creek. Turn south, cross the bridge, and head up into Wearyman Creek along the road. Climb for 0.8 mile to the right (west), then turn into the Hornsilver Mountain Road and begin the 2,270-foot ascent of Hornsilver Mountain. Remain on the marked ski route that follows a four-wheel-drive trail, continue past a left turn at Elevation Point 10,080' and past several right turns near Elevation Point 10,800'. Traverse up to the west ridge of Hornsilver Mountain, then turn east and ascend along the ridge to the summit.

Continue along the ridge over Hornsilver Mountain, cross a small hill and a saddle, and ascend the west side of the ridge to the northwest corner of Resolution Mountain. From this flat shoulder, turn east and drop into the large gully, Resolution Narrows, on the north side of the mountain. Ski through this passage, avoiding any potential avalanche slopes on both sides of the gully, and exit up and out of the southeast side of the narrows. After climbing onto the large saddle/ridge on the northeast side of Resolution Mountain, continue east for several hundred feet to the Fowler/Hilliard Hut.

TOUR 14B   PANDO TRAILHEAD

Difficulty:	Advanced	
Time:	4 to 7 hours	
Distance:	5 miles	
Elevations:	Trailhead 9,200', Hut 11,500', +2,500'/-200'	
Avalanche Note:	Some avalanche terrain encountered; easily avoided	
Maps:	USGS 7.5': Pando, 1987	
	National Forest: White River	
	Trails Illustrated: Map #109 (Breckenridge/Tennessee Pass)	
	10th Mountain: Chicago Ridge; Resolution Mountain	
	See map pages 88-89 and 114-115	

McAllister Gulch is the shortest, most direct route to the Fowler/Hilliard Hut. Although it follows a road and is relatively short, it gains a considerable amount of elevation in a short distance, climbing very steeply through its middle portion. Also it is makes for a very fast descent. Consequently, this route gets a nudge into the advanced category. Getting an early start and using climbing skins will help make this tour more manageable. Also, since the trail has a northwest exposure, it normally has better snow than the more south-facing routes, especially important when descending to Camp Hale. Nevertheless, snow conditions can vary widely.

To reach the trailhead from I-70, take the Minturn exit (Exit 171) which is 5.4 miles west of Vail, and proceed south for 17 miles. From Leadville drive north on US 24 from the intersection of CO 91 for 16.3 miles over Tennessee Pass to Pando. Park on the east side of the road by the concrete foundations immediately south of the railroad crossing. As there is no bridge, mountain bikers should use the Camp Hale Trailhead.

From the parking area, ski east and cross the Eagle River either via a snow bridge or by fording the stream. Continue toward the mountains, then turn north (left) at the intersection at the foot of the mountain. Ski north along this road into for 0.5 mile, then traverse to the McAllister Gulch Road (FR 708). Climb for 2 miles along the south side of the creek until the route turns to the southeast. Continue climbing steeply until you leave the trees and intersect the Resolution Creek Trail. Look for trail markers on trees at this intersection.

Follow the trail up the ridge and begin an ascending traverse north across the open west face of Resolution Mountain. (Note views of the Mount of the Holy Cross!) This ascent is 200 to 300 feet beneath the summit of Resolution Mountain through islands of evergreens.

From the flat shoulder on the northwest corner of the mountain, turn east and drop into the large cleft, or gully, on the north side of the mountain. This is Resolution Narrows. Ski through this passage, avoiding potential avalanche slopes on both sides, and exit up and out of the southeast side of the narrows. After climbing onto the large saddle/ridge on the northeast side of Resolution Mountain, continue east to the hut.

TOUR 14C   CAMP HALE TRAILHEAD

Difficulty:	Intermediate/Advanced
Time:	5 to 8 hours
Distance:	6.5 miles
Elevations:	Trailhead 9,250', Hut 11,500', +2,450'/-200'
Avalanche Note:	Route crosses avalanche runout zones; can be dangerous during high-hazard periods
Maps:	USGS 7.5': Pando, 1987
	National Forest: White River
	Trails Illustrated: Map #109
	(Breckenridge/Tennessee Pass)
	10th Mountain: Chicago Ridge
	See map pages 88-89 and 114-115

This route leaves Camp Hale and ascends to the Fowler/Hilliard Hut via Resolution Creek. The upper section of this tour is often combined with the

Pearl Creek route to the Jackal Hut (Tour 14D) to create the hut-to-hut route between the Jackal Hut and the Fowler/Hilliard Hut. However, when the sun has been at work hardening the south-facing slopes, descending this route can be thrilling.

While all three Camp Hale trailheads are starting points for this trail, only directions from the main Camp Hale parking area are given. From I-70, exit at Minturn (Exit 171), which is 5.4 miles west of Vail, and proceed south on US 24 for 18.5 miles. From the Leadville area, drive north on US 24 from the intersection with CO 91 for 14.7 miles, across Tennessee Pass to the main Camp Hale road. Park on the east side of the road.

There are two possible routes to Resolution Creek. The first goes straight across Camp Hale to the road on the far, east side. This entails crossing the Eagle River, which may be simple or difficult, depending on whether there are any snow bridges. Either cross a snow bridge or ford the stream. Once you have reached the road (FR 714), turn north and proceed to Resolution Creek. If crossing the Eagle River is too difficult, it is also possible to ski to the river, then turn north and ski along the river for 0.8 mile, until you reach the first turn to the east. Follow this road east over the river via a bridge until you reach the Resolution Creek Road and turn left.

Pass Forest Service signs, then ski up the Resolution Creek Road for 1.4 miles to a fork in the road. Continue along the left fork (the right fork leads to the Jackal Hut), traveling north for 1 mile. The first significant drainage since the Pearl Creek fork is on the left. Turn up this creek and ski along the south side. After climbing 300 feet, the route leaves the creek and ascends a series of switchbacks to the southwest ridge of Resolution Mountain. This climb follows a trail that, at times, is a little difficult to track, for the blue diamond trail markers are spaced far apart. Pay attention.

(Bicyclists should continue straight up Resolution Creek on FR 702 toward Ptarmigan Pass, then turn west 400 feet below the pass onto FR 751, which leads up to the forested pass directly east of the hut.)

When you reach a tiny forested saddle on top of the ridge, turn northeast and climb 360 feet directly up the ridge, passing the McAllister Gulch Trail at 11,300 feet. Continue up the ridge via the trail, gaining another 100 feet of elevation. Ascend, traversing north across the open west face of Resolution Mountain. The trail heads through evergreens, about 250 feet below the summit.

From the flat shoulder on the northwest corner of the mountain, turn east and drop into the large gully, Resolution Narrows, on the north side of the mountain. Ski through this passage, avoiding potential avalanche slopes on either side. Exit out of the southeast side of the narrows. After climbing onto the large saddle/ridge on the northeast side of Resolution Mountain, continue east for several hundred feet to the Fowler/Hilliard Hut.

TOUR 14D   FOWLER/HILLIARD HUT TO JACKAL HUT

Difficulty:	Advanced
Time:	6 to 9 hours
Distance:	7.8 miles
Elevations:	F/H Hut 11,500', J Hut 11,610', +2,202'/-2,022'
Avalanche Note:	Route crosses avalanche runout zones; can be dangerous during high-hazard periods
Maps:	USGS 7.5': Pando, 1987
	National Forest: White River
	Trails Illustrated: Map #109 (Breckenridge/Tennessee Pass)
	10th Mountain: Chicago Ridge
	See map pages 88-89 and 114-115

This classic route combines the Camp Hale to Fowler/Hilliard Hut via Resolution Creek route (Tour 14C) and Camp Hale to Jackal Hut via Pearl Creek route (Tour 15A) into a long, hut-to-hut day. Because this route requires several thousand feet of descent and ascent (in either direction), it is a very challenging tour. Skiers wearing backpacks must be able to descend long, steady drops. The climb to the huts adds a final kicker to the day.

Described from north to south, this trail starts from the Fowler/Hilliard Hut and heads west through Resolution Narrows, the gully due west of the hut on the north side of Resolution Mountain. From the northwest shoulder of Resolution Mountain, the trail then traverses gradually down across the west face of the mountain through sparse islands of trees, following the occasional blue diamond trail marker. The route then follows the southwest ridge of the mountain down past the marked right turn (blue and orange diamonds) to McAllister Gulch.

Continue dropping down the ridge until you reach a small, wooded saddle. Turn to the southeast and begin a long and treacherous descent into the Resolution Creek drainage. Follow a somewhat obscure trail as it switchbacks wildly down through the forest. There are blue trail markers, but you must keep an eye out for them. This descent stays on the southwest side of the creek all the way to the Resolution Creek Road.

Drop down the Resolution Creek Road (FR 702) for 1 mile until you reach the turnoff to Pearl Creek, marked by a bridge and mileage sign. Cross the bridge and follow the road south on a gradual climb. After a few hundred feet, the road divides into two logging roads. The road of choice veers sharply to the southeast and heads upstream past old logging cuts. Stay on the south side of the stream, and after a few hundred feet begin an ascending traverse above the creek. Watch for blue trail markers. Do not follow any of the trails that lead down to the creek. The road climbs steadily, then begins to steepen and turn south along a tiny creek. Follow the road uphill until you spot a road branching sharply to the east/southeast. Cross the creek and follow this road 1 mile to a creek crossing in a small, willowy bog. This stretch of trail from Resolution Road to the creek crossing makes for a joyous descent.

Cross to the north side of the creek and follow a distinct trail 0.3 mile upstream to a faint trail crossing to the south side of the creek. This poorly marked crossing is in a large clearing along the creek, at a point where the drainage begins to contour to the northeast. From this point, you can start to see Sugarloaf Peak, high to the northeast. There is also a small stream flowing in from the south, usually marked by old ski tracks. There are usually many tracks popping out of the woods throughout this area.

Cross the creek and ski up along the west side, keeping an eye out for blue markers! Skins are recommended for the climb to the hut. After a few hundred feet, the trail climbs steeply to the right, then becomes well defined. After 800 feet, the gradient relaxes as you reach a picturesque ridge. Ski west through the woods. Continue west into a ridge-top clearing, ascend up over the last 200-foot climb, then glide easily to the Jackal Hut.

TOUR 14E   FOWLER/HILLIARD HUT TO JACKAL HUT VIA HIGH TRAVERSE

Difficulty:	Advanced
Time:	7 to 9 hours
Distance:	9 miles
Elevations:	F/H Hut 11,500', J Hut 11,610', +2060'/-1,700'
Avalanche Note:	Route crosses avalanche slopes; prone to skier-triggered avalanches during high-hazard periods
Maps:	USGS 7.5': Copper Mountain, 1988; Pando, 1987
	National Forest: Arapaho, White River
	Trails Illustrated: Map #108 (Vail/Frisco/Dillon)
	10th Mountain: Chicago Ridge
	See map pages 88-89 and 114-115

The High Traverse is a backcountry skiing experience that is more ski-mountaineering than cross-country skiing. This unofficial 10th Mountain Division route is a committing, high-altitude, hut-to-hut ridge traverse between the Fowler/Hilliard Hut and the Jackal Hut. It is one of the most scenic tours in Colorado, overlooking deep, forested valleys with unobstructed 360-degree views of central Colorado's mountains, including the Gore Range to the north, the Tenmile Range to the east, the Sawatch Range to the south, and 14,005-foot Mount of the Holy Cross to the west. If you have done the Resolution Creek/Pearl Creek hut-to-hut route one too many times, then give this super alternative a try.

Competent, experienced groups will find the route finding straight forward, the technical difficulty minimal, and the avalanche hazard low under normal conditions. Parties interested in doing this tour will need a clear day, because most of the route follows a treeless, and therefore unprotected, ridge that is exposed to the full fury of storms coming out of the west or north.

The route's snowpack is usually scoured by westerly winds and so most of the route is either over hard sastrugi with occasional patches of talus or grass. Keep an eye out for cornices overhanging the eastern flank, small wind-deposited pockets, and the steep traverse around the western and southern flanks of 12,545-foot Sugarloaf Peak. Be sure to carry safety equipment

To begin the tour, leave the Fowler/Hilliard Hut and head east over a small hill to the main trail. Turn to the east and follow the roadbed around the southern flank of 12,143-foot Ptarmigan Hill. Ski down to a switchback, where the road swings to the south and west down into Resolution Creek. Leave the road at the apex of the switchback and ski northwest up to Ptarmigan Pass.

From the pass, climb to the southeast, up toward the top of the ridge. It is not necessary to climb straight up to the ridge; you can take a long traverse across the moderate and windswept west slopes of Elevation Point 12,370', gaining the ridge at the flat saddle immediately south of this point.

From the saddle, the route takes the path of least resistance south along the crest of the ridge, steering clear of any avalanche hazards, especially the cornices overhanging the eastern aspect of the ridge. Exercise caution on the exposed western and southern flanks of Sugarloaf Peak. Generally this slope is wind-scoured and is normally a walk across stones and crusty snow, so be careful.

Continue southeast along the ridge up and over the high point of the trip, 12,693-foot Elk Mountain. From the summit of this peak, drop south off the summit to the first minor saddle at 12,540 feet, then begin a descent southwest across a broad, moderate slope to the saddle immediately northeast of Pearl Peak. From here ascend directly up the ridge and over Pearl Peak, staying well away from the huge cornices that often form on the southeastern aspect of this peak. Descend west/southwest along the broad ridge crest to the intersection with the Jackal Hut Trail. Continue west on the trail for 0.6 mile to the hut.

Doug Seyb en route from the Fowler/Hilliard Hut to the Jackal Hut on the High Traverse, with the Gore Range in the distance.

15   JACKAL HUT

Perched on the edge of a towering ridge, the Jackal Hut is like an eagle's nest overlooking the Eagle River Valley, Tennessee Pass, and nearly the entire length of the Sawatch Range to the south and west. The hut offers a view from its porch that is one of the finest of any hut in the state. The view you get by climbing directly north onto the hill behind the hut gets even better: a 360-degree panorama that includes the Gore Range to the north and the Tenmile Range to the east and southeast. Every route to the hut gains over 2,000 feet — there are no "easy" ways. With an early start, most skiers, even novice backcountry skiers with good endurance, can reach the hut.

The Jackal Hut opened in 1988 and was formerly called the Schuss/Zesiger Hut. Now it bears the monikers of a man named Jack (Schuss) and a man named Al (Zesiger). Get it?

The hut sleeps up to 16 people and is laid out on the same basic floor plan as its sister hut, the Fowler/Hilliard. Upstairs are the sleeping areas, which include several private rooms and an assortment of sleeping benches. The view out of the upstairs window rivals the one from the front porch. Whether you are sipping tea on the deck or inside curled up in a sleeping bag near the picture windows, this is great place to watch the sun set behind Homestake Peak. Make reservations through the 10th Mountain Division Hut Association (see Appendix A).

TOUR 15A   CAMP HALE TRAILHEAD VIA PEARL CREEK

Difficulty:	Intermediate/Advanced
Time:	5 to 8 hours
Distance:	6.6 miles
Elevations:	Trailhead 9,250', Hut 11,610', +2,360'/-40'
Avalanche Note:	None
Maps:	USGS 7.5': Pando, 1987
	National Forest: White River
	Trails Illustrated: Map #109
	(Breckenridge/Tennessee Pass)
	10th Mountain: Chicago Ridge
	See map pages 88-89 and 114-115

The trail up Pearl Creek is my favorite tour to the Jackal Hut. While each route to the hut has its own advantages and disadvantages, this one remains special for one reason — good snow. Pearl Creek lies deep in a valley, far below and to the north of the Jackal Hut. This route tends to harbor better snow for longer periods of time because it receives less direct solar radiation than its southern counterparts. This is especially obvious when you are descending from the hut.

This route covers the first 2.6 miles of the Fowler/Hilliard via Resolution Creek route (Tour 14C) to the bridge over Resolution Creek and the last 4 miles of the Fowler/Hilliard-Jackal Hut route (14D). Refer to those routes for detailed descriptions and for specific directions.

RECOMMENDED DAY TOURS: When the powder is fresh, great telemark skiing is right out the front door on the south-facing slopes. Be careful not to drop too far down! On the north side of the hut, ski over Elevation Point 11,716' where there is tree skiing on advanced downhill descents of 1,400 vertical feet. Winter mountaineers will delight in traversing the ridge to the east and climbing Pearl Peak, Elk Peak, or Corbett Peak.

TOUR 15B SOUTH CAMP HALE TRAILHEAD VIA RANCH CREEK

Difficulty:	Intermediate/Advanced
Time:	4 to 6 hours
Distance:	4 miles
Elevations:	Trailhead 9,280', Hut 11,610', +2,330'
Avalanche Note:	Some avalanche terrain encountered; easily avoided
Maps:	USGS 7.5': Pando, 1987
	National Forest: White River
	Trails Illustrated: Map #109 (Breckenridge/Tennessee Pass)
	10th Mountain: Chicago Ridge
	See map pages 88-89 and 114-115

The Ranch Creek trail is the beeline to the Jackal Hut. Gaining over 2,300 feet of elevation in 4 miles, this route holds very few surprises. While the tour is described as starting from South Camp Hale, a start from Camp Hale works just as well, although it does lengthen the trip by roughly 0.6 mile and increase the elevation gain by a formidable 30 feet.

To reach the trailhead from I-70, exit at Minturn (Exit 171), which is

5.4 miles west of Vail, and proceed south on US 24 for 19.3 miles. From Leadville, drive north on US 24 from the intersection with CO 91 for 13.9 miles, across Tennessee Pass to the main Camp Hale road. Park on the east side in a plowed turnout near a fishing pond marked by a sign reading "Fisherman Parking."

Leave the parking area and drop down a few feet onto the main valley floor. Travel directly across the valley on an east/northeast course, aiming for the south side of a rocky cliff that has power lines running over it. On the south side of the cliff is a low-angled, fan-shaped slope, covered only with shrubs. This is where the trail begins its climb. After crossing the Eagle River by locating a snow bridge, or by fording the stream, continue across the valley until you reach a road (FR 714) below the mountainside. Turn south and follow the road for 0.25 mile, until you reach a marked left turn (northeast) onto the Ranch Creek Road.

Begin the ascent gradually into Ranch Creek, switchback up the road west and then due north. Climb 200 feet, then turn east and traverse across a clearing, back toward the creek. As you approach the creek, start to parallel it at the beginning of a steep, consistent ascent to the top of the ridge. Cross a meadow between 10,700 and 10,800 feet, passing some old cabins, and continue upward.

As you approach the ridge, search for the trail leading up to the east/southeast. Follow the trail into a large meadow, change your direction to east/northeast, then exit the meadow and climb back to the crest of the ridge. From here

Cully Culbreth views the distant Sawatch Range from Jackal Hut.

the trail ascends on a moderate traversing climb to the hut, which is below the summit on the south at Elevation Point 11,716'. If you miss any turns, the easiest route to the hut would be to ski north directly onto the ridge crest and follow it to the top of Elevation Point 11,716'. From there it is easy to locate the hut by descending south off the top into the large meadow on the southeast side.

TOUR 15C   SOUTH CAMP HALE TRAILHEAD VIA CATARACT CREEK

Difficulty:	Intermediate/Advanced
Time:	5 to 7 hours
Distance:	6 miles
Elevations:	Trailhead 9,280', Hut 11,610', +2,440'/-40'
Avalanche Note:	Some avalanche terrain encountered; easily avoided
Maps:	USGS 7.5': Pando, 1987
	National Forest: White River
	Trails Illustrated: Map #109 (Breckenridge/Tennessee Pass)
	10th Mountain: Chicago Ridge
	See map pages 88-89 and 114-115

This is the most scenic trail to the Jackal Hut. It is south-facing, so the snow tends can be heavy and/or develop a crust. Some sections may even be rocky. With a deep snowpack or new snow, this route is as good as the other Jackal routes. It is also the most direct route to Vance's Cabin.

To reach the trailhead from I-70, exit at Minturn (Exit 171), which is 5.4 miles west of Vail, and proceed south on US 24 for 19.3 miles. From Leadville, drive north on US 24 for 13.9 miles across Tennessee Pass to the south Camp Hale parking area. Park in a plowed turnout near a fishing pond, marked by a sign reading "Fisherman Parking."

Leave the parking area and drop down onto the main valley floor. Travel across the valley on an east/northeast course, aiming for the south side of a rocky cliff with power lines running over it. Cross the Eagle River via a snow bridge or by fording the stream. Continue across the valley to a road (FR 714). Turn south and follow the road for 2 miles.

Uphill to the north, a road leads into Cataract Creek. This road, marked by a sign, climbs almost continuously to the Jackal Hut. (It also joins with the Colorado Trail for 1.8 miles.) Climb the road as it gains altitude rapidly, switchback around a rocky promontory, then switchback again and head north to Cataract Creek. Cross the creek, climb around another large switchback, then traverse northeast across a wide, south-facing slope.

Traverse into the moderately steep, forested upper valley, then search for a narrow, rocky, treeless swath that runs directly uphill to the north. Begin the laborious task of climbing this hill and up a drainage, through a series of clearings. Follow the clearings back to the northwest, up to the top of the ridge. Ski west through the forest, following the crest of the ridge. Pass over a small saddle (where the Pearl Creek route, Tour 15A, attains the ridge from the north), continue west along the crest of the ridge, then begin climbing the last 260 feet through a large, ridge-top clearing. The Jackal Hut is 0.6 mile away from this saddle. As you near the summit of Elevation Point 11,716', gently traverse downward toward the southwest and the Jackal Hut.

TOUR 15D   JACKAL HUT TO VANCE'S CABIN

Difficulty:	Intermediate/Advanced
Time:	6 to 9 hours
Distance:	8.6 miles
Elevations:	J Hut 11,610', V Cabin 10,980', +1,700'/-2,275'
Avalanche Note:	Some avalanche terrain encountered; easily avoided
Maps:	USGS 7.5': Pando, 1987
	National Forest: White River
	Trails Illustrated: Map #109 (Breckenridge/Tennessee Pass)
	10th Mountain: Chicago Ridge
	See map pages 88-89 and 114-115

The northern 3.6 miles of this tour follow the Cataract Creek-Jackal Hut route, (Tour 15C) down the steep, south face from Elevation Point 11,716' through Cataract Creek. South of the East Fork of the Eagle River, the trail enters the forest, following a sinuous trail. Skiing this route can take a long time, particularly when new snow forces you to break trail.

From the Jackal Hut, ski east along the ridge and make the 260-foot drop to the 11,400-foot saddle. Pass the north turn to Pearl Creek and continue east through the trees. Ski 0.4 mile along the south side of the ridge until the forest opens into a broad, treeless, bowl-shaped drainage. Contour southeast through the meadow, dropping to Cataract Creek.

Ski downstream along the Cataract Creek Road/Colorado Trail for 1.8 miles to the East Fork of the Eagle River Road (FR 714). Turn upstream and ski southeast 0.25 mile along the road to the river. Cross the river, leave the road and head for the forest, following a south/southwest course. Enter the forest via a marked trail. For the next 2.2 miles, ski through the woods, following a secluded trail on a long traverse up to Jones Gulch. As the trail nears the gulch, it climbs steeply south along the creek until it reaches a beautiful and remote willow-filled meadow.

Follow the trail west, returning to the forest along the meadow's northern edge to an old road. (There are many old logging roads in the area that do not appear on the latest USGS topo maps, so be careful and remain alert.) Traverse west on a moderate climb for 0.4 mile and gain the forested, north ridge of Taylor Hill. Turn sharply uphill and follow a distinct trail (the old Trail of the 10th) straight up the ridge for roughly 400 feet to a junction with a road at 11,033 feet. Turn right onto this road and ski along it for 0.6 mile to a tiny clearing and a fork in the trail. Continue traversing along the left, or higher, trail and ski the last 0.7 mile to Vance's Cabin, which is near the top of a clearing and faces west.

16 VANCE'S CABIN

Vance's Cabin is an unusual 10th Mountain Division structure in that it is privately owned and resembles a hunting lodge. Constructed out of logs and featuring a large, south-facing deck, the cabin overlooks the Ski Cooper downhill area. It has a tri-level design, with sleeping for 16 upstairs and down, with a main living and cooking area. The basement also contains a sauna fired by a wood-burning stove. Make reservations through the 10th Mountain Division Hut Association (see Appendix A).

TOUR 16A   TENNESSEE PASS TRAILHEAD

Difficulty:	Novice/Intermediate
Time:	3 to 4 hours
Distance:	3.1 miles
Elevations:	Trailhead 10,424', Hut 10,980', +776'/-200'
Avalanche Note:	None
Maps:	USGS 7.5': Leadville North, 1970; Pando, 1987
	National Forest: White River
	Trails Illustrated: Map #109
	(Breckenridge/Tennessee Pass)
	10th Mountain: Chicago Ridge
	See map pages 88-89 and 114-115

From Tennessee Pass, the Piney Gulch Trail to Vance's Cabin is one of the shortest routes to a 10th Mountain Division hut. It is a great introduction to hut skiing for those not yet ready for more rigorous trips. Skiers attempting this trail still should be prepared for winter weather; there have been mishaps here where skiers had to spend the night on the trail.

To reach the trailhead from I-70, exit at Minturn (Exit 171), which is 5.4 miles west of Vail. Drive south on US 24 for 24.4 miles to the top of Tennessee Pass. From Leadville, drive north on US 24 from the junction of CO 91 for 8.8 miles to the top of Tennessee Pass. Park on the west side.

From the Ski Cooper parking lot, walk to the nordic center office. Begin skiing east along a snow-packed aqueduct road. This is the beginning of the Piney Gulch/Cooper Loop nordic center trails, so don't become confused. After 0.6 mile, search for a trail and a marker to the north. Cross the creek and begin climbing through a clearing on the west side of Piney Creek, following the north branch of the creek 0.3 mile. Look northeast for an uphill clearing, and ascend through it. If you begin to contour northeast along the

Beth Smith views Mount Elbert and Mount Massive, Sawatch Range, 10th Mountain Division Hut System.

114

CHICAGO RIDGE

WHITE RIVER NATIONAL FOREST

10th Mountain Division Hut System

10th Mountain Division Hut System is located in the White River and San Isabel National Forests under agreement with the Forest Service, USDA.
Scale 1:24,000 Contour Interval: 40 Feet

SCALE IN MILES

MN 12°

Hut
Trailhead
Wilderness Boundary

© 1994 • 10th Mountain Division Hut Association

3.63 miles to Jackal Hut
3.70 miles to Camp Hale
4.94 miles to Vance's Cabin

2.77 miles to Vance's Cabin
5.78 miles to Jackal Hut
5.87 miles to Camp Hale

1.33 miles to Vance's Cabin
7.22 miles to Jackal Hut
7.31 miles to Camp Hale

2.12 miles to Vance's Cabin
6.43 miles to Jackal Hut
6.52 miles to Camp Hale

7.14 miles to Margy's Cabin

0.71 miles to Vance's Cabin
7.84 miles to Jackal Hut
7.90 miles to Camp Hale

0.29 miles to Vance's Cabin
2.84 miles to Tennessee Pass

1.06 miles to Tennessee Pass
2.06 miles to Vance's Cabin

15D

16A
16B

Vance's Cabin
(10,980')

1.46 miles to Vance's Cabin
1.66 miles to Tennessee Pass

Tennessee Pass Trailhead
(10,424')

16B

Crane Park Trailhead
(10,137')

creek, you've missed the turn. After gaining 300 feet in elevation, the trail reaches a saddle north of Elevation Point 10,963'. Begin climbing northeast into the forest. Watch for the blue diamond markers to confirm that you are on course. Soon the trail starts traversing north at about 11,120 feet. Ski due north and then west. Vance's Cabin is 0.3 mile west and 200 feet down a short but thrilling descent.

RECOMMENDED DAY TOURS: The skiing around the cabin is somewhat limited. One possibility is to climb up behind the cabin and explore the woods on the west side of Taylor Hill. Another choice is to explore an older cross-country trail, called the Trail of the 10th. From the Ski Cooper parking lot, this trail ascends Piney Gulch to Taylor Hill. From Taylor Hill, the trail travels down the northwest ridge to the Taylor Hill Road at 11,033 feet. From this point, skiers can return south 1.3 miles to Vance's Cabin. From the top of Taylor Hill, it is also quite reasonable to climb onto Chicago Ridge, where there's great skiing after storms.

TOUR 16B   VANCE'S CABIN TO 10TH MOUNTAIN DIVISION HUT

Difficulty:	Intermediate	🚶 🚲 👫
Time:	6 to 8 hours	
Distance:	8.9 miles	
Elevations:	V Cabin 10,424', 10th Mtn Hut 11,370',	
	+1,410'/-1,066'	
Avalanche Note:	None	
Maps:	USGS 7.5': Homestake Reservoir, 1970;	
	Leadville North, 1970; Pando, 1987	
	National Forest: San Isabel, White River	
	Trails Illustrated: Map #109 (Breckenridge/	
	Tenn. Pass); Map #126 (Holy Cross/Ruedi Res.)	
	10th Mountain: Chicago Ridge, Galena Mountain	
	See map pages 88-89, 114-115, and 128-129	

For skiers wishing to ski from Vance's Cabin to the 10th Mountain Division Hut, this is the only game in town. This trail combines the Tennessee Pass Trailhead to Vance's Cabin route (Tour 16A) and the Tennessee Pass Trailhead to the 10th Mountain Division Hut route (Tour 17A). The route is long but not difficult — mostly long stretches of pleasant touring. The trail west of Tennessee Pass uses 2.6 miles of a well-used Forest Service nordic trail (the Mitchell Creek/Old Railroad Run). Please be courteous to day skiers in the area. Summer bicyclists will want to descend south on US 24 for 1.8 miles to Crane Park, then follow Tour 17A.

17   10TH MOUNTAIN DIVISION HUT

Built in 1989, the 10th Mountain Division Hut and Uncle Bud's Hut initiated the latest round of construction. Along with the Skinner Hut and the Betty Bear, these four huts created the link that finally connected the Camp Hale/Vail Pass huts with the Aspen/Edwards huts — a bridge between east and west.

The trails to the hut, while suitable for strong beginners, are solid, classic intermediate trails. Novice skiers who are ready to push their limits a little and folks who are ready to lead their own trip would do well to head for this hut. The surroundings are magnificent. Above the hut to the west is Homestake Peak and a glacially carved cirque. A gem of a trail follows the Slide Lake four-wheel-drive road 0.6 mile to Slide Lake. If you get up early and ski to the lake, you'll enjoy a special treat at sunrise.

Industrious backcountry skiers will want to climb Homestake Peak. By skiing southwest from the hut, it is possible to traverse up on to the East Ridge. Once on the ridge, simply head straight up 1,400 feet to the top. This ridge is remarkably free of avalanche danger and often is covered with fine snow perfect for carving turns. The glades to the west of the hut make for fun runs close to the cabin.

10th Mountain Division Hut in early morning light.

The large hut sleeps 16 and has all the standard amenities. The porch is perfect for snoozing in the sun and dreaming about bottomless powder. Make reservations through the 10th Mountain Division Hut Association (see Appendix A).

TOUR 17A   TENNESSEE PASS TRAILHEAD

Difficulty:	Intermediate	🚶 🚴 🚶🚶
Time:	5 to 7 hours	
Distance:	5.7 miles	
Elevations:	Trailhead 10,424', Hut 11,370', +1,210'/-140'	
Avalanche Note:	None	
Maps:	USGS 7.5': Homestake Reservoir, 1970;	
	Leadville North, 1970	
	National Forest: San Isabel, White River	
	Trails Illustrated: Map #109 (Breckenridge/	
	Tennessee Pass); Map #126 (Holy	
	Cross/Ruedi Reservoir)	
	10th Mountain: Galena Mountain	
	See map pages 88-89 and 128-129	

This trail begins on the summit of Tennessee Pass and heads west along a Forest Service nordic trail and the Colorado Trail into the massive West Fork of the Tennessee Creek drainage. After the route meets the Crane Park/Slide Lake Trail, the trails merge and climb to the hut.

To reach the trailhead from I-70, take the Minturn exit (Exit 171), which is 5.4 miles west of Vail, and drive on US 24 south 24.4 miles to the top of Tennessee Pass. Approaching from Leadville, drive north on US 24 from the junction with CO 91 for 8.8 miles to the summit of Tennessee Pass. Park on the west side of US 24.

From the parking area, begin traveling southwest on the nordic trail that joins the Colorado Trail. Begin a long, descending traverse to the southwest, into the West Fork of the Tennessee Creek drainage. After 2.3 miles, the trail crosses a creek, then turns south and climbs to the Wurt's Ditch Road. The intersection is marked with trail signs for the 10th Mountain Trail, Colorado Trail, and Mitchell Creek.

Cross the road, following the Colorado and 10th Mountain trails south and west over a hill and down a quick descent to another junction. The left (southeast) trail heads to the gravel pit, the trail to south/southwest heads up West Tennessee Creek to Uncle Bud's Hut, while the right (west/northwest) trail heads to the 10th Mountain Division Hut. Take the right-hand trail, which then leaves the Colorado Trail and heads toward Lily Lake.

Traverse northwest through the woods into a creek drainage, eventually crossing the creek. Ascend along the southern side of the creek to another trail junction, between the north side of Lily Lake and the south edge of a large meadow. Follow the trail that crosses northwest through a willow bog.

Climb a steep, but short hill (around 200 feet of elevation gain) on the far side, then begin the long but moderate ascent along the north side of Slide Creek. This climb travels through open clearings, and among occasional tree stumps and evergreen trees for 1.6 miles until you reach a flat meadow. Veer right (north) into the meadow and the 10th Mountain Division Hut.

The greatest challenge on this route is to avoid turning off onto one of the many confusing, well-traveled, and errant trails in the area. Pay close attention to map, compass, and trail markers, especially at intersections.

TOUR 17B   CRANE PARK TRAILHEAD

Difficulty:	Intermediate
Time:	4 to 6 hours
Distance:	4.4 miles
Elevations:	Trailhead 10,137', Hut 11,370', +1,343'/140'
Avalanche Note:	None
Maps:	USGS 7.5': Homestake Reservoir, 1970; Leadville North, 1970
	National Forest: San Isabel, White River
	Trails Illustrated: Map #109 (Breckenridge/ Tennessee Pass); Map #126 (Holy Cross/Ruedi Reservoir)
	10th Mountain: Galena Mountain
	See map pages 88-89 and 128-129

Crane Park/Slide Lake Trail is the most popular route to the 10th Mountain Division Hut, gaining 1,300 feet in 4.4 miles. This route weaves through a network of back roads, so keep your map and compass handy. Note that the first mile of trail has been relocated and more stringent parking rules apply. The designated plowed parking area is near the main highway. The trail used to leave the parking area and follow the plowed dirt road west through a small group of houses. Now the trail exits the road just west of the parking area (near a 10th Mountain sign) and parallels the road on the north through a meadow and then up into the woods, where it meets Wurt's Ditch Road (Tennessee Pass/10th Mountain Hut Trail — also the Colorado Trail).

From there the trail turns left (south) and proceeds over a hill to the cabin. Refer to the shared Tennessee Pass route (see Tour 17A) for a description of the trail between Wurt's Ditch Road and the hut.

To reach the trailhead from I-70, exit at Minturn (Exit 171, 5.4 miles west of Vail) and go south on US 24 for 24.4 miles to the top of Tennessee Pass. Continue 1.6 miles to the Crane Park turnoff (FR 100), turning west at a large curve in the road. Traveling north from Leadville, drive from the junction of CO 91 on US 24 for 7.2 miles to the Crane Park turnoff (FR 100). A yellow piece of machinery marks the turn. Park near US 24, being careful not to block the road.

Ski west along the road from the official parking area. In a few hundred feet, you'll see a 10th Mountain trailhead on the right. Leave the road and ski into the meadow. The trail heads west and follows the creek until it reaches the Tennessee Pass/10th Mountain Hut Trail. Turn left (south), following the Colorado Trail and 10th Mountain trails south and west over a hill to another junction. The left (southeast) junction heads to a gravel pit, the south/southwest trail heads up West Tennessee Creek to Uncle Bud's Hut, and the right (west/northwest) trail heads to the 10th Mountain Division Hut. Take the right-hand trail, which then leaves the Colorado Trail and heads to Lily Lake and the Slide Lake four-wheel-drive road. Follow Tour 17A for the last 2.7 miles to the hut.

A final note: As this book goes to print, the 10th Mountain Division maps do not reflect the trail changes. These will be corrected in the future.

TOUR 17C   10TH MOUNTAIN DIVISION HUT TO UNCLE BUD'S HUT

Difficulty:	Intermediate
Time:	5 to 8 hours
Distance:	7.2 miles
Elevations:	10th Mtn Hut 11,370', UB Hut +1,380', +1,520'/-1,500'
Avalanche Note:	Some avalanche terrain encountered; easily avoided
Maps:	USGS 7.5': Homestake Reservoir, 1970
	National Forest: San Isabel, White River
	Trails Illustrated: Map #109 (Breckenridge/ Tennessee Pass); Map #126 (Holy Cross/Ruedi Reservoir)
	10th Mountain: Galena Mountain
	See map pages 88-89 and 128-129

The trail between the 10th Mountain Division Hut and Uncle Bud's is a spectacular and geologically interesting section of trail. Running north-south, parallel to the Continental Divide on the east side of the Sawatch Range, the trail passes through an area that was heavily scoured during the Pleistocene glacial period (around three million years ago), and it is a stone's throw from textbook cirques, alpine tarns, and rock outcrops shaped and smoothed by the massive weight of glacial ice. The many creeks, descents, and climbs make for interesting and enjoyable route finding. This route crosses the Holy Cross Wilderness and is closed to bikes.

From the 10th Mountain Hut, the trail heads south through a meadow, past a dead tree with a trail marker. Ski up over a flat ridge with a tiny, snow-covered pond, then drop into the North Fork of West Tennessee Creek below the east ridge of Homestake Peak. Continue south up and over a small, forested ridge and down to West Tennessee Creek. At the clearing in the valley bottom, correct your direction of travel and head slightly southwest. Cross the creek and pick up the trail as it climbs south into the forest along the west side of a small creek. Enter a flat meadow, turn east, cross the clearing and re-enter the woods.

Follow the trail east and then south over another ridge with a tiny lake, then begin a distinct drop into a marshy creek. Head south/southeast from this marsh past a trail junction (joining the Colorado Trail), then ski around the east scarp of Elevation Point 11,375' and begin a long, traversing descent to the southwest into Long's Gulch. Follow the creek upstream past the wilderness boundary (1.5 miles west of the trail junction), then begin a rising traverse out of the valley to the southwest.

The trail climbs through rocky terrain onto a promontory that overlooks the valley and the peaks to the west. Contour to the east and drop easily down and across Porcupine Gulch. Begin the 600-foot ascent of the steepest and most demanding 1 mile of trail. From here, the route switchbacks up a steep and at times rocky trail until it gains the east ridge of Galena Mountain, near treeline. (This portion of the route presents very difficult telemark skiing for those headed north to the 10th Mountain Division Hut. You may wish to leave climbing skins on to slow the descent through this area.) Make a gentle traverse east down to a forested saddle. Descend to the hut by curving sharply to the southwest, following trail markers down a drainage and into a clearing. After dropping 400 feet, the trail leaves the creek and traverses southeast along the Colorado Trail up to Uncle Bud's Hut.

18   UNCLE BUD'S HUT

This hut is named for Burdell "Bud" Winter, a 10th Mountain Division soldier killed in action in the Italian Alps during World War II. A display tells the story of a young man who died young, already a seasoned mountaineer.

Completed in 1989, Uncle Bud's Hut is unique in that the first level is constructed of stone, with a traditional wood-sided second story. Uncle Bud's Hut sleeps 16. Day skiing around the hut is extensive and varied, with a little bit of everything for everyone. Make reservations through the 10th Mountain Hut Association (Appendix A).

TOUR 18A   TURQUOISE LAKE TRAILHEAD

Difficulty:	Novice/Intermediate
Time:	4 to 7 hours
Distance:	5.8 miles
Elevations:	Trailhead 10,030', Hut 11,380', +1,620'/-40'
Avalanche Note:	None
Maps:	USGS 7.5': Homestake Reservoir, 1970; Leadville North, 1970
	National Forest: San Isabel, White River
	Trails Illustrated: Map #109 (Breckenridge/ Tennessee Pass); Map #126 (Holy Cross/Ruedi Reservoir)
	10th Mountain: Galena Mountain
	See map pages 88-89, 128-129, and 132-133

Due to acts of vandalism at the traditional trailhead, the trailhead has been moved down the road 2.1 miles into the main Tennessee Creek/Arkansas River Valley. Located on the eastern side the river and the railroad tracks, this new parking lot is more open and lighted. Try not to leave valuables in your car — or valuable cars — here.

The trail now gains an additional 270 feet of elevation and is 5.8 miles long. It is still an easy-to-follow road for the entire distance. Novice skiers will be challenged by the climb to the hut, but will enjoy cranking turns (or snowplowing!) back down to the parking area. For skiers, bikers, and hikers, this steep route climbs continuously from the parking area to the hut and features nice views of the Mosquito Range to the east.

The Turquoise Lake Trailhead is a little difficult to locate, so follow the directions closely. The road to the trailhead begins on the north end of Leadville near Safeway. From the junction of US 24 and Mountain View Drive, turn west and drive 2.8 miles to a T junction. Turn north (right), cross a fork of the Arkansas River and proceed to the parking lot, which is near where the road veers west to cross the main river and the railroad tracks.

Ski or walk west over the railroad tracks. Cross the main stem of the Arkansas River, then head west past the entrance to Turquoise Lake. When you reach another intersection, turn north again. Follow FR 104, passing a picnic area, campgrounds and boat ramps on the left between the road and the lake. Continue along the road, above the lake on the northeast, to a fork in the road.

Take the north fork onto FR 107 and start climbing. Pass a right turn to Saint Kevin Gulch after 0.3 mile. Continue climbing north, ski under a power line, and then contour west up to a flat shoulder and small clearing with great views of the Arkansas Valley. Traverse west along the south aspect of the ridge for another 0.3 mile, then gain another flat shoulder.

Follow the trail north across gentle terrain, then begin the final 340-foot climb to the hut. Follow the road northwest up a forested ridge and across a clearing, eventually leaving the road near Elevation Point 11,285'. Ski northwest through thinning trees to Uncle Bud's Hut.

RECOMMENDED DAY TOURS: To the west of the hut is a large basin between Saint Kevin, Galena, and Bear lakes. It is easy to drop down from the hut and spend a full day touring up and down this gully. Behind the hut to the north, skiers can climb back to the east ridge of Galena Mountain and ascend west to Elevation Point 12,313' for a brief and noncommitting introduction to winter mountaineering. Around the northeast corner of the hut is Saint Kevin Gulch, which has many acres of treeless terrain offering nice and easy telemark skiing, especially after a storm.

Finally, Galena Mountain's south ridge makes for a very safe and classic winter climb. From the hut, the route drops down to the Colorado Trail/Skinner Hut Trail, then west to the foot of the south ridge of Galena Mountain and a safe route up, out of the forest. Once on the south ridge, the route is straightforward and ascends north up a broad ridge to the 12,893-foot summit. If you attempt this route, remember that although easy for a climb to a 12,000-foot peak, it is a committing day excursion.

Beth Smith in front of Uncle Bud's Hut,
10th Mountain Division Hut System

TOUR 18B UNCLE BUD'S HUT TO SKINNER HUT

Difficulty:	Advanced
Time:	6 to 9 hours
Distance:	7 miles
Elevations:	UB Hut 11,380', S Hut 11,620', +1,985'/-1,760'
Avalanche Note:	Some avalanche terrain encountered; easily avoided
Maps:	USGS 7.5': Homestake Reservoir, 1970
	National Forest: San Isabel, White River
	Trails Illustrated: Map #126 (Holy Cross/ Ruedi Reservoir)
	10th Mountain: Continental Divide
	See map page 88-89 and 132-133

The route climbs to the Skinner Hut via one of the steepest and most physically taxing sections of trail in the 10th Mountain Division system. The ascent of Glacier Creek seems to catch people off guard, and pushes them to the limit. Get an early start so that you can travel at a comfortable pace.

Leave Uncle Bud's and descend into the basin west of the hut, Bud's Gulch. Proceed to the wilderness area boundary sign and intercept the Colorado Trail. Follow the trail west over a small rise, then drop down across the Bear Creek drainage. Cross the basin north of Galena and Bear lakes and ski southwest for 0.5 mile. Climb a series of switchbacks to treeline, across a shoulder of Galena Mountain.

Traverse west for a few hundred feet, then begin the long, switchbacking descent into Lake Fork valley through a clearing. After descending roughly 150 feet, traverse west through the trees, below a large ridge south of Galena Mountain. Continue on switchbacks near Mill Creek, then head southeast under the power lines, and finally turn west into the Lake Fork valley.

The fun begins when you start the ascent to the Skinner Hut. Finding the trail can be a little tricky. Basically, the arduous ascent begins about 500 feet south of several Forest Service/Colorado Trail signs, located in a clearing near Lake Fork Creek, west of Turquoise Lake. (If you happen to be coming from the Turquoise Lake Trailhead, follow that road west until it turns south to cross the creek. From this spot, ski west along the creek on a trail through the woods — after a few hundred feet you will see several signs.)

From the signs, ski southwest, following the trail into the woods and across the creek to a trail junction. The right fork is the Timberline Lake Trail. Take the left fork, which heads south through some tightly spaced trees and begins climbing immediately. From here, the trail switchbacks to the southwest without respite as it heads up and into Glacier Creek. The trail, marked by blue diamonds, remains on the west side of the creek. After climbing nearly 600 feet, the trail enters a flat basin below large cliffs and avalanche slopes to the west. The Skinner Hut is on top of the ridge to the south. Ski directly up the valley along the creek and enter the woods on the far southwest end. Climb the west side of the creek, gaining an impressive 400 feet in elevation, and enter a second, smaller basin. Ski past the east edge of the meadow and follow the trail southwest, gaining approximately 160 feet in elevation. Turn to the southeast and climb the last grueling 200-foot slope to the ridge top. Once on the ridge, turn to the northeast and traverse the ridge crest for 0.3 mile to the Skinner Hut.

19   SKINNER HUT

The Skinner Hut is on probably the most precipitous site of any hut in the state. The hut is unique among the 10th Mountain Division huts in that it deviates from the traditional two-story floor plan. Instead, it is laid out in a one-story ranch style. The handsome, stone building appears to have been carved from the underlying crags, and it blends well with the high, alpine landscape. This shelter has a decidedly European flavor.

Inside the hut, the living and cooking area is set apart from sleeping quarters, which accommodate 19. Numerous windows provide abundant light and views of Leadville and the Arkansas Valley.

Protected from the wind by stands of rugged spruce trees, this hut is the most remote, hardest to reach hut in the system. But those able to get here are in for a treat. Make reservations through the 10th Mountain Division Hut Association (Appendix A).

The Skinner Hut, a one-story hut with stone exterior.

10th Mountain Hut & Trail System

The 10th Mountain Division Hut System is located in the White River and San Isabel National Forests under agreement with the Forest Service, USDA.

Scale 1:24,000 Contour Intervals: 40 Feet

0   .25   .50   .75   1
SCALE IN MILES

MN 12°

Hut
Trailhead
Wilderness Boundary

Trails are marked intermittently by blue diamonds, except in Wilderness Areas where trails are marked by tree blazes. Trail heads are not marked. USFS trails and roads are not maintained and their exact location may vary. This map is not a substitute for good route-finding skills. This map is an aid to help locate routes. There are suggested routes only. Hazards exist in the backcountry, including avalanches. Common sense and good judgment can reduce but not eliminate these hazards.

© 1994 • 10th Mountain Division Hut Association

WHITE RIVER NATIONAL FOREST

HOLY CROSS WILDERNESS

Tennessee Pass Trailhead
10,424

Crane Park Trailhead
10,137

10th Mountain Division Hut

16B
17A
17B
17C
16B

CONTINENTAL DIVIDE

1.30 miles to Crane Park
2.64 miles to Tennessee Pass
3.07 miles to 10th Mountain Division Hut
7.00 miles to Uncle Bud's Hut

2.74 miles to 10th Mountain Division Hut
2.97 miles to Tennessee Pass
6.67 miles to Uncle Bud's Hut

1.72 miles to 10th Mountain Division Hut
3.96 miles to Tennessee Pass

1.46 miles to 10th Mountain Division Hut
5.79 miles to Uncle Bud's Hut

2.75 miles to 10th Mountain Division Hut
4.50 miles to Uncle Bud's Hut
5.29 miles to Tennessee Pass

3.00 miles to Uncle Bud's Hut
4.22 miles to 10th Mountain Division Hut

SAN ISABEL

NATIONAL FOREST

GALENA MOUNTAIN

TENNESSEE

PARK

Turquoise Lake
Trailhead
9,780

Turquoise Lake Trailhead

From Highway 24 and Mountain View Drive at
the N end of Leadville, drive 2.8 miles west on
Mountain View Drive to the multi-use trailhead
parking lot at the end of the paved road.

18 A
19 A

18 A

19 A

18 B

17 C

Uncle Bud's Hut
11,380'
Lat: 80° 15.066 N
Long: 106° 24.396 W

6.95 miles to Uncle Bud's Hut
6.90 miles to 10th Mountain Division Hut

1.82 miles to Uncle Bud's Hut
5.43 miles to 10th Mountain Division Hut

5.50 miles to Turquoise Lake Trailhead
2.54 miles to Uncle Bud's Hut
7.25 miles to Skinner Hut

1.25 miles to Uncle Bud's Hut
4.50 miles to Turquoise Lake Trailhead

1.99 miles to Uncle Bud's Hut
6.08 miles to Skinner Hut

TURQUOISE   LAKE

SEE 10TH MOUNTAIN MAP NO. X CONTINENTAL DIVIDE

TOUR 19A   TURQUOISE LAKE TRAILHEAD

Difficulty:	Advanced
Time:	7 to 11 hours
Distance:	8.6 miles
Elevations:	Trailhead 10,030', Hut 11,620', +2,170'/-580'
Avalanche Note:	Some avalanche terrain encountered; easily avoided
Maps:	USGS 7.5': Homestake Reservoir, 1970; Leadville North, 1970
	National Forest: San Isabel, White River
	Trails Illustrated: Map #109 (Breckenridge/ Tennessee Pass); Map #126 (Holy Cross/Ruedi Reservoir)
	10th Mountain: Continental Divide
	See map pages 88-89 and 132-133

This is the standard trail to the Skinner Hut. The first 7.7 miles, which follow the Turquoise Lake Road, pass easily. Near the end of the road, at Lake Fork Creek, the character of the route changes dramatically, climbing directly up to the hut via Glacier Creek. Gaining over 1,500 feet of elevation in just under 3 miles, this route provides navigation and route-finding challenges, giving the trail its advanced rating. The route should be attempted only by skiers who are physically prepared to work hard at high altitudes.

This trail shares the climb to the hut with the Uncle Bud's to the Skinner Hut route. See Tour 18B for detailed directions for the last 3 miles from Lake Fork Creek to the Skinner Hut.

The Turquoise Lake Trailhead is a little difficult to locate, so follow directions closely. The road to the trailhead begins on the north end of Leadville, near Safeway. From the junction of US 24 and Mountain View Drive, turn west and drive toward Mount Massive (on the horizon). After 2.8 miles, you'll reach a T road junction. Turn north (right), cross a fork of the Arkansas River and proceed to the parking lot, which is near where the road veers west to cross the main river and the railroad tracks.

Ski or walk west over the railroad tracks. Cross the main stem of the Arkansas River, then head west, past the entrance to Turquoise Lake. When you reach another intersection, turn north again. Follow FR 104, passing a picnic area, campgrounds, and boat ramps that are on the left between the road and the lake. Continue along the road, above the lake on the northeast. Ski west along the Turquoise Lake Road (FR 104/105) for 7.7 miles, passing the right (north) turn to Uncle Bud's Hut at 3.4 miles.

Basically, the first part of the tour just follows this popular summer road. Is very obvious and traverses through the woods above the lake, gradually climbing for the first half, then beginning a long descent into the Lake Fork Creek valley. Just be careful not to turn off into any of the campgrounds or boat ramps.

At the 7.7 miles, where the road turns sharply and heads southeast back along the creek, leave the road and ski west into the woods, following a trail that leads to a small clearing and a large Forest Service sign. Refer to Tour 18B for a detailed description of the trail between the sign and the hut.

RECOMMENDED DAY SKI TOURS: Skiing around the Skinner Hut is more alpine than the skiing around most other huts. Since it is so high and exposed to the westerly winds over Hagerman Pass, the surrounding snowpack tends to be less forgiving. Intermediate and advanced skiers can tour up to Hagerman Pass and onto the Continental Divide. From the pass, you can climb to the north and south onto the surrounding peaks. Telemark skiing near the summit is limited due to the steep nature of the terrain.

RECOMMENDED DAY BIKE TOURS: During the summer, the Skinner Hut can be reached directly from the Fryingpan River drainage (west) and from Turquoise Lake (east) by riding up the Hagerman Pass road (FR 105).

To reach the hut from the Leadville area, proceed to the east entrance to Turquoise Lake. See Tour 18A for directions to the entrance. Turn left (south) and follow the road over the dam. Proceed 5 miles to the turnoff to the Hagerman Pass Road. Park and bike up toward the pass for 7 miles and a gain of 1,400 feet. The Skinner Hut is directly on top of a spectacular ridge above the final, sharp switchback. It is roughly 100 feet north from the road, marked by a dirt driveway and rock cairn. Keep an eye out, as this shelter can be difficult to see from the road. This optional, summer route consists of strenuous, intermediate bike touring.

From the Fryingpan River, leave from the trailhead for the Betty Bear Hut via FR 505. See Tour 20A for directions to the trailhead. From the parking area, bike along Hagerman Pass Road for 14.7 miles to the top of Hagerman Pass (be sure to follow the road above Ivanhoe Lake to the north). From there, drop 1 mile down the east side of the pass to the left turn. Ride out on the ridge 0.3 mile to the hut.

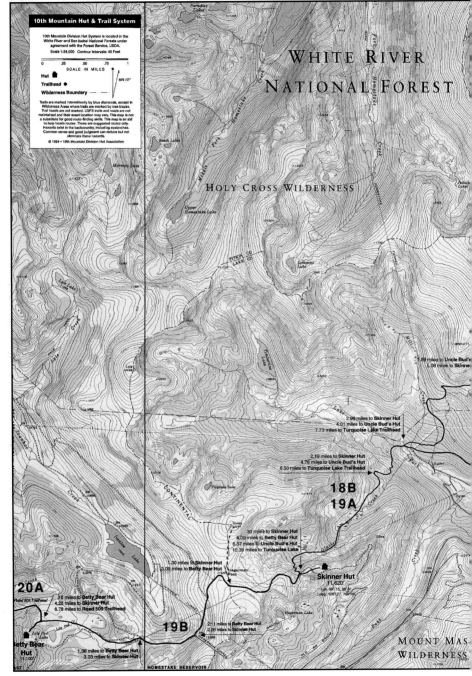

10th Mountain Hut & Trail System

10th Mountain Division Hut System is located in the
White River and San Isabel National Forests under
agreement with the Forest Service, USDA.

Scale 1:24,000   Contour Intervals: 40 Feet

0   .25   .50   .75   1
SCALE IN MILES

MN 12°

Hut   🏠
Trailhead   ●
Wilderness Boundary — — —

Trails are marked intermittently by blue diamonds, except in
Wilderness Areas where trails are marked by tree blazes.
Trail heads are not marked. USFS trails and roads are not
maintained and their exact location may vary. This map is not
a substitute for good route-finding skills. This map is an aid
to help locate routes. These are suggested routes only.
Hazards exist in the backcountry, including avalanches.
Common sense and good judgment can reduce but not
eliminate these hazards.

© 1994 • 10th Mountain Division Hut Association

WHITE RIVER
NATIONAL FOREST

HOLY CROSS WILDERNESS

1.89 miles to Uncle Bud's
5.08 miles to Skinne

2.96 miles to Skinner Hut
4.01 miles to Uncle Bud's Hut
7.73 miles to Turquoise Lake Trailhead

2.19 miles to Skinner Hut
4.78 miles to Uncle Bud's Hut
8.50 miles to Turquoise Lake Trailhead

**18B
19A**

.30 miles to Skinner Hut
4.09 miles to Betty Bear Hut
6.57 miles to Uncle Bud's Hut
10.39 miles to Turquoise Lake

1.30 miles to Skinner Hut
3.09 miles to Betty Bear Hut

20A

Road 505 Trailhead

.18 miles to Betty Bear Hut
4.29 miles to Skinner Hut
6.78 miles to Road 505 Trailhead

Skinner Hut
11,620
Lat. 39° 15' 38" N
Long. 106° 27' 76" W

19B

2.11 miles to Betty Bear Hut
2.26 miles to Skinner Hut

**Betty Bear
Hut**
11,100

1.36 miles to Betty Bear Hut
3.03 miles to Skinner Hut

HOMESTAKE RESERVOIR

MOUNT MAS
WILDERNESS

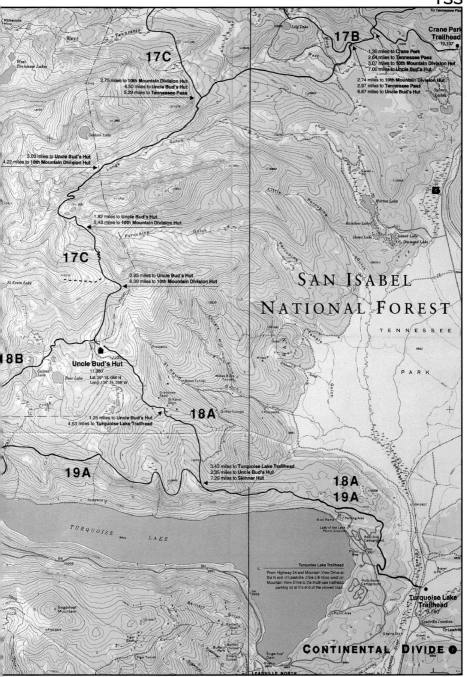

To Tennessee Pass

17B

Crane Park
Trailhead
10,137

17C

West Tennessee Lakes
West

2.75 miles to 10th Mountain Division Hut
4.50 miles to Uncle Bud's Hut
5.29 miles to Tennessee Pass

1.30 miles to Crane Park
2.64 miles to Tennessee Pass
3.07 miles to 10th Mountain Division Hut
7.00 miles to Uncle Bud's Hut

2.74 miles to 10th Mountain Division Hut
2.97 miles to Tennessee Pass
6.67 miles to Uncle Bud's Hut

Sylvan Lakes

Dexters Lake

3.03 miles to Uncle Bud's Hut
4.22 miles to 10th Mountain Division Hut

Longs Gulch

Little Porcupine

Morton Lake

Rainbow Lake

1.82 miles to Uncle Bud's Hut
5.43 miles to 10th Mountain Division Hut

Porcupine Gulch

Home Lake

Island Lake
Diamond Lake

17C

St Kevin Lake

0.95 miles to Uncle Bud's Hut
6.30 miles to 10th Mountain Division Hut

SAN ISABEL
NATIONAL FOREST

TENNESSEE

PARK

8B

Galena Lake

Uncle Bud's Hut
11,380
Lat. 39° 18.082' N
Long. 106° 24.298' W

Bear Lake

St Kevin Gulch

Wildes Boarding Tunnel

Glacialene Shaft

St Kevin Shaft

Griffith Tunnels

Prospects

1.25 miles to Uncle Bud's Hut
4.53 miles to Turquoise Lake Trailhead

18A

19A

3.43 miles to Turquoise Lake Trailhead
2.35 miles to Uncle Bud's Hut
7.26 miles to Skinner Hut

18A
19A

TURQUOISE LAKE

Boat Ramp
Parking Area

Lady of the Lake
Picnic Grounds

Baby Doe
Campground

Turquoise Lake Trailhead
From Highway 24 and Mountain View Drive at the N end of Leadville, drive 2.8 miles west on Mountain View Drive to the multi-use trailhead parking lot at the end of the plowed road.

Molly Brown
Campground

Turquoise Lake Trailhead
9,760

Leadville Junction

To Leadville

Sugarloaf Mountain

Bartlett Gulch

Tiger Shaft

Bartlett Shaft

Buffalo Peak

Bartlett Park

Picnic Area

Sugarloaf Dam

CONTINENTAL DIVIDE

LEADVILLE NORTH

TOUR 19B   SKINNER HUT
                    TO BETTY BEAR HUT

Difficulty:	Advanced	🚶 🚴 🚶‍♂️
Time:	4 to 6 hours	
Distance:	4.4 miles	
Elevations:	S Hut 11,620', BB Hut 11,100', +410'/-900'	
Avalanche Note:	Some avalanche terrain encountered; easily avoided	
Maps:	USGS 7.5': Homestake Reservoir, 1970; Nast, 1970	
	National Forest: San Isabel, White River	
	Trails Illustrated: Map #126 (Holy Cross/ Ruedi Reservoir)	
	10th Mountain: Upper Fryingpan	
	See map pages 88-89, 132-133, and 140-141	

The 4-mile trail between the Skinner Hut and the Betty Bear Hut is significant because it is one of only two points in the 10th Mountain Division system where a hut-to-hut route crosses the Continental Divide, thus connecting the eastern section of the 10th Mountain Division huts with the western section.

This trail crosses Hagerman Pass at an elevation of 11,925 feet and is exposed to mountain storms. Fifty percent of the total mileage is above treeline. Under settled skies, skilled skiing parties can successfully complete this route in a few hours while those with less route-finding experience could easily wander about for longer. Navigation can be very difficult in blizzards and whiteouts. Compass bearings and altimeters are helpful on this tour.

Leave the Skinner Hut and return southwest along the ridge to the Hagerman Pass Road. Follow the road west, above treeline, on an ascent around the north side of a low, rocky hill. Contour southwest on the road to a narrow passage overlooking Busk Creek and Mount Massive. Turn west and ascend moderate terrain to Hagerman Pass, which is marked by a large wooden Forest Service sign.

Ski west from the sign and begin to descend gradually to the south/southwest. Either follow the summer road down to the first sharp switchback, losing 150 feet of elevation, or ski across the tundra toward the trees and the roadbed (the Hagerman Tunnel grade) that traverses west around the upper Lake Ivanhoe drainage at 11,450 feet.

At the road, ski west 0.7 mile until the road crosses the earthen "bridge," or saddle, separating Lily Pad Creek from the Ivanhoe drainage. Follow a well-traveled trail that drops off the road to the west down into the Lily Pad drainage. Proceed west through the center of a long meadow for 1.2 miles, crossing Lily Pad Creek. Continue along the south edge of the meadow until you reach the junction of the FR 505 trail. Turn left (south) and descend a short distance to the Betty Bear Hut.

Many skiers take a workable, but unofficial, alternate route that exits the meadow a little prematurely and follows the Lily Pad Creek Road around the south side of Lily Pad Lake, then down a steep hill to a switchback. From there, it is possible to turn north and ski up to the Betty Bear Hut on a short climb. If you descend too far down, this road begins to drop into the Fryingpan River via a long series of switchbacks. During the winter, the descent to the Fryingpan River becomes an avalanche deathtrap — do not descend this way! This hazard is why the marked ski route drops to the Fryingpan River via the more protected Lily Pad Creek to the west of the Betty Bear Hut.

20   BETTY BEAR HUT

Opened in 1991, the Betty Bear Hut is the newest hut in the 10th Mountain Division system. Named for the wives of Jack Schuss and Al Zesiger, this hut gets my vote for having the best panorama in the system. From the second-story deck, you can see the magnificent Hunter-Fryingpan Wilderness and the glacially carved gorge of Marten Creek.

The standard two-story floor plan is inverted: The sleeping quarters, for 16, are on the first level, while the spacious upper level serves as the lounging, cooking, and eating area. The second story has a very open feel, thanks to a cathedral ceiling and a long bank of windows along its south side. During the day, the upper level warms up considerably just from the passive solar effects of the sun. A final nicety of the second level is a glassed-in dining nook that provides an expansive vista to the south and west. Make reservations through the 10th Mountain Division Hut Association (Appendix A).

TOUR 20A   FOREST ROAD 505 TRAILHEAD

Difficulty:	Intermediate
Time:	6 to 8 hours
Distance:	6.9 miles
Elevations:	Trailhead 9,120', Hut 11,100', +1,980'/-40'
Avalanche Note:	Route crosses avalanche runout zones; can be dangerous during high-hazard periods
Maps:	USGS 7.5': Nast, 1970
	National Forest: White River
	Trails Illustrated: Map #126 (Holy Cross/ Ruedi Reservoir)
	10th Mountain: Upper Fryingpan
	See map pages 88-89 and 140-141

This route is as straightforward as they come. After leaving the trailhead, it follows a forest road (FR 505) for 4.7 miles to the Lily Pad Creek drainage. The ascent along the road is very gradual, while the climb up Lily Pad Creek is steep and abrupt. This trail was laid out this way to avoid the dangerous avalanche slopes along the Lily Pad Lake Trail (FR 1907). The hazardous slopes are southeast of the cabin, directly above the gauging station and the Fryingpan Lakes Trailhead, where the trail climbs to Lily Pad Lake.

The new winter trail ascends steeply through the forest along the east side of the creek, thereby avoiding any potential threat. In summer, ... , Pad Lake Trail is the recommended route for mountain bikes.

To reach the trailhead, drive east from the town of Basalt on FR 105 for 32.2 miles, passing Ruedi Reservoir en route. Drive carefully on this slow, twisting road; the surrounding hillsides are composed of structurally unsound bedrock that often falls onto the road. This road may also be very slick, and the drive can take 45 minutes or more. Drive past the turnoff to FR 505 to the winter road closure and park.

Walk back to the FR 505 junction. Follow FR 505 down across Ivanhoe Creek and begin the long ascent into the upper Fryingpan River drainage. Continue 4.7 miles up the valley along the road to the spot where it crosses Lily Pad Creek, immediately east of the second rock outcrop on the south side of the road.

Search for a trail marker on the uphill side of the road. Climb a steep series of south-facing switchbacks along the east side of Lily Pad Creek. Watch for trail markers. After gaining roughly 500 feet in elevation, enter a clearing near the creek. Follow the trail eastward on a 500-foot climb to the west edge of the Lily Pad Creek meadow. After entering the clearing, turn to the south and follow the trail 300 yards to the hut.

When returning to the trailhead, ski in control (possibly even using skins) on the descent from Lily Pad Creek to FR 505.

RECOMMENDED DAY TOURS: There are many fine cross-country ski routes in the upper Lily Pad Creek and Ivanhoe drainages. Feel free to explore and even climb up to Hagerman Pass for a high-altitude lunch.

Sunny and spacious interior of Betty Bear Hut.

21   POLAR STAR INN & CARL'S CABIN

The Polar Star Inn is like a "stretch" version of a typical 10th Mountain Division hut. Named after a local mine, the Polar Star Inn sleeps 19, is equipped with a muscle-melting sauna and has running spring water, and a propane barbecue. Conveniently located on the northwest corner of New York Mountain, the inn, which is privately owned, fits well into the overall 10th Mountain Division scheme. The inn is open year round and is often combined with the Peter Estin Hut and the Harry Gates Hut for great hut-to-hut ski and mountain bike trips.

Carl's Cabin is a new satellite hut that is a very short walk from the Polar Star Inn. This diminutive shelter is completely equipped for a group of six — the idea being to provide a smaller structure that can easily be rented by a single group. This cozy cabin cost slightly more that a typical 10th Mountain hut fee. A small price to pay to enjoy the privacy of you own hut. Make reservations through the 10th Mountain Division Hut Association (see Appendix A).

TOUR 21A   WEST LAKE TRAILHEAD

Difficulty:	Intermediate/Advanced
Time:	6 to 9 hours
Distance:	7 miles
Elevations:	Trailhead 8,220', Hut 11,040', +2820'/-200'
Avalanche Note:	None
Maps:	USGS 7.5': Fulford, 1987; Grouse Mountain, 1987
	National Forest: White River
	Trails Illustrated: Map #121 (Eagle/Avon)
	10th Mountain: New York Mountain
	See map pages 88-89 and 144-145

The route from West Lake Trailhead is the longest way to the Polar Star Inn and is a textbook exercise in gear hauling. Many skiers use this trailhead as a jumping-off point for a multi-day traverse of the western half of the system, ending their trip in Aspen. Other skiers choose to begin in Aspen and end their expedition at the inn. Without question, it is easier to ski out than to ski in due to the considerable elevation gain. This route is not open to mountain bikers because it crosses the Holy Cross Wilderness Area.

To reach the trailhead, turn off I-70 at the Edwards exit (Exit 163). Head south across the Eagle River to US 6. Turn west for 0.7 mile to the Lake Creek Road. Turn south on Lake Creek Road for 1.8 miles to a fork in the road. Take the right fork onto West Lake Creek Road and proceed 2.8 miles to a sharp hairpin curve. Park at the apex of the turn, where FR 423 heads south. The road is marked with a national forest welcome sign and a sign for East Lake Trail Baryetta Cabins.

From the parking area, ski south along the east side of the creek on FR 423, then cross a bridge and make a rising traverse across the steeply angled

Moon and high clouds in late evening light, Polar Star Inn.

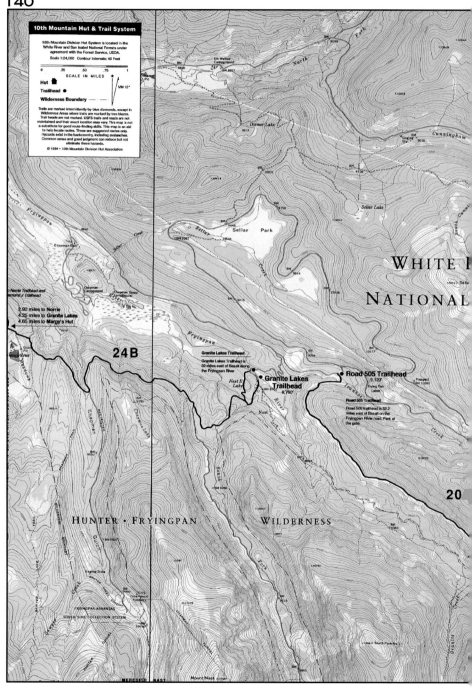

10th Mountain Hut & Trail System

10th Mountain Division Hut System is located in the White River and San Isabel National Forests under agreement with the Forest Service, USDA.

Scale 1:24,000   Contour Intervals: 40 Feet

SCALE IN MILES

0   .25   .50   .75   1

Hut 🏠

Trailhead ●

Wilderness Boundary

MN 12°

Trails are marked intermittently by blue diamonds, except in Wilderness Areas where trails are marked by tree blazes. Trail heads are not marked. USFS trails and roads are not maintained and their exact location may vary. This map is not a substitute for good route-finding skills. This map is an aid to help locate routes. These are suggested routes only. Hazards exist in the backcountry, including avalanches. Common sense and good judgment can reduce but not eliminate these hazards.

© 1994 • 10th Mountain Division Hut Association

to Norrie Trailhead and
Diamond J Trailhead

2.92 miles to Norrie
4.25 miles to Granite Lakes
4.65 miles to Margy's Hut

24B

WHITE

NATIONAL

Granite Lakes Trailhead

Granite Lakes Trailhead is 32 miles east of Basalt along the Fryingpan River

Granite Lakes
Trailhead
8,760'

Road 505 Trailhead
9,120'

Road 505 Trailhead

Road 505 trailhead is 32.2 miles east of Basalt on the Fryingpan River road. Park at the gate.

20

HUNTER · FRYINGPAN   WILDERNESS

MEREDITH   NAST

HOLY CROSS
WILDERNESS

ER

OREST

Paradise
Lakes

Bench Lakes

Mormon Lake

Upper
Homestake Lake

Lonesome
Lake

Lyle Lake

Lyle Creek

PITKIN CO
LAKE CO

Timberline
Lake

Hell Gate
Gaging Sta

Ireland Creek

WILDCAT MOUNTAIN

Virginia Lake

CONTINENTAL

FRYINGPAN-ARKANSAS
NORTH SIDE COLLECTION SYSTEM

Ivanhoe Lake

Lily Pad Creek

Divide

.30 miles to Skinner Hut
4.09 miles to Betty Bear Hut
6.37 miles to Uncle Bud's Hut
10.39 miles to Turquoise Lake

To Turquoise Lake Trailhead
and Uncle Bud's Hut

PITKIN CO
LAKE CO

Hagerman
Pass

Skinner Hut
11,620'
Lat 39° 15.98 N
Long. 106° 27. 767' W

1.30 miles to Skinner Hut
3.09 miles to Betty Bear Hut

.16 miles to **Betty Bear Hut**
4.23 miles to Skinner Hut
6.78 miles to Road 505 Trailhead

2.11 miles to Betty Bear Hut
2.28 miles to Skinner Hut

2.19 miles to Betty Bear Hut
.75 miles to Road 505 Trailhead

Lily Pad Lake

**Betty Bear
Hut**
11,100'
Lat. 39° 15.370' N
Long. 106° 31. 372' W

1.36 miles to **Betty Bear Hut**
3.03 miles to Skinner Hut

19B

Hagerman Lake

UPPER FRYINGPAN

slopes on the west side of the creek. At the 1-mile mark, the road heads back across the creek to the east, to a trail junction. Stay on the right fork as it climbs up and around to the west. From here the road contours east through a meadow past some old cabins and then begins the climb straight south up along a forested ridge.

Eventually the trail reaches an intersection at 9,370 feet, near an old faded Forest Service trail sign attached to a tree. The Card Springs Trail is the right fork and is marked with a blue diamond. It leaves the main trail and crosses south, then west into a forested basin.

Follow the trail west, cross into the wilderness boundary near the creek, and continue ascending along a road until it fades out in an aspen forest. The route switchbacks cross-country, heading west, straight up through aspen trees to a small meadow on the Card Creek Saddle at 9,980 feet. Finding the proper route through this stretch is probably the most tricky section of route finding on the tour, although it is usually marked with a few pieces of colored plastic flagging. Don't be misled by ski trails through the aspen trees that have been left by skiers coming downhill or by an old road that heads directly north through the aspen trees, just before you climb up onto the Card Creek Saddle.

Once at the small, protected meadow (a nice break or lunch spot), ski straight through it to the west, re-enter the woods, then begin a descending traverse into Squaw Creek. The trail contours into the Squaw Creek drainage and ascends all the way up it, first along the west side, then, after making a very sharp dogleg turn at 9,980 feet, on the east. After crossing the creek the trail climbs steadily through the forest and exits the wilderness area and the Squaw Creek drainage near a sign at 10,700 feet.

Continue to the south/southeast to an intersection with a switchback on a logging road. The trail follows the road for a short while, then it strikes off through the woods above the road along its northeast side. It eventually regains the road and follows it the last few hundred yards to the Polar Star Inn. This last few hundred yards of trail travels through open meadows and sporadic trees and can be a little bit difficult to navigate through during snowstorms.

For those leaving the inn, ski north to the road, past a tree with a blue diamond. Be sure to keep an eye out for the places where the trail deviates from the switchbacking road, during the first 1 mile and don't be surprised by the abrupt dogleg turn at the 2.1 mile mark as it shows up quickly. Also this is a very fast descent for most of its length, so exercise caution.

RECOMMENDED DAY TOURS: The area around the Polar Star Inn is laced with many old logging and mining roads that offer many days of skiing. A recommended day trip climbs New York Mountain by the north ridge. The route up the mountain is quite direct. Leave the inn and ascend east to the ridge. Follow the crest of the north ridge, just south to the summit. This is a great mountaineering trip and is one of the most straightforward climbs to a 12,000-foot peak that is available to hut skiers. Carry appropriate safety equipment and be wary of snowy cornices overhanging the northeast face.

TOUR 21B   YEOMAN PARK TRAILHEAD VIA FULFORD ROAD

Difficulty:	Intermediate	🏃 🚴 🏃🏃
Time:	5 to 7 hours	
Distance:	6.2 miles	
Elevations:	Trailhead 9,060', Hut 11,040', +2,033'/-140'	
Avalanche Note:	None	
Maps:	USGS 7.5': Fulford, 1987	
	National Forest: White River	
	Trails Illustrated: Map #121 (Eagle/Avon)	
	10th Mountain: New York Mountain	
	See map pages 88-89 and 144-145	

There are two routes from the Yeoman Park Trailhead to the Polar Star Inn: Fulford Road and Newcomer Spring. Both routes ascend through similar terrain, switchback and traverse a great deal, and gain roughly the same amount of elevation. What differentiates the two is that the Fulford Road route follows a wide, well-traveled road for the initial 4.4 miles, while the Newcomer Spring route is a trail through the forest. At the point where they meet, the two routes converge and ascend more steeply to the inn. The Fulford Road is better for folks who want to follow an obvious road and like lots of space for snowplow turns, although it is traveled by snowmobilers.

To reach the trailhead, drive on I-70 to the Eagle exit (Exit 147). Head south across the Eagle River, then turn right onto US 6. Proceed into Eagle and turn left on Broadway. Drive to the intersection of Broadway and 6th Street, and turn left onto 6th Street. Drive for one block, then turn right onto the Brush Creek Road (FR 400). Drive to a fork in the road near where the pavement ends. Take the left fork to East Brush Creek Road (to Fulford and Yeoman Park) and proceed 5.6 miles, then turn right, cross the creek and turn into an obvious plowed parking area.

To begin the tour, leave the parking lot, return to the East Brush Creek Road and head southeast. Ski or walk along the road for 0.4 mile to the turnoff to the Fulford Road (FR 418). Follow the Fulford Road for 4.2 miles

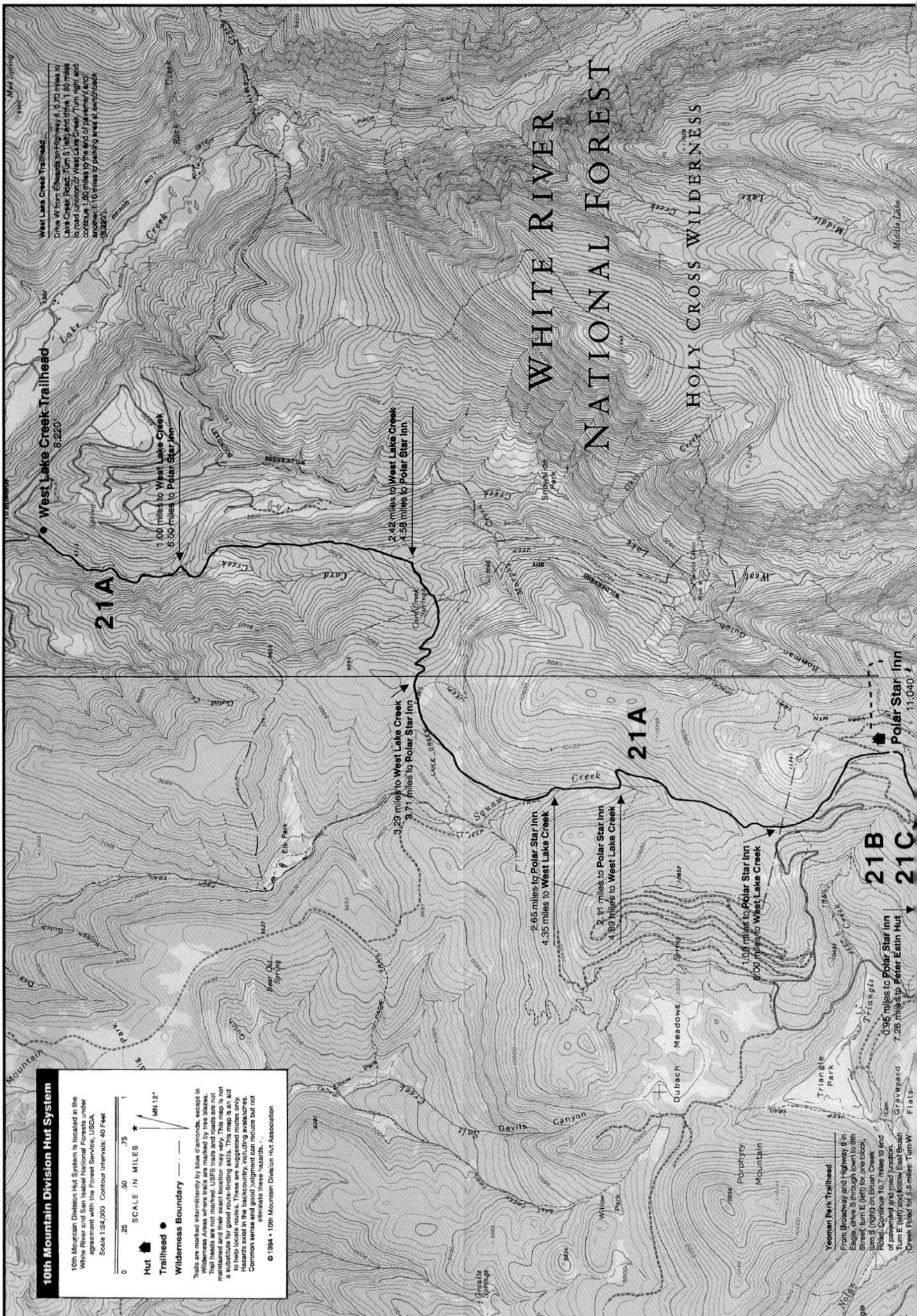
10th Mountain Division Hut System
10th Mountain Division Hut System is located in the White River and San Isabel National Forests under agreement with the Forest Service, USDA.
Scale 1:24,000 Contour Intervals: 40 Feet
0 .25 .50 .75
SCALE IN MILES
MN 12°
Hut
Trailhead
Wilderness Boundary
Trails are marked intermittently by blue diamonds, except in Wilderness Areas where trails are marked by tree blazes. Trail heads are not marked. USFS trails and roads are not maintained and their exact location may vary. This map is not a substitute for good route-finding skills. This map is an aid to help locate routes. These are suggested routes only. Hazards exist in the backcountry, including avalanches. Common sense and good judgment can reduce but not eliminate these hazards.
© 1994 • 10th Mountain Division Hut Association
West Lake Creek Trailhead
Drive W from Edwards on Highway 6, 0.70 miles to Lake Creek Road. Turn S (left) and drive 1.80 miles to road junction of West Lake Creek. Turn right and continue 1.80 miles to the end of pavement and another 1.10 miles to parking area at switchback (8,220').
West Lake Creek Trailhead
8,220'
1.00 miles to West Lake Creek
6.00 miles to Polar Star Inn
2.42 miles to West Lake Creek
4.58 miles to Polar Star Inn
3.29 miles to West Lake Creek
3.71 miles to Polar Star Inn
2.65 miles to Polar Star Inn
4.35 miles to West Lake Creek
2.11 miles to Polar Star Inn
4.89 miles to West Lake Creek
1.00 miles to Polar Star Inn
6.00 miles to West Lake Creek
0.96 miles to Polar Star Inn
7.26 miles to Peter Estin Hut
21A
21B
21C
Polar Star Inn
11,040'
WHITE RIVER
NATIONAL FOREST
HOLY CROSS WILDERNESS
Yeoman Park Trailhead
From Broadway and Highway 6 in Eagle, drive S through town to 5th Street, turn E (left) for one block, turn S (right) on Brush Creek Road. Continue 10.7 miles to end of pavement and road junction. Turn E (left) and follow East Brush Creek Road for 5.5 miles. Turn W
Lake
Creek
Card Creek
Squaw Creek
Snowslide Park
Elk Park
Bear Cat Spring
Dubach Meadows
Devils Canyon
Salt Creek
Willow Park
Porphyry Mountain
Triangle Park
Graveyard Flats
Granite Springs
Middle Lake
West
Bowman Gulch
Dry
Mountain
Mud Spring
WILDERNESS
BOUNDARY
PACK TRAIL
JEEP TRAIL
to Eagle
East

NEW YORK MOUNTAIN

Creek

Upper Camp Lake

East

Gold Dust Lakes

Big Lake

Horseshoe Lake

Big Spruce Lake

Mystic Island Lake

Gold Dust Pass

Mesa Basin

Lake Charles

Finnegan Peak

New York Lake

New York Mountain

GROUSE MOUNTAIN

MOUNT JACKSON

FULFORD CREEK PASS

CROOKED CREEK PASS

Gold Dust Basin

Craig Peak

Nolan Lake

Nolan Creek

21C
21D

1.79 miles to Polar Star Inn
6.42 miles to Peter Estin Hut

3.57 miles to Polar Star Inn
4.54 miles to Peter Estin Hut

1.40 miles to Yeoman Park
3.00 miles to Peter Estin Hut
6.21 miles to Polar Star Inn

22A
21D

3.40 miles to Peter Estin Hut
4.81 miles to Polar Star Inn

0.40 miles to Yeoman Park
5.00 miles to Fulford Creek Campground

2.30 miles to Yeoman Park
6.02 miles to Peter Estin Hut

Yeoman Trailhead
9,080

1.70 miles to Yeoman Park
4.55 miles to Polar Star Inn

Yeoman Park

Hat Creek

22B

22C

0.72 miles to Peter Estin Hut
6.60 miles to Yeoman Park via Hat Creek Road
7.46 miles to Polar Star Inn

Peter Estin Hut
11,200

0.71 miles to Peter Estin Hut
3.40 miles to Crooked Creek Pass
6.22 miles to Harry Gates Hut

22D

as it gradually traverses, switchbacks, and climbs to the isolated, tiny community of Fulford.

There are two sections where skiers can deviate from the road to avoid snowmobile traffic. The first is near the 1.4-mile mark after the road veers back to the southeast into a creek drainage. Here skiers can parallel the road down near the creek. The second spot is actually a shortcut at the head of this creek, where the main road switchbacks sharply back to the west. At this point a logging road heads southeast up into the upper stretches of the creek. Turn onto it and climb up along the creek before regaining the primary route southeast of the little forested hill, marked 9,953 feet. Both of these alternatives are marked with blue diamonds

From here the route contours around a sharp, northwest-running ridge before it traverses into the Nolan Creek drainage. The route intersects another road just upstream from the little community of Fulford, near an outhouse and a sign that reads "Upper Town & Nolan Lake." Turn here at a blue diamond into Nolan Creek, and take a short but steep ascent up to a clearing with several cabin ruins.

Head straight east, past the ruins, to a trail that is marked with blue diamonds. This is where the Newcomer Spring route meets this trail. From here, the route leaves the road and switchbacks up through the aspen forest, gaining elevation quickly. Watch for diamonds on the trees here. At 5.3 miles the trail intercepts another road, the New York Mountain jeep road at 10,520 feet. Switchback onto this trail and head south, then east on the final approach to the hut.

Climb steadily up the road for 0.5 miles until you reach another intersection with signs for the Polar Star Mine and New York Mountain. Take the left fork (northeast) and follow this marked trail for the last 0.5 mile to the Polar Star Inn and Carl's Cabin.

TOUR 21C YEOMAN PARK TRAILHEAD VIA NEWCOMER SPRING

Difficulty:	Intermediate	🚶 🚲 🏃🏃
Time:	5 to 7 hours	
Distance:	6 miles	
Elevations:	Trailhead 9,060', Hut 11,040', +2,180'/-160'	
Avalanche Note:	None	
Maps:	USGS 7.5': Crooked Creek Pass, 1987; Fulford, 1987	
	National Forest: White River	
	Trails Illustrated: Map #121 (Eagle/Avon)	
	Map #126 (Holy Cross/Ruedi Reservoir)	
	10th Mountain: New York Mountain	
	See map pages 88-89 and 144-145	

Of the two Yeoman Park routes to the Polar Star Inn, Newcomer Spring is slightly more challenging and is also the route of choice, when combined with the Ironedge Trail (Tour 22A), for traveling between the inn and the Peter Estin Hut. The Newcomer Spring route shares the last 1.8 miles with the Fulford Road route and also shares the same trailhead and parking area. Refer to the Yeoman Park Trailhead to Polar Star Inn via Fulford Road (Tour 21B) for trailhead directions.

To begin the tour, leave the parking area, return to the East Brush Creek Road and head southeast. Ski or walk up the road, past the turnoff to Fulford, for 1 mile to the Newcomer Spring Trailhead, which is indicated by a trail marker. Begin the steep, initial climb by leaving the road and following the trail up through a series of large switchbacks.

After gaining 600 feet of elevation, the angle of ascent begins to lessen, and the trail, beginning on a road, traverses due north for 1 mile on a very gradual climb. This stretch of trail provides the most challenging route finding as it leads through nondescript forests interspersed with clearings and woods. It also crosses a logging road at 10,160 feet that is occasionally plowed. Keep map, compass, and altimeter at the ready here and watch closely for trail markers.

Switchback to the southeast around a sharp, forested ridge and then descend to Nolan Creek. The trail contours across the head of this creek and descends slightly to a road above the cabin ruins on the Fulford Road route. From here follow the route to the inn as described in Tour 21B.

TOUR 21D   POLAR STAR INN TO PETER ESTIN HUT

Difficulty:	Intermediate/Advanced
Time:	6 to 8 hours
Distance:	8.3 miles
Elevations:	PS Inn 11,040', PE Hut 11,200', +2,120'/-2,080'
Avalanche Note:	None
Maps:	USGS 7.5': Crooked Creek Pass, 1987;
	Fulford, 1987
	National Forest: White River
	Trails Illustrated: Map #121 (Eagle/Avon);
	Map #126 (Holy Cross/Ruedi Reservoir)
	10th Mountain: New York Mountain
	See map pages 88-89 and 144-145

This inter-hut route makes a large V down and across East Brush Creek, whether heading south from the Polar Star Inn or north from the Peter Estin Hut. There is considerable elevation gain and loss in both directions. Get an early start, for this passage can take more time than one would expect. Skiers without minimal experience descending steep and narrow trails should consider substituting either the Hat Creek Trail or the Fulford Road Trail. These trails are much easier to descend.

This route is a combination of the Newcomer Spring Trail and the Ironedge Trail, which meet on the East Brush Creek Road, 1 mile upstream from the Yeoman Park Trailhead. Refer to the Newcomer Spring route (Tour 21C) and the Ironedge Trail (Tour 22A) for specific directions.

22 PETER ESTIN HUT

The Peter Estin Hut is a favorite in the 10th Mountain Division system —
and for good reasons. The hut is on a forested ridge and looks south over
Lime Park and the Elk Mountains. Telemark skiing around the hut is first-
rate, with thinly forested glades dominating the landscape. There are also
many north- and west-facing slopes to explore. Beginners and expert skiers
alike will find a staggering selection of possible downhill runs. Above the
hut to the east is a treeless slope on the northwest ridge of Charles Peak. The
skiing along the ridge is outstanding. Individuals interested in a little ridge-
running can traverse the spine of the ridge all the way to Fool's Peak.

   The Peter Estin Hut is open year round and sleeps 16. Make reservations
through the 10th Mountain Division Hut Association (see Appendix A).

TOUR 22A   YEOMAN PARK TRAILHEAD VIA IRONEDGE TRAIL

Difficulty:	Intermediate/Advanced
Time:	4 to 7 hours
Distance:	4.4 miles
Elevations:	Trailhead 9,060', Hut 11,200',+2,140'/-80'
Avalanche Note:	None
Maps:	USGS 7.5': Crooked Creek Pass, 1987; Fulford, 1987
	National Forest: White River
	Trails Illustrated: Map #121 (Eagle/Avon); Map #126 (Holy Cross/Ruedi Reservoir)
	10th Mountain: New York Mountain
	See map pages 88-89 and 144-145

The Ironedge Trail is the direct route to the Peter Estin Hut. The trail
ascends a moderate road before beginning a stiff climb to the hut. Skiers
with climbing skins and well-developed lungs and calves will make quick
work of this trail. Returning, however, is a different matter. The trail down
is steep and narrow and has many switchbacks. Competent skiers will enjoy
this route; skiers with less experience should consider the Hat Creek Trail
(Tour 22B) as an alternative. For directions to the Yeoman Park Trailhead,
see Tour 21B.

   Leave the parking lot and ski onto the East Brush Creek Road (FR 415) and head southeast. Ski up the road, past the turnoff to Fulford at 0.4 mile and the Newcomer Spring Trailhead near the 1-mile mark until you finally reach the Fulford Cave Campground at 1.4 miles. Continue past the campground and a small lake, following the road as it turns west and passes some cabins, until it finally crosses East Brush Creek.

Enter the deep forest and begin climbing the seemingly interminable series of short switchbacks that head south. Eventually, the narrow "valley of the switchbacks" begins to open up into a logged area near the 10,400-foot level. The trail soon widens into a road that climbs south through open terrain up to the 11,100-foot ridge immediately west of the hut. At the ridge, turn east and follow a Peter Estin Hut sign as you ski through a stand of spruce trees to the hut.

RECOMMENDED DAY TOUR 1: The area north of the hut was once logged and today is covered with a thin forest, perfectly suited for intermediate-level tree skiing. Ski north and west from the hut along the Ironedge Trail. By remaining east of the trail, it is possible to drop 400 to 600 feet across rolling, stepped topography, crossing a series of old logging roads in the process. When the drainage begins to constrict, it is very easy to traverse west to the upper part of the Ironedge Trail and return to the hut.

RECOMMENDED DAY TOUR 2: From the hut, ski south to the edge of the steep drainage. Contour east around the edge of the trees, then begin climb-

Departing the Peter Estin Hut for a day of powder skiing.

ing into the forest. Follow the path of least resistance up to the east until you reach a clearing. Switchback up to treeline and the top of the ridge. Be sure to catch the view into East Brush Creek and the Holy Cross Wilderness before you telemark back down through the clearing to the hut.

TOUR 22B   YEOMAN PARK TRAILHEAD VIA HAT CREEK TRAIL

Difficulty:	Intermediate
Time:	6 to 8 hours
Distance:	7.4 miles
Elevations:	Trailhead 9,060', Hut 11,200', +2,180'/-40'
Avalanche Note:	None
Maps:	USGS 7.5': Crooked Creek Pass, 1987; Fulford, 1987
	National Forest: White River
	Trails Illustrated: Map #121 (Eagle/Avon); Map #126 (Holy Cross/Ruedi Reservoir)
	10th Mountain: New York Mountain
	See map pages 88-89 and 144-145

Although it is several miles longer than the Ironedge Trail, the Hat Creek Trail is the recommended Peter Estin Hut tour for strong novice and intermediate skiers as well as for mountain bikers, especially for the return run down to Yeoman Park. The route follows a road and should present very few navigation problems. For directions to the Yeoman Park Trailhead, see Tour 21B.

From the parking area, this route heads to the southwest, away from East Brush Creek. Begin skiing (or riding, as the case may be) southwest, then southeast along FR 416, past a campground. Begin climbing in earnest by ascending to Hat Creek via a long traverse to the northwest. After gaining about 400 feet of elevation, the road switchbacks sharply to the southeast into the Hat Creek drainage. Climb along the east side of Hat Creek, passing a right (southwest) turn onto FR 436 at the 5-mile mark.

Remain on the northeast side of Hat Creek, enter a logged area and climb through one series of switchbacks. Continue traversing upward, then go through another, much larger series of switchbacks. Contour around the south flank of Elevation Point 11,110', and intersect the Ironedge Trail on a saddle at 6.6 miles. Turn south up onto the top of the 11,200-foot ridge, gaining 400 feet of elevation from the trail junction. Once you have reached the top of the ridge, turn east and follow a Peter Estin Hut sign as you ski through a stand of spruce trees to the hut.

TOUR 22C   SYLVAN LAKE TRAILHEAD VIA CROOKED CREEK PASS

Difficulty:	Intermediate
Time:	7 to 10 hours
Distance:	9.5 miles
Elevations:	Trailhead 8,558', Hut 11,200', +2,702'/-60'
Avalanche Note:	None
Maps:	USGS 7.5': Crooked Creek Pass, 1987
	National Forest: White River
	Trails Illustrated: Map #126 (Holy Cross/ Ruedi Reservoir)
	10th Mountain: Burnt Mountain
	See map pages 88-89 and 154-155

This is the longest route to the Peter Estin Hut and is the preferred route for people who are skiing between this hut and the Harry Gates Hut. Most of the route follows a moderate road and is a classic intermediate trail. It then jaunts 1 mile cross country up to the hut via the last bit of Lime Ridge Trail, which connects the Peter Estin Hut to the Harry Gates Hut.

To reach the trailhead, drive on I-70 to the Eagle exit (Exit 147). Drive south across the Eagle River, then turn right onto US 6. Proceed into Eagle and turn left on Broadway. Drive to the intersection of Broadway and 6th Street and turn left onto 6th Street. Drive for one block, then turn right onto the Brush Creek Road (FR 400). Drive to a fork in the road near the end of the pavement. Take the right fork to Sylvan Lake and proceed 4.7 miles along West Brush Creek to a parking area on the east side of the lake.

To begin the tour, ski from the parking area, following the West Brush Creek Road around the east side of Sylvan Lake, then southeast up into Brush Creek. Follow FR 400 up through Brush Creek on a long, steady 5.3-mile climb to the top of the pass, skiing around several switchbacks en route.

From the top of the pass, leave the main road and follow a road (FR 428) that switchbacks sharply up toward the northwest across a clearing. Reaching the crest of a ridge, switchback to the southeast around the top of a drainage (Spine Creek). Follow the trail as it traverses west and north above Spine Creek. Enter a logged area and continue due east, dropping across a flat depression, or pass, until you reach a switchback along a creek where the road heads back to the northeast.

Exit the road at the switchback and follow the shallow drainage east on a moderate climb onto the top of Lime Ridge. Turn left (north) and follow the Lime Ridge Trail through sparse timber along the crest of the ridge, with a steep drainage on the east. Contour slightly to the northeast to reach the Peter Estin Hut, which is set back several hundred feet from the edge of the clearing at the head of the drainage.

TOUR 22D PETER ESTIN HUT TO HARRY GATES HUT

Difficulty:	Intermediate
Time:	5 to 7 hours
Distance:	7 miles
Elevations:	PE Hut 11,200', HG Hut 9,700', +734'/-2,180'
Avalanche Note:	None
Maps:	USGS 7.5': Crooked Creek Pass, 1987
	National Forest: White River
	Trails Illustrated: Map #126 (Holy Cross/ Ruedi Reservoir)
	10th Mountain: Burnt Mountain
	See map pages 88-89 and 154-155

This is the most direct path connecting these huts. The route is long but not too severe. With a net loss of 2,180 feet from the Peter Estin Hut (on the north) to the Harry Gates Hut (on the south), the most taxing portion of the trail is descending the ridge between Lime Creek and the Peter Estin Hut. The route crosses the wide and treeless Lime Park, which may present navigation difficulties during blizzards and whiteouts. Keep navigation tools handy. Due to elevation gain, skiing north from the Gates Hut to the Estin Hut is harder.

From the Peter Estin Hut, begin skiing southwest into the trees above the steep drainage to the south. Follow a marked trail that descends straight south through sparse timber along the ridge that forms the east boundary of Middle Creek. Some skiers may want to bypass this ridge completely by dropping straight down from the hut through the unnamed tributary on the east side of the ridge along the summer pack trail. Attempt only when avalanche danger is low! (Note: Bikes are not allowed on the ridge.)

After dropping 1,300 feet to very steep terrain and aspen trees directly above Lime Creek, the trail switchbacks north into an unnamed tributary of Lime Creek and then south across the Lime Creek basin. Cross the creek and ascend to the southeast to a flat, low ridge. Turn right and follow the four-wheel-drive road to the southwest along the forested ridge crest (very narrow at times). Finally the ridge begins to spread out, and the trail eventually enters a meadow. Head due south across the clearing on a slight descent to the intersection with the Woods Lake Road (FR 507) and Burnt Mountain Road (FR

SEE 10TH MOUNTAIN MAP NO. 4 • NEW YORK MOUNTAIN

Sylvan Lake Trailhead
8,558'

Sylvan Lake Trailhead

From Broadway and Highway 6 in Eagle, drive S
through town to 6th Street, turn S (left) for one block,
then left on Brush Creek Road. Continue for
10.7 miles to end of pavement and road junction.
Follow right fork 4.7 miles on the West Brush Creek
Road to Sylvan Lake. Park on E side of the Lake.

To Fulford Cave Campground

Dust Basin Gulch

HOLY CROSS WILDERNESS

WILDERNESS BOUNDARY

22A
21D

0.72 mile to Peter Estin Hut
6.60 miles to Yeoman Park via Fulford Creek Road
7.49 miles to Polar Star Inn

Peter Estin Hut
11,200'

0.74 mile to Peter Estin Hut
3.40 miles to Crooked Creek Pass
4.28 miles to Harry Gates Hut

22B

22C

22C

23A

23A
22C

3.17 miles to Peter Estin Hut
3.76 miles to Harry Gates Hut

22D

Woods Lake

3.30 miles to Crooked Creek Pass
5.60 miles to Spring Creek

4.17 miles to Peter Estin Hut
5.30 miles to Sylvan Lake
8.90 miles to Spring Creek

1.80 miles to Harry Gates Hut
3.70 miles to Crooked Creek Pass
5.13 miles to Peter Estin Hut
via Little Lime Creek Ridge Trail

Crooked Creek

Crooked Creek Reservoir

Middle Creek

Lime Creek

Crooked Creek

WHITE RIVER
NATIONAL FOREST

TABLE MOUNTAIN

West Brush Creek

10th Mountain Division Hut System

10th Mountain Division Hut System is located in the
White River and San Isabel National Forests under
agreement with the Forest Service, USDA.

Scale 1:24,000 Contour Interval: 40 Feet

SCALE IN MILES
0   25   50   75   1

● Hut
● Trailhead
- - - Wilderness Boundary

© 1994 • 10th Mountain Division Hut Association

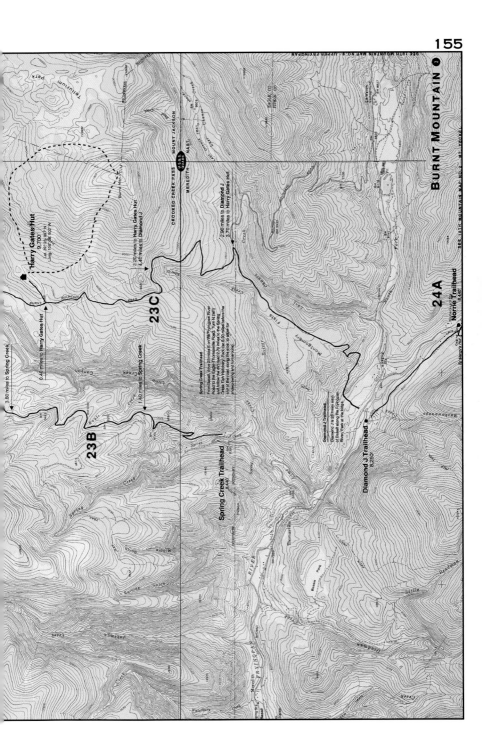

506). This intersection is in wide-open meadow, so keep an eye out for signs and trail markers and keep maps and compass handy.

From the intersection of Burnt Mountain and Woods Lake roads, turn sharply south onto the Burnt Mountain Road and descend across the Lime Creek drainage. Follow the Burnt Mountain Road south for 1.4 miles to a small clearing in the midst of evergreen and aspen trees, on top of a tiny ridge. Exit the road to the northeast onto a trail that follows the ridge, ski through stands of aspen trees and continue 0.4 mile to the Harry Gates Hut, which is hidden in the trees.

Note: Bicyclists should consider descending into Lime Park via Crooked Creek Pass (see Tour 22C) and continuing to the Harry Gates Hut via the route described in Tour23A.

23   HARRY GATES HUT

The Harry Gates Hut is one of the lower-elevation destinations in this guide-book, which makes it a nice choice for beginning hut-to-hut excursions. Aside from the elevation gain and a few possible route-finding problems in Lime Park, all of the trails follow wide roads.

The Harry Gates Hut is the quintessential log cabin. It sleeps 16, with plenty of room to spread out and relax. For reservations call the 10th Mountain Division Hut Association (see Appendix A).

TOUR 23A   SYLVAN LAKE TRAILHEAD

Difficulty:	Intermediate
Time:	8 to 11 hours
Distance:	10.7 miles
Elevations:	Trailhead 8,558', Hut 9,700', +2,140'/-895'
Avalanche Note:	None
Maps:	USGS 7.5': Crooked Creek Pass, 1987
	National Forest: White River
	Trails Illustrated: Map #126 (Holy Cross/
	Ruedi Reservoir)
	10th Mountain: Burnt Mountain
	See map pages 88-89 and 154-155

At 10.7 miles, this is a marathon route across Crooked Creek Pass to the Harry Gates Hut and is recommended only if you intend to travel back to Sylvan Lake, to Yeoman Park (via the Peter Estin Hut), or possibly to the West Lake Trailhead. This trail follows secondary roads for its entire length. As long as you pay attention to your surroundings and keep your map and compass handy for routine checks, you should have very little trouble nav-igating. The first 8.6 miles of this route simply climb up and over Crooked Creek Pass into Lime Park. Car shuttles are necessary if you plan to ski to the north or south ends of the system.

To reach the trailhead, drive on 1-70 to the Eagle exit (Exit 147). Head south across the Eagle River and turn right onto US 6 in Eagle. Turn left on Broadway. Drive to the intersection of Broadway and 6th Street and turn left onto 6th Street. Drive for one block, then turn right onto the Brush Creek Road (FR 400). Drive to a fork in the road near the end of the pavement and take the right fork to Sylvan Lake, proceeding 4.7 miles along West Brush

Creek to a parking area on the east side of the lake.

From the parking lot, ski along FR 400, following it around the east side of Sylvan Lake and then southeast up into the Brush Creek drainage. Follow the road along Brush Creek on a long, steady 5.3-mile climb to the top of Crooked Creek Pass via several switchbacks.

Cross directly over the pass and continue on a southeast course down the north side through scenic aspen forests. Skirt the west side of Crooked Creek Reservoir and head south for 0.7 mile downstream to an intersection. Take the left (southeast) fork onto Burnt Mountain Road (FR 506), climb over a small rise, then drop down to a second junction with the Woods Lake Road (FR 507).

From the Burnt Mountain Road/Woods Lake Road intersection, remain on Burnt Mountain Road through a sharp south turn and head across the Lime Creek drainage. Follow the Burnt Mountain Road for 1.4 miles to a small clearing in the midst of evergreen and aspen trees, on top of a tiny knoll. Exit via the road to the northeast onto a trail along the ridge, through stands of aspen, skiing 0.4 mile to the Harry Gates Hut.

Note: Do not shortcut across Lime Park; there are many hidden cliffs along the creek that can be very dangerous in whiteout conditions.

RECOMMENDED DAY TOURS: Day skiing around the hut mostly consists of long, moderate trail excursions into Lime Park. The exception is the tour up Burnt Mountain, the 11,178-foot peak southeast of the cabin. The top of Burnt Mountain provides a great panorama and many acres of glade skiing. It is recommended for intermediate and advanced skiers.

Departing the Harry Gates Hut for the Peter Estin Hut.

TOUR 23B   SPRING CREEK TRAILHEAD

Difficulty:	Intermediate	🚶 🚲 🚶‍♂️🚶
Time:	7 to 9 hours	
Distance:	8.1 miles	
Elevations:	Trailhead 8,440', Hut 9,700', +1,795'/-520'	
Avalanche Note:	None	
Maps:	USGS 7.5': Crooked Creek Pass, 1987; Meredith, 1987	
	National Forest: White River	
	Trails Illustrated: Map #126 (Holy Cross/ Ruedi Reservoir)	
	10th Mountain: Burnt Mountain	
	See map pages 88-89, 154-155, and 160-161	

The Spring Creek Trail begins downriver from the Diamond Joy Retreat (formerly known as Diamond J Ranch). After an initial steep climb, the Spring Creek/Crooked Creek Pass Road becomes more gentle, allowing for moderate nordic skiing through Lime Park.

To reach the Spring Creek Trailhead, drive 25 miles east from Basalt on the Fryingpan/Ruedi Reservoir Road (FR 105). Take your time on FR 105, because the narrow, twisting road is often snow packed and littered with fallen rocks. Turn left (north) onto the Eagle/Thomasville Road (FR 400) and drive 2.7 miles to a parking area near the Spring Creek Fish Hatchery. Park about 300 yards below the hatchery, leaving room for snowplows and vehicles turning around.

Get ready to work. Begin by skiing around a switchback, past the fish hatchery buildings, and proceed uphill for 1.4 miles until the grade begins to moderate. Continue climbing north along the road toward Lime Park, passing under power lines at the 3.6-mile mark. Begin descending to Lime Park at 4.3 miles.

Drop 300 feet to the junction of Burnt Mountain and Crooked Creek Pass roads. Take the right fork onto Burnt Mountain Road (FR 506) over a small rise, then drop down to a second junction with the Wood Lake Road. From this intersection, turn sharply south onto the Burnt Mountain Road and head down across the Lime Creek drainage. Follow the Burnt Mountain Road south for 1.4 miles to a small clearing on top of a tiny ridge in the midst of evergreen and aspen trees. Exit the road to the northeast onto a trail that follows the ridge. Ski through stands of aspen for 0.4 mile to the Harry Gates Hut, which is hidden among the trees.

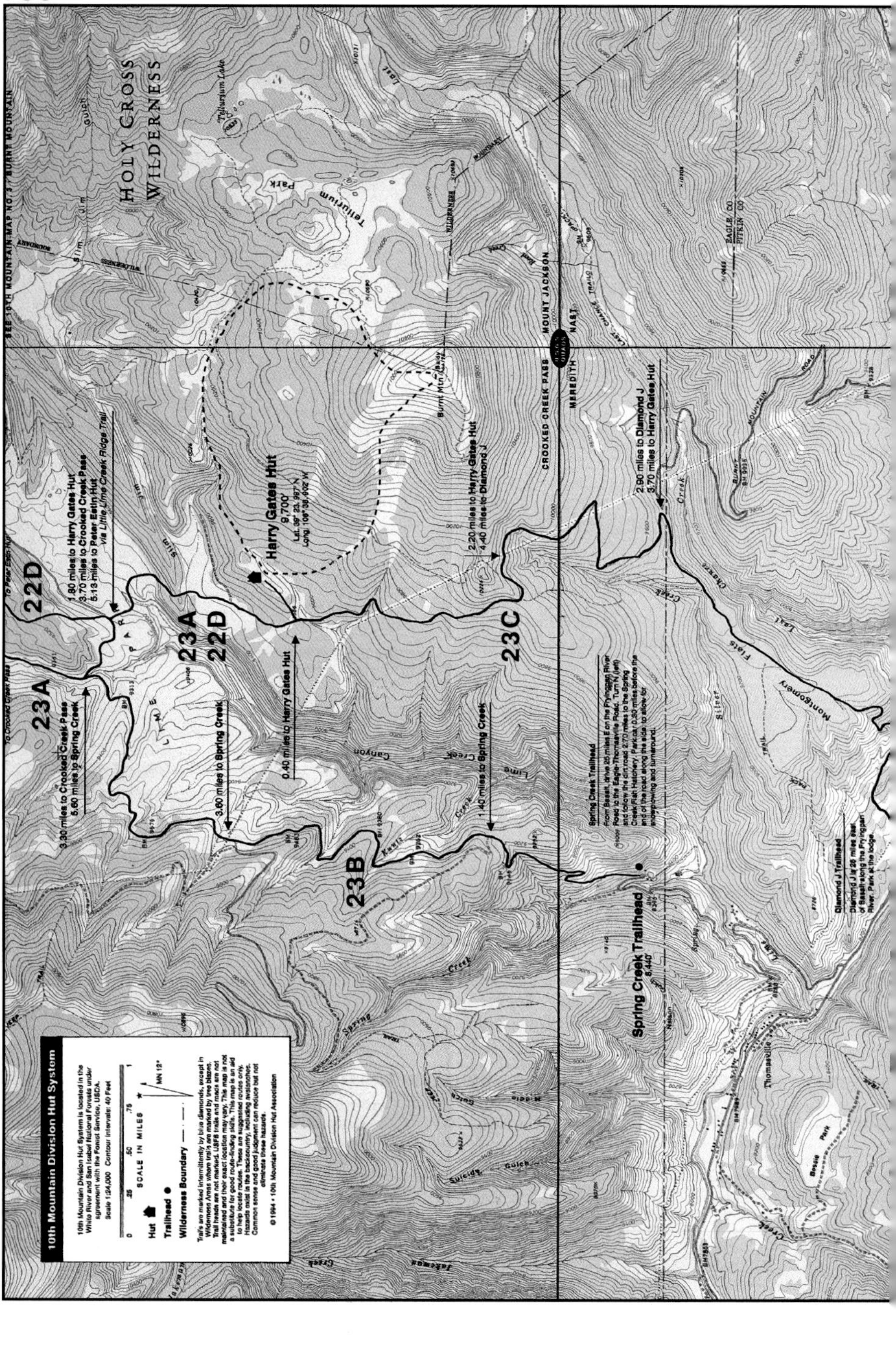
10th Mountain Division Hut System
10th Mountain Division Hut System is located in the White River and San Isabel National Forests under agreement with the Forest Service, USDA.
Scale 1:24,000 Contour interval: 40 Feet
SCALE IN MILES
Hut
Trailhead
Wilderness Boundary
© 1994 - 10th Mountain Division Hut Association
HOLY CROSS
WILDERNESS
Tellurium Lake
Tellurium
Park
22D
23A
23A
22D
23B
23C
1.80 miles to Harry Gates Hut
3.70 miles to Crooked Creek Pass
5.13 miles to Peter Estin Hut
via Little Lime Creek Ridge Trail
3.30 miles to Crooked Creek Pass
5.60 miles to Spring Creek
3.60 miles to Spring Creek
0.40 miles to Harry Gates Hut
1.40 miles to Spring Creek
2.20 miles to Harry Gates Hut
4.40 miles to Diamond J
2.90 miles to Diamond J
3.70 miles to Harry Gates Hut
Harry Gates Hut
9,700'
Burnt Mtn
CROOKED CREEK PASS
MOUNT JACKSON
MEREDITH
NAST
Spring Creek Trailhead
8,440'
Spring Creek Trailhead
Diamond J Trailhead
Montgomery
Flats
Lime
Creek
Canyon
Spring
Creek
Suicide
Gulch
Middle
Gulch
Bessie
Park
Thomasville
EAGLE CO
PITKIN CO
SEE 10TH MOUNTAIN MAP NO. 3 - BURNT MOUNTAIN

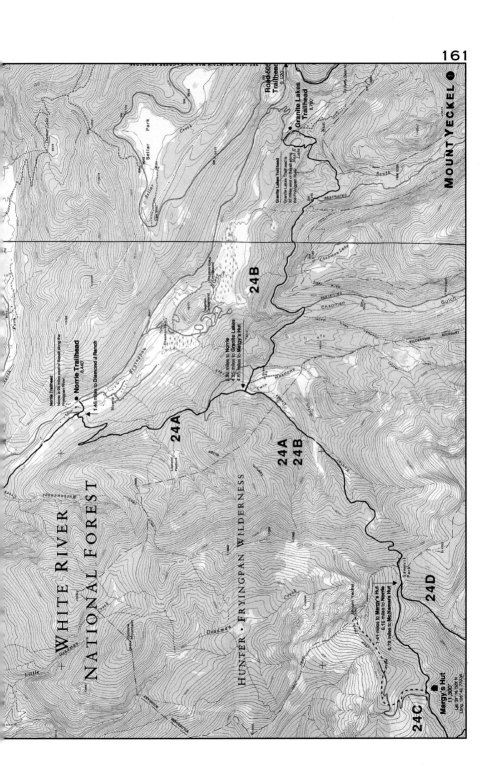

M O U N T Y E C K E L

SEE 10TH MOUNTAIN MAP NO. 23 - HODGE (USGS)

Road 505
Trailhead
9,120'

Granite Lakes
Trailhead

Granite Lakes Trailhead is
.02 miles east of Basalt along
the Fryingpan River.

South

RESTRICTED

24B

Chapman Lake

RESTRICTED

Chapman

Gulch

WILDERNESS
BOUNDARY

Norrie Trailhead is 28 miles east of Basalt along the
Fryingpan River.

Norrie Trailhead
8,440'

1.45 miles to Diamond J Ranch

2.92 miles to Norrie
4.25 miles to Granite Lakes
4.65 miles to Margy's Hut

24A

24A
24B

W H I T E   R I V E R

N A T I O N A L   F O R E S T

H U N T E R · F R Y I N G P A N   W I L D E R N E S S

1.41 miles to Margy's Hut
8.16 miles to Norrie
6.78 miles to McNamara Hut

24D

Margy's Hut
11,300'

24C

TOUR 23C   DIAMOND J TRAILHEAD

Difficulty:	Intermediate	🚶 🚲 👥
Time:	5 to 7 hours	
Distance:	6.6 miles	
Elevations:	Trailhead 8,320', Hut 9,700', +1,880'/-480'	
Avalanche Note:	None	
Maps:	USGS 7.5': Crooked Creek Pass, 1987; Meredith, 1987	
	National Forest: White River	
	Trails Illustrated: Map #126 (Holy Cross/ Ruedi Reservoir)	
	10th Mountain: Burnt Mountain	
	See map pages 88-89, 154-155, and 160-161	

The Diamond J Trailhead provides skiers with a relatively short and minimally difficult route to the Harry Gates Hut. This trail works well for travelers continuing through to Aspen, or for those spending the night in the upper Fryingpan River valley before heading north to the Yeoman Park/Edwards area.

To reach the trailhead, drive east from Basalt for 26 miles on the Fryingpan/Ruedi Reservoir Road (FR 105). Take your time on FR 105, for this narrow, twisting road is often snow packed and littered with fallen rocks. At the entrance to the Diamond Joy Retreat (formerly the Diamond J Ranch), turn right (south) into the ranch, cross the river and park in the plowed area on the left.

Return to the road from the parking area. Cross the road, go through a fence and begin ascending to the northeast for 0.3 mile to a road above the Diamond J Trailhead, passing under a power line en route. Once you have reached the road, follow it uphill onto Montgomery Flats, gaining 750 feet of elevation. Ski to the northeast along the southeast edge of Montgomery Flats above Last Chance Creek until you cross a constriction between Silver Creek (to the northwest) and Last Chance Creek (to the southeast). After crossing the constriction, traverse off the ridge, heading east toward the Burnt Mountain Road (FR 506), which you will intercept 1.4 miles from the south edge of Montgomery Flats.

From here, the route climbs the road for 1.5 miles, crossing back and forth under the power lines, until you begin descending and pass around the southwest ridge of Elevation Point 10,224'. Continue descending northerly for a little under 2 miles, crossing two tributaries of Lime Creek en route. After crossing the second tributary, climb onto a tiny clearing on a ridge surrounded by evergreen and aspen trees. Exit the road to the northeast onto a trail that follows the ridge, skiing through stands of aspen for 0.4 mile to the Harry Gates Hut.

24   MARGY'S HUT

Margy's Hut and the McNamara Hut were the first two huts constructed by the 10th Mountain Division Hut Association. Built in 1982, both of these huts were created and named to honor Margaret McNamara, the late wife of former Secretary of Defense Robert McNamara.

Margy's Hut occupies one of the loveliest sites in Colorado. High on the south ridge of Mount Yeckel at the edge of the Hunter-Fryingpan Wilderness, this hut has all of the qualities that make Colorado hut-to-hut skiing a special experience: It can be reached by several intermediate-rated tours; there is excellent telemark skiing directly below the front porch and on Mount Yeckel; and, finally, the hut overlooks the Williams, Sawatch, and Elk mountains.

Margy's Hut can be reached from the community of Lenado, from Aspen via the McNamara Hut, or from the north, out of the Fryingpan River valley. This hut, along with other huts situated on the west side of the Holy Cross Wilderness, tends to receive less traffic than it used to because of the increase

Enjoying the view, the morning sun, and the company at Margy's Hut.

in popularity of the Vail Pass/Tennessee Pass area huts. Make reservations through the 10th Mountain Division Hut Association (see Appendix A).

TOUR 24A   NORRIE TRAILHEAD

Difficulty:	Intermediate/Advanced
Time:	7 to 9 hours
Distance:	7.6 miles
Elevations:	Trailhead 8,440', Hut 11,300', + 2,917'/-60'
Avalanche Note:	None
Maps:	USGS 7.5': Meredith, 1987
	National Forest: White River
	Trails Illustrated: Map #126 (Holy Cross/
	Ruedi Reservoir)
	10th Mountain: Mount Yeckel
	See map pages 88-89 and 160-161

This trail has an elevation gain of nearly 3,000 feet, making for a very long climb to the hut or a long "cruise" if you are leaving the hut and descending north into the Fryingpan River valley. This route crosses the Hunter-Fryingpan Wilderness and is closed to bike travel.

To reach the Norrie Trailhead, drive 28 miles east from Basalt on the Fryingpan/Ruedi Reservoir Road (FR 105). Take your time driving on FR 105, because the narrow, twisting road is often snow packed and littered with fallen rocks. Pass the Diamond Joy Retreat (formerly the Diamond J Ranch) entrance at 26 miles, then arrive at the well-marked right turn into Norrie. Proceed a few hundred feet, crossing the river, and drive to the end of the plowed road to park.

The route ascends the obvious and unplowed section of road (FR 504) as it switchbacks above the valley to the southwest for the first 2.5 miles. Begin skiing along the road, gaining elevation immediately as you climb around a switchback. After two switchbacks, the road begins a long, ascending traverse to the trail to Twin Meadows. The trail to Twin Meadows is obvious and marked by a blue diamond. Nevertheless, it is possible to ski past it while climbing the road. Bear in mind that the trail is on the right after the third drainage crossing. If you miss the trail, the road does continue up into the meadow, but it is not as direct a route.

Once on the trail, climb a few hundred feet into the north edge of Twin Meadows. After entering the meadows, you will need to pay attention in order to locate the exit point to Deed's Creek and the Hunter-Fryingpan Wilderness Area. From the meadows' north edge, ski due south along the west edge of the meadows, passing to the west of a tiny pond and a road that meets the trail from the east. (Both of these features may be partially obscured by snow.) Continue for a few hundred yards until the trail exits into the forest and Deed's Creek drainage, the first drainage on the west.

Pass a large wilderness area information sign and begin a long, steep climb. Ski up Deed's Creek for about a mile, then follow the trail over into Foster Gulch. Continue upward on a well-traveled trail that ascends Foster Gulch along its northwest bank, then up through the forest for a final steep climb through several switchbacks. After 4.2 miles, you will reach the flat saddle of Sawmill Park.

From here it is important to locate the trail accurately to the hut. To find it, continue over the Sawmill Park saddle, skiing along the right (north) edge of the forest on a very gradual descent. Keep searching on the edge of the trees for old ski tracks or for trail markers, but also be careful that you do not mistake someone's day-touring telemark tracks for the trail. If you begin dropping into Spruce Creek, you have gone too far.

After finding the trail, ski to the hut via a 1.4-mile gradual traverse. This section of trail is heavily used, but you still need to keep an eye out for trail markers. Margy's Hut sits near the top of a low-angled clearing just below the northwest ridge of Mount Yeckel.

RECOMMENDED DAY TOURS: There is a nice, south-facing slope directly below the front porch of the hut that is perfect for practicing free-heel skiing. Some of the finest backcountry powder skiing in the 10th Mountain Division system is on Mount Yeckel. A large, open meadow lies northwest of the hut on the west ridge of the mountain. The road that leads across this clearing begins on the west side of the cabin and travels northwest, past the turnoff to Lenado. Skiers can follow this road to the summit ridge of Mount Yeckel. The northwest face of Mount Yeckel offers supreme telemark skiing. It is easy to spend a full "rest" day cutting fresh tracks down into this bowl. Anyone skiing off Mount Yeckel should be well versed in avalanche-terrain travel.

TOUR 24B   GRANITE LAKES TRAILHEAD

Difficulty:	Intermediate	🏃 🏃🏃
Time:	7 to 9 hours	
Distance:	8.9 miles	
Elevations:	Trailhead 8,760', Hut 11,300', +2,780'/-240'	
Avalanche Note:	Some avalanche terrain encountered; easily avoided	
Maps:	USGS 7.5': Meredith, 1987; Nast, 1970	
	National Forest: White River	
	Trails Illustrated: Map #126 (Holy Cross/ Ruedi Reservoir)	
	10th Mountain: Mount Yeckel	
	See map pages 88-89 and 160-161	

The Granite Lakes Trailhead is 6 miles upstream from the Diamond Joy Retreat (formerly the Diamond J Ranch). It is essentially an alternate start from the Norrie Trailhead and is often used by people staying at the Fryingpan River Ranch or by those descending from the Betty Bear Hut.

To reach the trailhead from the town of Basalt, drive east on the Fryingpan/Ruedi Reservoir Road (FR 105). Take your time on FR 105, for the narrow, twisting road is often snow packed and littered with fallen rocks. Pass the Diamond Joy Retreat at 26 miles, turn right at the fork in the road, pass Norrie at 28 miles, turn right into the ranch at 32 miles, which is well marked. Proceed down the curvy road past the main buildings to the south end of the retreat, near the last cabins. Park in assigned visitors' spots.

Begin skiing up the trail, through dense forest on a curving climb into the South Fork of the Fryingpan River, crossing a creek via a small bridge en route. Ski west across the South Fork and continue up to a wide road (FR 504) by contouring slightly to the northwest. Once on this road, follow it west/northwest, traversing high above the Fryingpan River (to the north) toward Twin Meadows. Intercept the Norrie Trailhead route on the north edge of the meadows and follow that route 4.6 miles to the hut. See Tour 24A for directions to the hut.

TOUR 24C   LENADO TRAILHEAD

Difficulty:	Intermediate/Advanced
Time:	5 to 7 hours
Distance:	6.3 miles
Elevations:	Trailhead 8,649', Hut 11,300', +2,660'
Avalanche Note:	Route crosses avalanche slopes; prone to skier-triggered avalanches during high-hazard periods
Maps:	USGS 7.5': Aspen, 1987; Meredith, 1987
	National Forest: White River
	Trails Illustrated: Map #126 (Holy Cross/Ruedi Res.); Map #127 (Aspen/Independence)
	10th Mountain: Bald Knob
	See map pages 88-89 and 170-171

The route from the Lenado Trailhead up Johnson Creek is the most direct route to Margy's Hut. The trail climbs steadily, gaining over 2,600 feet in elevation in a little over 6 miles. Be prepared for some labored breathing when you ski to the hut and some exciting schusses on the way back down.

To reach the trailhead, drive on CO 82 to the Woody Creek Canyon turn, which is 6.5 miles west of Aspen. Cross the Roaring Fork River and continue to an intersection. Turn left (north) and drive on CR 17 for 1 mile to the Woody Creek Tavern. Drive another 0.25 mile and take a sharp right turn (east) onto the Woody Creek Road (CR 18/FR 103). Proceed 8.5 miles to Lenado and park near the end of the plowed road. This road is narrow and often snow packed so drive carefully.

The turnoff onto the Woody Creek Road (CR18/FR 103) is north of the Woody Creek Tavern and may also be reached from Glenwood Springs or Basalt by turning onto Lower River Road at Old Snowmass or a little farther upstream across from the Aspen Village Trailer Park. From here drive across to the Lower River Road, on the north side of the Roaring Fork River. Now follow Lower River Road upstream to the Woody Creek turn.

Leave the parking area and start climbing east on the unplowed road (FR 103). Follow the road as it crosses Woody Creek and contours to the northwest. After gaining roughly 100 feet of elevation, search for a marked trail to the north. Follow this trail up the Silver Creek drainage. The trail switchbacks sharply to the southeast and begins to climb generally eastward, up and into the Johnson Creek drainage. Climb the drainage until you reach a road near Johnson Creek, gaining a steep 1,200 feet.

Follow this road east, then north, on a long, 2.3-mile traverse around

Elevation Point 11,376'. Pass a clearing above the road, take a left turn and climb onto a saddle near the top of Elevation Point 11,376'. Upon reaching an intersection, turn northeast, following this road 0.7 mile upward to a point where the road begins to turn out into a massive, low-angled, south-facing meadow. Turn east, then ski through a stand of spruce trees and descend to Margy's Hut. If you miss this turn, you will be on your way across the meadow toward the west ridge of Mount Yeckel.

TOUR 24D   MARGY'S HUT
TO McNAMARA HUT

Difficulty:	Intermediate	
Time:	5 to 8 hours	
Distance:	8.2 miles	
Elevations:	M Hut 11,300', McN Hut 11,360', +2,020'/-1,000'	
Avalanche Note:	None	
Maps:	USGS 7.5': Meredith, 1987; Thimble Rock, 1987	
	National Forest: White River	
	Trails Illustrated: Map #126 (Holy Cross/	
	Ruedi Res.) Map #127 (Aspen/Independence)	
	10th Mountain: Bald Knob	
	See map pages 88-89 and 170-171	

The section of trail between these two huts was the first hut-to-hut trail in the 10th Mountain Division system. It is generally well traveled and, because the route follows a well-marked and obvious path, navigation is not too difficult.

Leave Margy's Hut and ski down to Sawmill Park. Enter this tiny clearing, turn southwest and begin the long and treacherous drop down to Spruce Creek. Follow the trail along the creek for 3.3 miles, remaining on the northwest side of Spruce Creek all the way down to the confluence of Woody Creek and Spruce Creek. This spot is marked by the obvious narrowing of the two drainages; make sure you do not drop down into Woody Creek here.

Cross Spruce Creek via a quick, steep drop. Ski south, traversing up across steep, timbered slopes above the precipitous confluence. Pass some trail signs, then contour sharply east into the Woody Creek drainage. Climb Woody Creek for 0.8 mile. Switchback across the creek and begin climbing due west for a few hundred yards, then due south upward along Woody Creek. Follow the trail across this creek, then traverse west (crossing two more tributaries) until you cross a large drainage. Follow the trail south, then west, across this creek and continue 0.4 mile to the McNamara Hut, which is on the north side of the trail.

25 MCNAMARA HUT

The McNamara Hut was built in 1982 and, like Margy's Hut, is a memorial to Margaret McNamara, the wife of former Secretary of Defense Robert McNamara. The closest hut to Aspen, this hut was one of the most frequently used huts in the early days of the 10th Mountain Division system, and it still provides access to classic cross-country ski adventures.

The hut is set back into the woods below and north of 11,092-foot Bald Knob. Skiers can climb to the summit of Bald Knob for a 360-degree top-of-the-world panorama of Colorado's most famous peaks, including the Maroon Bells. Telemark skiing on the slopes between the hut and Bald Knob can be excellent.

McNamara Hut, with its beautiful, wood-burning stove, sleeps 16 and is open only for winter use. The area is closed in the summer because it is a calving area for elk. Make reservations through the 10th Mountain Division Hut Association (see Appendix A).

TOUR 25A HUNTER CREEK TRAILHEAD

Difficulty:	Intermediate
Time:	5 to 8 hours
Distance:	5.7 miles
Elevations:	Trailhead 8,380', Hut 11,360', +1,980'/-40'
Avalanche Note:	None
Maps:	USGS 7.5': Aspen, 1987; Thimble Rock, 1987
	National Forest: White River
	Trails Illustrated: Map #127
	(Aspen/Independence Pass)
	10th Mountain: Bald Knob
	See map pages 88-89 and 170-171

This tour begins at Hunter Creek on the north edge of Aspen. The trail is spectacular for it overlooks the town of Aspen, the downhill ski areas, and the Elk Mountains. If you can find the parking area and the trailhead (in the middle of a hillside residential area), you should have no problem navigating on this route.

To reach the trailhead, locate the intersection of Mill Street and Main Street in Aspen. Go north on Mill Street and proceed across the Roaring Fork River. Turn left onto Red Mountain Road and climb north for roughly 1 mile

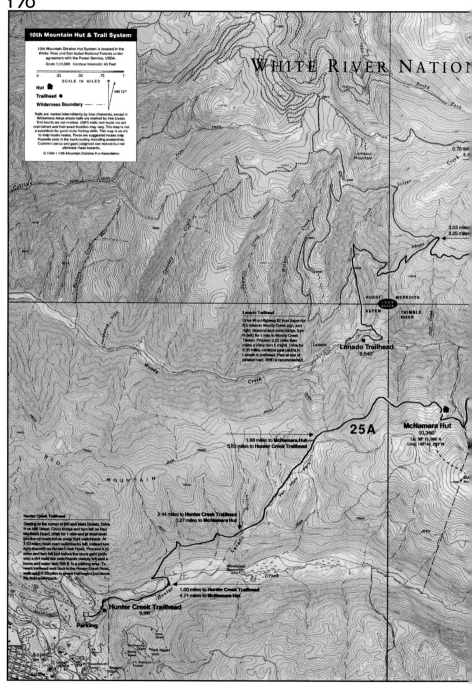

10th Mountain Hut & Trail System

10th Mountain Division Hut System is located in the White River and San Isabel National Forests under agreement with the Forest Service, USDA.

Scale 1:24,000 Contour Interval: 40 Feet

0   .25   .50   .75   1

SCALE IN MILES

Hut ⌂
Trailhead ●
Wilderness Boundary — — —

MN 12°

Trails are marked intermittently by blue diamonds, except in Wilderness Areas where trails are marked by tree blazes. Trail heads are not marked. USFS trails and roads are not maintained and their exact location may vary. This map is not a substitute for good route-finding skills. This map is an aid to help locate routes. These are suggested routes only. Hazards exist in the backcountry, including avalanches. Common sense and good judgment can reduce but not eliminate these hazards.

© 1994 • 10th Mountain Division Hut Association

WHITE RIVER NATION

0.70 mil

3.03 miles
3.25 miles

RUEDI   MEREDITH

U.S.G.S.
QUADS

ASPEN   THIMBLE
ROCK

Lenado Trailhead

Drive W on Highway 82 from Aspen for 6.5 miles to Woody Creek sign, turn right, descend and cross bridge, turn N (left) for 1 mile to Woody Creek Tavern. Proceed 9.25 miles then make a sharp turn E (right). Drive for 6.95 miles, continue past cabins in Lenado to trailhead. Park at end of plowed road. 4WD is recommended.

Lenado Trailhead
8,640'

McNamara Hut
10,360'
Lat: 39° 13.996' N
Long: 106° 44.292' W

25 A

1.88 miles to McNamara Hut
3.83 miles to Hunter Creek Trailhead

2.44 miles to Hunter Creek Trailhead
3.27 miles to McNamara Hut

Hunter Creek Trailhead

Starting at the corner of Mill and Main Streets, Drive N on Mill Street. Cross bridge and turn left on Red Mountain Road, climb for 1 mile and at short trail junction of roads follow sharp right switchback. At 1.50 miles, main road switchbacks left, instead turn right downhill on Hunter Creek Road. Proceed 0.25 miles and turn left just before the stone gate posts onto a dirt road that switchbacks steeply left past a home and water tank 300 ft. to a parking area. To reach trailhead walk back to the Hunter Creek Road, walk uphill 0.33 miles to where trail begins just above the road switchback.

1.00 miles to Hunter Creek Trailhead
4.71 miles to McNamara Hut

Hunter Creek Trailhead
8,360'

Parking

Aspen

FOREST

SEE 10TH MOUNTAIN MAP NO. 2 - MT. YECKEL

To Norrie

Mount Yeckel

24A
24B

4.41 miles to Margy's Hut
6.16 miles to Norrie
6.78 miles to McNamara Hut

Sawmill Park

Margy's Hut
11,300'
Lat. 39° 16. 520' N
Long. 106° 42. 770' W.

Hut

24C

24D

Spruce Creek

PROPOSED
SPRUCE CREEK ADDITION

Sieger Lake

3.51 miles to McNamara Hut
4.68 miles to Margy's Hut

Woody

2.62 miles to McNamara Hut
5.57 miles to Margy's Hut

Creek

Slab Park

Horse Park

Deer Park

Hunter

Hunter Flats

HUNTER · FRYINGPAN WILDERNESS

Hunter

Thimble Rock

Creek

BALD KNOB ●

to an intersection on a flat bench. Turn sharply right (downhill) on the Hunter Creek Road. Drive south, then east, for 0.25 mile to a left turn before a stone gate. Turn left and drive a few hundred feet to a parking area near a water tank. From this point, walk back to the Hunter Creek Road and continue along it to the northeast (toward the creek). Walk up and around a steep switchback to the trailhead on the right. Watch for traffic on this road!

After locating the trailhead, ski or walk along this south-facing trail (which is often without snow for the first few hundred feet) as it travels above Hunter Creek and below some houses. Follow the trail as it turns east and crosses the creek via a bridge. Now climb a very steep trail, deep in the woods along the south side of Hunter Creek. Follow this trail for roughly 0.9 mile, until you can cross Hunter Creek via the 10th Mountain Division Bridge. Be sure not to cross the creek on any of several private bridges; these lead to large homes with even larger dogs. Ski well past these estates as you look for route markers.

Cross the bridge and climb north, away from the creek around a curve to the west. Pass a large Forest Service information sign near barbwire fences. Follow the steep road on a rising traverse to the northeast, eventually crossing Lenado Creek. Just before you reach the creek, you'll pass an obvious left turn, marked by a wooden sign that reads "Red Mountain/Lenado" to the left and "Van Horn Park" to the right.

Turn right and ski sharply to the northeast, passing through a gate before entering Van Horn Park. Climb through the treeless park, following a road on the northwest side. Continue following the road as it leads into the woods at the northeast corner of the park. From here follow the steep, well-traveled trail through the forest for 1.9 miles to the McNamara Hut. Enjoy!

Memorial to Margaret McNamara.

ALFRED A. BRAUN
MEMORIAL HUT SYSTEM

The Alfred A. Braun Memorial Hut System is the oldest system of its kind in Colorado, created specifically as an alpine, backcountry shelter system for ski mountaineers and nordic skiers. Pitkin County residents Jay Laughlin and Stuart and Isabel Mace are credited with the idea for the system: a network of cabins to provide outdoor enthusiasts the opportunity to live in Colorado's winter wilderness in relative comfort and safety.

Work on the first huts, the early Tagert and the Lindley, began in the 1940s and '50s; construction on the present Tagert Hut, as well as on additional huts, began in 1963. The huts are a wonderfully eclectic collection of refuges, ranging from small A-frames to log cabins; each one is unique.

The not-for-profit Braun hut system recently changed hands and is now run by a local Aspen-based group. With new energy and vision, the group intends to refurbish and remodel all of the huts during the next five years, and may build a limited number of additional huts in the future. Simple architectural modifications, such as relocating outhouses away from the

Kurt Lankford skiing above the Goodwin–Greene Hut above Ashcroft, Alfred A. Braun Memorial Hut System.

main structures and creating new windows, will greatly enhance the ambiance and liveability of these classic backcountry shelters. The original planners did their homework when choosing sites, for each hut features five-star vistas and trails for all levels of backcountry skiers. The system is named for Alfred Braun, who was the hut system manager for many years.

The Braun hut system is located in the Elk Mountains, in the midst of some of Colorado's most scenic and most photographed peaks. Ancient red and maroon sedimentary rocks have weathered into precipitous, crumbling cliffs, delicately balanced towers, and graceful peaks. Outstanding nordic trails, unparalleled treeline bowls, and an endless array of 13,000- and 14,000-foot mountains offer enough skiing and mountaineering challenges to fill many vacations.

The skiing, especially off-trail, is for more experienced skiers. All skiers using this system should have substantial experience traveling in the mountains in winter, for the Elk Mountains contain an ever-present avalanche danger due to their steep topography. Ideally, each skier heading into this hut system will have completed at least an introductory level avalanche class. Less-experienced skiers are encouraged to join a group of advanced skiers or to employ one of the many excellent guide services operating in the area (see Appendix D).

All of the Braun huts are fully stocked with the usual assortment of hut paraphernalia: wood and wood-burning stoves, matches, propane stoves, electric lights, cookware, axes, outhouse facilities, and beds and mattresses. It is highly recommended that skiers bring shovels, transceivers, probes, compasses, bivouac gear, and altimeters.

The routes to the huts are not marked, although some trails do have old hiking, skiing, and even snowmobile markers that may aid in navigation. Plan on route finding. Also, due to the remoteness and degree of serious skiing within the Braun system, a minimum of four skiers is required to reserve a hut. However, with four skiers, the huts are rented exclusively to one group. (The Lindley Hut requires a minimum of six skiers for exclusive occupancy.) To reserve a Braun hut, call the 10th Mountain Division Hut Association (see Appendix A).

All of the Braun hut trails share the same parking area in Ashcroft, a defunct mining community that has been a favorite Colorado nordic ski area for decades. To reach Ashcroft, turn south off CO 82 and onto Maroon Creek Road (CR 13/FR 125). This is a marked intersection at a stoplight on the west edge of Aspen. After turning onto Maroon Creek Road, immediately turn left onto the Castle Creek Road (CR 15/FR 102) and drive 11 miles along this winding and often snow-packed road. The overnight parking lot in Ashcroft is across the road from the Toklat Gallery. It is the first lot on the east (or left) side of the road and is marked by a sign.

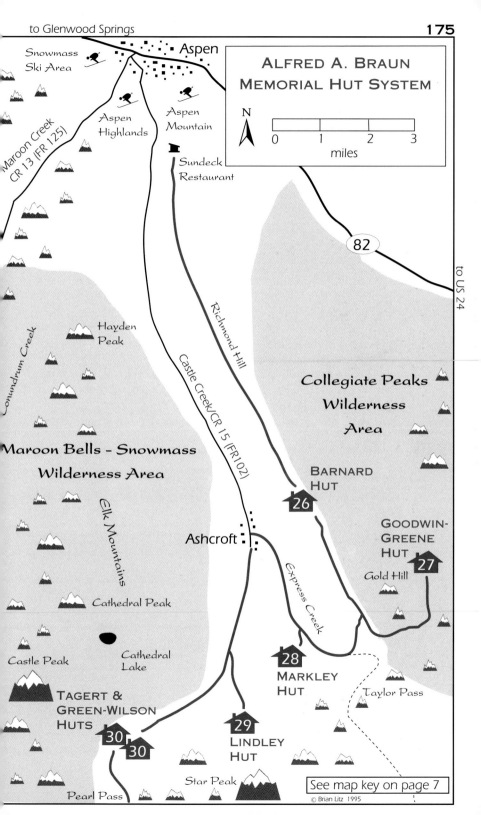

Snowmass
Ski Area

Aspen

ALFRED A. BRAUN
MEMORIAL HUT SYSTEM

N

0   1   2   3
miles

Aspen
Highlands

Aspen
Mountain

Maroon Creek
CR 13 (FR 125)

Sundeck
Restaurant

82

to US 24

Conundrum Creek

Hayden
Peak

Richmond Hill

Collegiate Peaks
Wilderness
Area

Castle Creek/CR 15 (FR 102)

Maroon Bells – Snowmass

Wilderness Area

Elk Mountains

BARNARD
HUT

26

GOODWIN-
GREENE
HUT

27

Gold Hill

Cathedral Peak

Ashcroft

Express Creek

Castle Peak

Cathedral
Lake

28

MARKLEY
HUT

Taylor Pass

TAGERT &
GREEN-WILSON
HUTS

30

30

29

LINDLEY
HUT

Star Peak

Pearl Pass

See map key on page 7

© Brian Litz 1995

26 BARNARD HUT

The Barnard Hut is hidden in a stand of evergreens on Richmond Hill, which is more of a ridge than a hill. The northern end of Richmond Hill is Aspen Mountain (still called Ajax Mountain by long-time locals). The southern end blends into alpine uplands near Taylor Pass. To the west and east are dramatic drops into the Castle Creek and Difficult Creek valleys. Both skiers and photographers will find Richmond Hill a delight. A great slope for telemark skiing drops off below and to the west of the southwest-facing front porch of the hut. Due south, the 12,139-foot summit of McArthur Mountain is a nice destination for day skiers experienced in ski mountaineering, route finding, and avalanche protocol.

Whether you ski to the Barnard Hut from the north (Aspen Mountain) or from the south and west (Ashcroft), be prepared for a long journey. Many skiers ride the gondola to the top of Aspen Mountain, ski to the Barnard and Goodwin-Greene huts, and then to Ashcroft via Express Creek (returning to Aspen by car shuttle). Skiers from Ashcroft might consider spending the first night at the Markley Hut, reducing the first day's mileage.

The Barnard Hut sleeps nine. For information on reservations and riding the Aspen Mountain Gondola, refer to Appendix A.

Liz Knapp, Jamal Maloo, Doug Johnson, Beth Smith, and Dave Muir at the Barnard Hut.

TOUR 26A   ASHCROFT TRAILHEAD

Difficulty:	Advanced 🚶
Time:	6 to 9 hours
Distance:	8.8 miles
Elevations:	Trailhead 9,422', Hut 11,480', +3,048'/-980'
Avalanche Note:	Route crosses avalanche runout zones; can be dangerous during high-hazard periods
Maps:	USGS 7.5': Aspen, 1987; Hayden Peak, 1987
	National Forest: White River
	Trails Illustrated: Map #127 (Aspen/ Independence Pass)
	Alfred A. Braun System: Richmond Hill
	See map pages 175 and 186-187

Ashcroft is the traditional trailhead for the Barnard Hut. This route is very long and gains considerable elevation through the Express Creek valley; however it is the most desirable trail if you wish to start and finish your tour in Ashcroft. Express Creek has incredible views of Castle Peak and the high summits around Taylor Pass.

This valley has conspicuous avalanche runs. The slopes face west into the prevailing winds which normally scour the ground of snow. Remember to call for information concerning current avalanche conditions and exercise proper avalanche protocol when traveling through this gorgeous valley (see Appendix E).

To reach the trailhead, park at the public overnight parking area across from the Toklat Gallery in Ashcroft (for directions, see Alfred A. Braun Memorial Hut System introductory text). The road to Express Creek is visible from the parking lot, as it traverses southeast up through aspen forests. There are two ways to this road. You can leave the northeast corner of the parking lot (near a tiny, wooden building) by climbing over piled-up snow and crossing the field to the northeast to the Taylor Pass/Express Creek Road (FR 122). Or, you can walk north along the Castle Creek Road for a few hundred feet to the summer turnoff to the Taylor Pass/Express Creek Road. This area is part of the Ashcroft Ski Touring Center, so please respect their trails and skiers.

The Taylor Pass/Express Creek Road angles to the southeast, crosses Castle Creek via a bridge and then begins to traverse upward. The initial 5 miles of the tour follow this road until reaching a distinct pass above and to the east of the turnoff for Taylor Pass.

Avalanche paths are plentiful along the east side of Express Creek. There are three obvious avalanche paths within the first mile, with many more upstream, including a massive system of slide paths to be traversed around the 3-mile mark. If conditions warrant, skiers can avoid the upper two avalanche paths by dropping down to the bottom of Express Creek valley and skiing up through the relative safety of the forested drainage. This ascent is steep and climbing skins are recommended.

Once at 11,900-foot Taylor Pass (marked as the intersection to the Barnard and Goodwin-Greene huts), turn due north and ascend along the boundary of Pitkin and Gunnison counties to the unnamed summit immediately west of Gold Hill. At the top of this knoll is one of the most commanding views of the Elk Mountains in the Braun system.

The rest of the route to the hut follows a snowmobile trail that is tracked and at times marked by four-inch-square wooden poles. However, the area is exposed to storms and high winds, which may obliterate the snowmobile tracks.

Descend northwest and follow the crest of the ridge toward McArthur Mountain, aiming for the flat shoulder on the southeast side. The main route drops from this shoulder down a low-angle drainage below the east face of the mountain. This gully runs below several potential avalanche slopes. When conditions are questionable, drop down to the small, forested ridge immediately east of the creek bed — rather than down the gully itself — to avoid possible danger from the slopes above.

The gully opens into a flat meadow. Cross the meadow by skiing north, following the natural path of the clearing. Within 0.5 mile, the meadow narrows between two forested knobs. To the west, hidden in the trees on a tiny knob, is the Barnard Hut. The turnoff is usually marked by a small sign reading "Hut Touring Area." The brown building is just beyond the edge of the meadow and can be difficult to spot.

TOUR 26B   SUNDECK TRAILHEAD

Difficulty:	Intermediate/Advanced
Time:	5 to 7 hours
Distance:	7.2 miles
Elevations:	Trailhead 11,212', Hut 11,480' +1,260'/-1,050'
Avalanche Note:	Route crosses avalanche runout zones; can be dangerous during high-hazard periods
Maps:	USGS 7.5': Aspen, 1987; Hayden Peak, 1987
	National Forest: White River
	Trails Illustrated: Map #127 (Aspen/ Independence Pass)
	Alfred A. Braun System: Richmond Hill
	See map pages 175 and 186-187

While the mileage on this tour may seem daunting, the route is actually quite manageable for most skiers. Except for the long drop in the Difficult Creek drainage, most of the touring is moderate. The trailhead atop Aspen Mountain starts at the ski area's Sundeck Restaurant. The key to completing this tour successfully is to get an early start via Aspen Mountain's gondola. The logistics involved in leaving a shuttle vehicle in Ashcroft, finding parking in Aspen, getting one-way lift tickets, and, finally, riding up the gondola can consume a great deal of time. However, this is the easiest way to gain 3,000 feet of elevation between Aspen and Richmond Hill. Skiers must be equipped for a serious backcountry trip and be prepared for complicated route finding if the weather turns bad or if trail markers are obscured. (For information on gondola tickets see Appendix A)

From immediately behind the top of the gondola, two roads head south. One drops steeply to the south/southwest, while the other road leads off to the south/southeast. Avoid the first road to Little Annie Basin. The second choice, the Richmond Hill Road, is relatively flat and remains on the ridge. Traveled by both skiers and snowmobilers and marked by orange snowmobile diamonds, this trail is generally a straightforward trip, though at times snowmobile and ski trails crisscross, which can be confusing. Keep maps and compasses handy and remember to watch for the orange markers all the way to the hut.

Follow the Richmond Hill Road south, eventually passing several private cabins along the top of the ridge. The views here include Pyramid, Hayden, Cathedral, and Castle peaks to the west with the Sawatch Range to the east and the Holy Cross Wilderness far off to the northeast.

Approaching the 2-mile mark, the trail traverses down along the east side of Elevation Point 11,534', then contours to the southwest on a fun and moderate descent. Pleasant ski touring dominates as you follow the obvious road on a gentle ascent south through the forest for several miles. Eventually, the road enters a flat, wide clearing on top of the ridge. Continue southeast until the road approaches the forest.

At this point, the trail drops abruptly into the woods to the head of the Difficult Creek drainage. This very steep section of road has several blind curves, is traveled by snowmobilers, and often has a washboard surface. Solid intermediate skiers and advanced skiers will encounter little trouble on this descent, while those weak in downhill snowplows might consider walking or wearing skins.

The descent ends at Difficult Creek, 1.5 miles from the Barnard Hut. Once you enter the drainage, turn uphill and ascend along the west side of the creek via the snow-covered road. (Do NOT take the left fork in the trail, marked by an orange diamond, which splits off to the east at the bottom of the drop.) Ski a few hundred yards up the creek to a point where the terrain steepens and becomes forested. Climb up through a series of switchbacks (not well-indicated on maps) to the west of the creek, taking time to enjoy the great view of Hayden Peak to the west.

Follow the trail markers south, noting small clearings. Ski through rolling terrain, in and out of trees on a less-distinct path. Pass two small hills, drop down and across the head of a Castle Creek tributary and ascend gently into the north edge of a large, flat meadow. Snowmobilers often travel in this meadow, obscuring old nordic trails. However, the turnoff to the hut is usually marked by a sign reading "Hut Touring Area." The Barnard Hut is 100 feet farther in the trees, facing south on a small, forested knob.

TOUR 26C   BARNARD HUT TO GOODWIN-GREENE HUT

Difficulty:	Advanced	
Time:	5 to 7 hours	
Distance:	4.5 miles	
Elevations:	B Hut 11,480', GG Hut 11,680', +1,100'/-910'	
Avalanche Note:	Route crosses avalanche runout zones; can be dangerous during high-hazard periods	
Maps:	USGS 7.5': Aspen, 1987; Hayden Peak, 1987 National Forest: White River Trails Illustrated: Map #127 (Aspen/ Independence Pass) Alfred A. Braun System: Richmond Hill See map pages 175 and 186-187	

This high-altitude traverse is spectacular. Like many of the routes on and around Richmond Hill, this one is exposed to high-country weather patterns. While the distance between the Barnard Hut and the Goodwin-Greene Hut is not great, periods of inclement weather can drastically increase the difficulty of this tour.

The majority of the route follows the upper portion of the trail from Ashcroft to Barnard Hut (Tour 26A). Snowmobilers also use this route, and there generally are tracks to follow as well as a series of four-inch-square posts and orange trail diamonds.

The Goodwin-Greene Hut is at the head of Difficult Creek/Bruin Creek and lies at treeline northeast and below Gold Hill. Skiers must traverse south around Gold Hill. Be careful not to confuse a private cabin that lies on the northwest shoulder of Gold Hill with the Goodwin-Greene Hut. This cabin sits in a very prominent spot, and many people have skied to it in error.

From the Barnard Hut, return east into the large flat meadow and turn south. Ski through the center of the meadow heading south/southeast, following the natural contour of this subtle drainage. Continue south into a treeless corridor that marks the creek bed. Ascend a gully below the east face of McArthur Mountain and cross over a small, flat shoulder on the northeast corner of the mountain. (This gully traverses below possible avalanche slopes; during periods of high avalanche danger, ascend past McArthur Mountain by climbing along the forested ridge immediately to the east of the gully.)

From the top of the shoulder, you can see the rest of the route. Continue south/southeast along the crest of the ridge, then begin the 500-foot climb to an unnamed point immediately west of Gold Hill. Incredible vistas abound along this entire stretch. If you plan to descend to Express Creek when your trip is over, this is a good spot for orientation should clouds and/or snow enshroud the area when you are ready to depart.

From here head east toward Gold Hill. Drop down across a saddle, then begin a short climb up and over the gentle, south flank of Gold Hill. Once past the crest of this broad ridge, gradually contour slightly to the northeast as you drop 200 feet to a small pass immediately east of Gold Hill. Descend the north side of the pass and cross a small, flat bowl spilling into steeper slopes that drop to Bruin/Difficult Creek.

Tucked among a grove of spruce trees, the Goodwin-Greene Hut is at the base of these final, steep slopes. They may be bypassed in favor of more gradual terrain by traversing down to the northeast. Remember to avoid the avalanche slopes that cover the upper aspects of Gold Hill.

Sunrise on Castle Peak, Maroon Bells-Snowmass Wilderness.

27 GOODWIN-GREENE HUT

The Goodwin-Greene Hut is in one of the most extraordinary backcountry locations in Colorado and one of my favorite ski destinations. One ski trip to this hut was made memorable by copious amounts of fresh powder and sunshine each morning. This is truly a special place!

This cozy cabin was built during the 1970s as a memorial to two young men, Peter Goodwin and Carl Greene, who perished in a mountaineering accident. Situated at the head of Difficult Creek, it is surrounded by a tree-less bowl. Moderate, rolling terrain dominates the southern and eastern horizons. The cabin sleeps six to eight people on bunk beds. Two of the beds are doubles; if you do not have skiers in your group willing to share a bed, it is best to limit your group to six. Make reservations through the 10th Mountain Division Hut Association (see Appendix A).

Evening light at the Goodwin-Greene Hut below Gold Hill.

TOUR 27A   ASHCROFT TRAILHEAD

Difficulty:	Advanced	🚶
Time:	5 to 7 hours	
Distance:	6.6 miles	
Elevations:	Trailhead 9,422', Hut 11,680', +2,838'/-580'	
Avalanche Note:	Route crosses avalanche runout zones; can be dangerous during high-hazard periods	
Maps:	USGS 7.5': Hayden Peak, 1987; New York Mountain, 1987	
	National Forest: White River	
	Trails Illustrated: Map #127 (Aspen/ Independence Pass)	
	Alfred A. Braun System: Richmond Hill	
	See map pages 175 and 186-187	

You can ski to the Goodwin-Greene Hut from the Barnard Hut (Tour 26C) or from Ashcroft via Express Creek. The most direct route, though quite strenuous, is from Ashcroft.

It is possible to break the tour into two shorter days by skiing into the Markley Hut for the first night, then on to the Goodwin-Greene Hut on the second day. This itinerary works especially well if you are planning to arrive at the trailhead and ski the same day (rather than staying in Aspen or Glenwood Springs the night before you start). Compass bearings are very useful on this tour, as on any route above treeline.

The first 75 percent of this tour follows the route from the Ashcroft trailhead to Barnard Hut; follow the directions for Tour 26A to 11,900-foot Taylor Pass.

From Taylor Pass, contour northeast around the south flank of a blunt ridge connecting the saddle and an unnamed point immediately west of Gold Hill. Drop down across the creek drainage, then begin a short climb up and over the gentle, south flank of Gold Hill. Once past the crest of the south ridge, begin to gradually contour slightly to the northeast as you drop 200 feet down to a small pass, immediately east of Gold Hill.

Drop off the north side of the pass and cross a small, flat bowl that spills into steeper slopes down to the Bruin Creek/Difficult Creek drainage. The hut is at the base of these slopes, tucked into a grove of spruce trees on a small shelf. The steeper slopes may be bypassed in favor of more gradual terrain by traversing to the northeast. Be sure to avoid the avalanche slopes on the east and north aspects of Gold Hill.

RECOMMENDED DAY TOURS: The bowls surrounding this hut provide unsurpassed backcountry skiing. The high ridges to the east, as well as Gold Hill, make fine destinations for day trips.

28   MARKLEY HUT

PPPDeep in the Express Creek forest, the Markley Hut is a secluded A-frame set among evergreens. It is easy to reach, though the tour gains almost 1,000 feet of elevation and crosses a few avalanche gullies. Strong beginners can enjoy this tour and get a taste of skiing the Elk Mountains. Skiers should be able to recognize avalanche terrain.

Touring around the cabin is somewhat limited. The steep topography of Express Creek is better suited to tours along the valley bottom or to longer excursions up the road toward Taylor Pass. This hut can be a stopover en route to the Barnard or the Goodwin-Greene huts.

Built in 1967, the Markley is one of the older backcountry shelters in the state. The cabin sleeps eight and is equipped with a wood-burning stove for heating and cooking, cookware, firewood, and an outhouse. Make reservations through the 10th Mountain Division Hut Association (see Appendix A)

The Markley Hut at Express Creek.

TOUR 28A   ASHCROFT TRAILHEAD

Difficulty:	Novice/Intermediate 🚶
Time:	2 to 4 hours
Distance:	2.3 miles
Elevations:	Trailhead 9,422', Hut 10,400', +978'
Avalanche Note:	Route crosses avalanche runout zones; can be dangerous during high-hazard periods
Maps:	USGS 7.5': Hayden Peak, 1987
	National Forest: White River
	Trails Illustrated: Map #127 (Aspen/Indp.)
	Alfred A. Braun System: Richmond Hill, Star Peak
	See map pages 175, 186-187, and 196-197

The route to the Markley Hut follows the Taylor Pass/Express Creek Road. To reach the trailhead, park at the public overnight parking area across from the Toklat Gallery in Ashcroft. For directions to the parking area, see Alfred A. Braun Memorial System introductory text.

The road to Express Creek is visible from the parking lot as it traverses southeast up through the aspen forest. There are two ways to the road. Skiers can either leave the northeast corner of the parking lot (near a tiny, wooden building) by climbing over the piled-up snow and crossing the field northeast to the Taylor Pass/Express Creek Road (FR 122). Or they can walk north back along the Castle Creek Road for a few hundred feet to the summer turnoff to the Taylor Pass/Express Creek Road. This area is part of the Ashcroft Ski Touring Center so please respect their trails and skiers.

The hut is located below Express Creek Road, very near and to the west of the creek. The turnoff to the hut is at the 2-mile point. This intersection is usually tracked, but can be somewhat difficult to spot — especially if you are moving fast along Express Creek Road. At the marked intersection, cross the creek and follow small painted circles on trees as you enter the forest. The Markley Hut is nearly impossible to see until you ski up to its front porch.

Avalanche paths are numerous throughout the Express Creek drainage. Three major slide paths are crossed within the first mile of the trail. Under normal conditions these paths are blown clear of snow by the winds, but nevertheless you should always exercise caution. Bent trees indicate relatively recent slide activity. Call the Colorado Avalanche Information Center (see Appendix E) before you leave or stop at the Ashcroft Ski Touring Center to inquire about the latest avalanche activity.

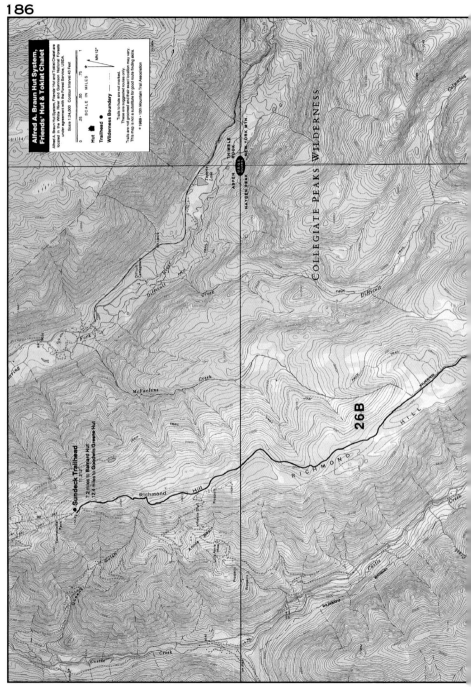

Alfred A. Braun Hut System, Friends' Hut & Toklat Chalet

Alfred A. Braun Hut System, Friends' Hut and Toklat Chalet are located in the White River and Gunnison National Forests under agreement with the Forest Service, USDA.

Scale 1:24,000   Contour Interval 40 Feet

SCALE IN MILES

0   .25   .50   .75

MN 12°

● Hut

▲ Trailhead

Wilderness Boundary ·········

Trails to huts are not marked.
These are suggested routes only.
Trails are not groomed and their exact location may vary.
This map is not a substitute for good route finding skills.

© 1999 • 10th Mountain Trail Association

COLLEGIATE PEAKS WILDERNESS

26B

RICHMOND HILL

● Sundeck Trailhead
2 miles to Barnard Hut
2.4 miles to Goodwin/Greene Hut

RICHMOND HILL

27A

Goodwin-Greene Hut
11,160'

1.5 miles to Goodwin-Greene Hut
3.7 miles to Barnard Hut
6.1 miles to Ashcroft

26A
26C

Barnard Hut
11,480'

26A
27A
28A

Overnight Parking
Waterfall

0.3 miles to Markley Hut
2.0 miles to Ashcroft

Markley Hut
10,400'

Ashcroft Mtn

Ashcroft Trailhead
9,600'

29A
30A

2.0 miles to Ashcroft
2.0 miles to Markley Hut
2.7 miles to Toklat Chalet
5.3 miles to Tagert/Wilson Huts

Avalanche Safety Detour
"Ava-Pass"

Tagert/Wilson Cookhouse

29A

WHITE RIVER
NATIONAL FOREST

MAROON BELLS • SNOWMASS
WILDERNESS

30A

29   LINDLEY HUT

The Lindley Hut is located in the Cooper Creek drainage and is a relatively easy destination with magnificent views of the surrounding country. The southern boundary of the Cooper Creek basin is an impenetrable wall of jagged ridges and summits that includes 13,521-foot Star Peak.

Largest of the Braun huts, the Lindley Hut sleeps 14. It is spacious and well equipped. The wood-burning stove is slow to produce heat, however, so be patient. This hut is unique in that it is built of painted cinder blocks. The Lindley Hut can be reserved through the 10th Mountain Division Hut Association (see Appendix A).

Navigation to this hut is straightforward. The first half of the tour crosses the Castle Creek valley and is essentially flat. The more demanding second half ascends by way of a moderately steep road.

Avalanche danger is minimal, but it does exist in several lightly timbered stretches on slopes east of the road. If avalanche danger is not extreme, you should be safe. Unfortunately, the upper reaches of Cooper Creek are filled with a complex network of dangerous avalanche slopes,

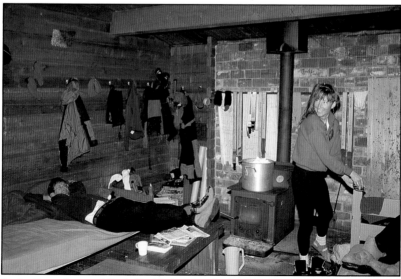

Craig Fournier and Beth Smith in a typical Braun hut.

which severely limit skiing possibilities. Even around the hut, the slopes are quite steep and prone to skier-triggered slides. Skiing up Cooper Creek to Pearl Pass or into any of the higher cirques is not recommended. Day skiing around the hut should be attempted only by skiers experienced in traveling across avalanche terrain.

TOUR 29A   ASHCROFT TRAILHEAD

Difficulty:	Novice/Intermediate
Time:	2 to 4 hours
Distance:	4 miles
Elevations:	Trailhead 9,498', Hut 10,440', +1,022'/-80'
Avalanche Note:	Route crosses avalanche runout zones; can be dangerous during high-hazard periods
Maps:	USGS 7.5': Hayden Peak, 1987
	National Forest: White River
	Trails Illustrated: Map #127 (Aspen/ Independence Pass)
	Alfred A. Braun System: Star Peak
	See map pages 175 and 196-197

To reach the Ashcroft Trailhead, park at the public overnight parking area near the Toklat Gallery in Ashcroft. For directions to the parking area, refer to the Alfred A. Braun Memorial Hut System introductory text.

The first 2 miles of the tour cross the Ashcroft Ski Touring Area and cover relatively flat terrain. There are two routes across the ski area. The traditional, and shorter, route simply follows the snow-covered Castle Creek Road (FR 102) to the large Forest Service information sign. At this spot, a trail marked by a Lindley Hut sign forks to the left (southeast). Turn left and cross the flat valley bottom, ski around a barricade and bridge, and then intercept a groomed nordic trail near a green building.

While this public access route is obvious and begins next to the ski touring center, it does have one serious drawback: It crosses the runout zones of some of the largest avalanche paths in the Castle Creek drainage. Most of the time these east-facing slide paths are safe to ski under. However, after storms and periods of high winds, they can be extremely dangerous. The Castle Creek Road turnoff to the Lindley Hut should be used only when conditions permit.

For those skiers who do not wish to run the gauntlet below dangerous gullies, the Ashcroft Ski Touring Center has created an Avalanche Path that avoids this hazardous section. Called the Ava-Pass, this route follows the

Castle Creek Road to the Pine Creek Cookhouse, then turns east at a trail intersection marked with signs warning skiers of avalanche hazards. It crosses Castle Creek, then continues south along the touring area trails to the above-mentioned green building.

While the Ava-Pass adds a little mileage to the trip, it does avoid the dangerous runout zones and is well worth the deviation. The trail, which is marked by orange discs, is provided as a courtesy by the nordic center area. Complimentary trail passes are required and can be picked up at the nordic center office, immediately south of the Toklat Gallery.

From the green building, the trail is straightforward as it steadily climbs the moderate Cooper Creek Road (FR 121) into the Cooper Creek drainage. At the first major switchback, leave the road and ski south, crossing the creek via a snow-covered bridge. The hut is only a few hundred feet away, but is hard to see and not well marked. Begin a descending traverse across the clearing, heading toward Cooper Creek and stands of evergreen trees. The large, white Lindley Hut sits near the creek.

Note: Keep an eye out for potential avalanche slopes on your left, especially near the 2.3- and 3-mile points.

30 TAGERT AND GREEN-WILSON HUTS

The very popular Tagert and Green-Wilson ski huts are in the heart of the Elk Mountains. These diminutive huts, located below Castle, Pearl, and Star peaks, provide skiers with a taste of genuine ski mountaineering. Either of these huts works well as a place to overnight when skiing on to the Friends Hut or on a longer expedition to Crested Butte via Pearl Pass.

Built in 1963, the A-frame Tagert Hut is one of the oldest backcountry shelters in the state. It was named for Billy Tagert, who drove stage and freight wagons over Taylor Pass during the mining era. Many skiers have done their first "real" skiing in the bowls of Pearl Basin and upper Castle Creek. The skiing potential is vast above both huts, as are opportunities for winter and spring ski mountaineering — and avalanches!

Sleeping capacity is seven for the Tagert and eight for the Green-Wilson. The cabins are within walking distance of each other and both may be booked for large groups. Make reservations through the 10th Mountain Division hut system (see Appendix A).

TOUR 30A   ASHCROFT TRAILHEAD

Difficulty:	Intermediate/Advanced
Time:	4 to 7 hours
Distance:	5.3 miles
Elevations:	Trailhead 9,498', T Hut 11,250', GW Hut, 11,280', +1,767'
Avalanche Notes:	Route crosses avalanche runout zones; can be dangerous during high-hazard periods
Maps:	USGS 7.5': Hayden Peak, 1987; Pearl Pass, 1961
	National Forest: White River
	Trails Illustrated: Map #127 (Aspen/ Independence Pass)
	Alfred A. Braun System: Star Peak
	See map pages 175 and 196-197

The route to the Tagert and Green-Wilson huts follows the Castle Creek Road through the Ashcroft Ski Touring Center, passing the turnoff to Cooper Creek and the Lindley Hut, and climbs toward upper Castle Creek. The first few miles are easy, while the last 3 miles ascend steadily until you arrive at the huts. This stretch can be taxing for skiers with heavy loads.

Also, Castle Creek is lined with massive avalanche paths. Groups heading to the huts must exercise all proper avalanche procedures.

To reach the trailhead, park across from the Toklat Gallery in Ashcroft; for directions see Alfred A. Braun Memorial Hut System introductory text. From the parking area, there are two routes: the traditional route and the avalanche safety path (Ava-Pass) through the Ashcroft Ski Touring Area.

The traditional route follows the road past the Pine Creek Cookhouse beneath avalanche runout zones. The alternate Ava-Pass route parts at the cookhouse on a marked route along the nordic trails. These two routes meet at the south end of the valley in an aspen forest near the turnoff to the Kellogg Cabin, a nordic area warming hut.

From this point, the Castle Creek Road (FR 102) is easy to follow. It is a steep climb past a pond, across the lower reaches of several huge avalanche gullies and through several large switchbacks into the upper valley. The road then drops down and crosses Castle Creek via a bridge. Once on the south side of the creek, following wand trail markers, ski west directly up the valley and across a large meadow. Be careful: There is a runout zone below a peak at 12,528 feet.

Re-enter the woods and continue up, following a small switchback in the trail. Cross several more avalanche runout zones. Above the Mace Hut, a private cabin, the trail becomes very steep through two switchbacks near the turnoff to the Montezuma Mine. After the switchbacks, the trail wanders southwest across the creek and ascends a small step to the huts.

Departing the Tagert Hut for Pearl Pass and the Friends Hut.

TOUR 30B TAGERT/GREEN-WILSON HUTS TO FRIENDS HUT VIA PEARL PASS

Difficulty:	Advanced
Time:	5 to 8 hours
Distance:	4.2 miles
Elevations:	T/G-W Hut 11,280', F Hut 11,500', +1,440'/-1,205'
Avalanche Note:	Route crosses avalanche slopes; prone to skier-triggered avalanches during high-hazard periods
Maps:	USGS 7.5': Hayden Peak, 1987; Pearl Pass, 1961 National Forest: White River, Gunnison Trails Illustrated: Map #127 (Aspen/ Independence Pass); Map #131 (Crested Butte/Pearl Pass) Alfred A. Braun System: Star Peak See map pages 175 and 196-197

Crossing Pearl Pass is one of Colorado's most challenging and exciting hut-to-hut trails. The route, from Ashcroft to Crested Butte, up Castle Creek and down through the Brush creeks, has long been a favorite winter adventure for experienced skiers. Ninety-nine percent of the terrain around the Tagert and Green-Wilson huts, as well as the Friends Hut, is above treeline. Rolling benches make for strenuous, yet not too technical, skiing in large glacial cirques. At 12,705 feet, Pearl Pass is one of the highest spots covered in this guide. The panoramas are beyond description.

The distance between the huts is just over 4 miles. However, the elevation gain and loss is considerable. Under ideal conditions, the tour can pass quickly and uneventfully. During storms, the lack of trail markers or a distinct trail can leave ski parties wandering aimlessly below major avalanche slopes. People have perished in this area under such less-than-ideal conditions.

Additionally, it is quite possible to cross Pearl Pass under pleasant weather only to be stranded by blizzards, unable to return over the pass to either Ashcroft or Crested Butte. Be sure to check avalanche and weather conditions before embarking on this journey.

All skiers attempting this route should be knowledgeable about winter travel and should carry shovels, transceivers, and bivouac equipment. Keep maps and compasses handy and consider carrying an altimeter to aid in navigation.

Some skiers travel straight from Ashcroft to the Friends Hut in one push. The less-committing plan calls for spending a night at the Tagert or Green-Wilson huts. This option is described below.

From the front door of the Green-Wilson Hut, begin the ascent into Pearl Basin by skiing up the snow-covered Pearl Pass Road. If this approach appears too dangerous, consider skiing along the creek for several hundred yards, then climbing out of the small basin in front of the cabins through the wide trough to the southwest. (This trough is also a popular ski slope). Follow the path of least resistance to the south, then southeast, by winding through small knolls and patches of willows and dwarf evergreen trees until you eventually gain the indistinct, flat saddle west/southwest of Elevation Point 12,528' (near the word "jeep" on the USGS 7.5-minute maps).

This is a good spot to take compass bearings and to memorize landmarks. Aim for the distinct, precipitous northeast ridge of Pearl Peak. The pass is barely hidden behind the ridge, at the head of the basin lying directly below and east of the peak.

From the flat saddle, it is necessary to contour across the head of the Cooper Creek valley below the toe of the jagged northeast ridge of Pearl Peak, thereby avoiding the avalanche slopes on the peak's north face. Here the route follows the summer road fairly closely, although it drops slightly lower near the corner of Pearl Peak.

It is important to avoid dropping into the head of Cooper Creek drainage. If you are skiing in from the south, the terrain naturally will draw you toward this very steep valley. A few weathered wooden trail markers mark the route along this leg of the tour, however, these markers may be hard to spot, are far apart, and should not be relied upon.

Ski across the moderately undulating terrain below Pearl Peak and begin to make your approach toward Pearl Pass proper. When visibility is good, it is possible to see the wooden sign atop the pass. The slope on the north side of the pass is the most dangerous portion of the tour, and astute route finding is required to ensure a safe crossing. Be prepared to assess the avalanche hazard before climbing this final slope. Also be ready to turn back if the conditions are questionable.

Many groups make the mistake of traversing too high to the west as they climb the last few hundred feet up to Pearl Pass, placing them directly below classic avalanche terrain. Try to ascend as directly to the pass as possible, yet slightly to the right (west). There are several small hills that facilitate this ascent. Make the final ascent one at a time and follow all avalanche hazard procedures.

The south side of Pearl Pass is not as treacherous as the north side, but it still possesses its share of hazards. The best route down follows the road for roughly 50 feet, then turns sharply southeast and descends onto a terrace that crosses the basin from the northwest to the southeast, along the path of least resistance. Ski across the basin, contouring around the steep slopes above the northwest fork of the creek. Descend into a subtle drainage immediately east of a low ridge covered with stunted trees. When you begin to see full-sized trees and the forest, head due south, skiing through sparse trees on steeper slopes. Eventually cross the northeast branch of East Brush Creek and ski up to the hut, which is visible on a small, forested hill at the edge of the forest.

During periods of poor visibility, compass bearings can be invaluable on this passage. Have readings ready before setting out, whether you are skiing north-to-south or in the reverse direction.

Culley Culbreth, Pete Stouffer, and John Fielder atop the "big hill," 12,705-foot Pearl Pass.

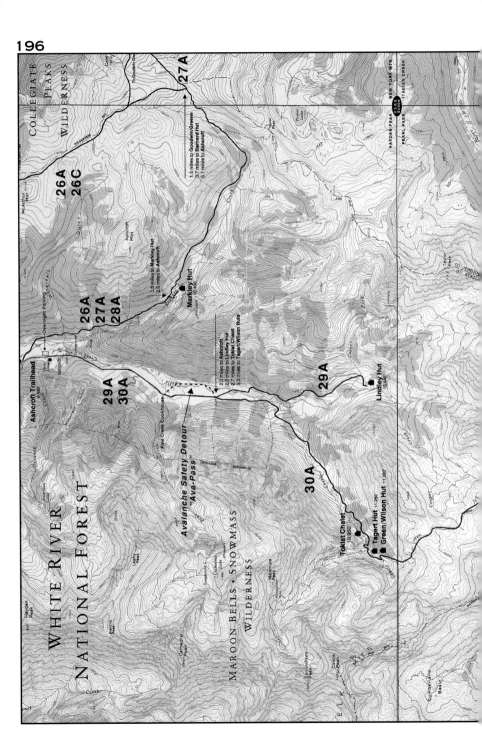

COLLEGIATE
PEAKS
WILDERNESS

27 A

26 A
26 C

1.5 miles to Goodwin/Greene
3.7 miles to Barnard Hut
5.1 miles to Ashcroft

Markley Hut
10,400'

0.9 miles to Markley Hut
2.0 miles to Ashcroft

26 A
27 A
28 A

2.0 miles to Ashcroft
2.0 miles to Lindley Hut
2.7 miles to Tokiat Chalet
3.3 miles to Tagert/Wilson Huts

Ashcroft Trailhead
9,485'

Overnight Parking

29 A
30 A

29 A

Lindley Hut
11,040'

Avalanche Safety Detour
"Ava-Pass"

Pine Creek Cookhouse

30 A

MAROON BELLS · SNOWMASS
WILDERNESS

WHITE RIVER
NATIONAL FOREST

Tokiat Chalet
10,850'

Tagert Hut 11,250'
Green/Wilson Hut 11,260'

ELK MTS

HAYDEN PEAK · NEW YORK MTN.
PEARL PASS · ITALIAN CREEK

Alfred A. Braun Hut System,
Friends' Hut & Toklat Chalet

197

STAR PEAK

GUNNISON NATIONAL FOREST

Friends' Hut 11,500'

1.60 miles to Friends Hut
2.60 miles to Tagert & Green-Wilson Huts

31A

CRESTED BUTTE AREA AND INDEPENDENT HUTS

Crested Butte is a conical peak surrounded by meandering rivers that course through rural and agriculturally rich valleys. A number of large valleys radiate away from Crested Butte like the spokes of a mountain bike wheel. Across the Elk Mountains from Aspen and Ashcroft, this area maintains a delicate balance among the demands of recreation, wilderness, and country living. The daily pace is slower, the smell of wild summer grasses stronger, and the people more inclined to stop and chat. The town of Crested Butte has grown relatively slowly and still possesses a blend of Victorian charm and Western cow town.

Encircled by the sweeping ridges of the Elk Mountains, the West Elks, and the Ruby-Anthracite ranges, the town and the downhill ski area lie at the center of an outdoor enthusiast's recreational mecca. Many people consider Crested Butte to be the place where the modern American telemark turn was born.

Old mining roads stripe the valleys, connecting abandoned mining camps and deserted townsites like delicate threads. During the summer, mountain bikers from all over the country converge here, huffing and puffing up 12,000-foot passes and white-knuckling their way back down. In the winter these same roads and trails become popular nordic routes.

Backcountry hut skiing in the southern Elks and in the Ruby-Anthracite ranges consist of four independent huts. What the area lacks in quantity of huts, however, it more than makes up in quality.

The huts are the Elkton Cabins, Cement Creek Yurt, the Gothic Cabin, and the Friends Hut. All the routes are very scenic, featuring pleasant touring to the huts as well as excellent backcountry skiing around them.

All of these huts are equipped for overnight skiers with an assortment of wood-burning stoves, beds with sleeping pads, cookware, and outhouse facilities. These huts are open only for the winter season.

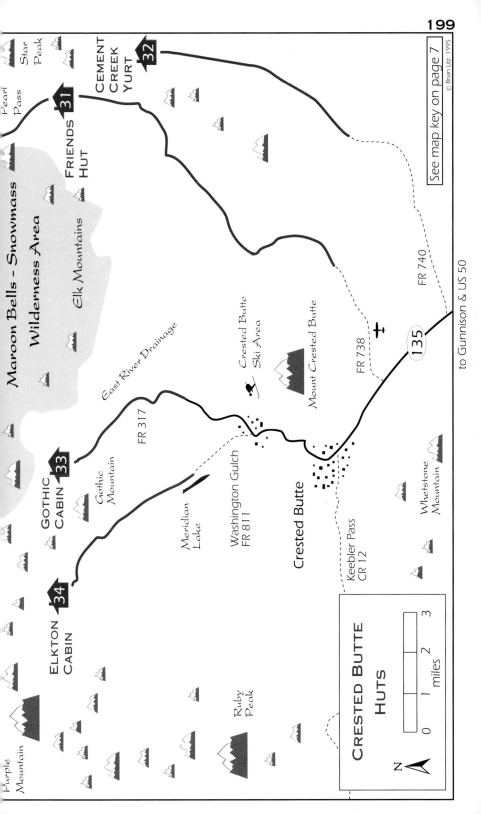

199

Maroon Bells - Snowmass
Wilderness Area

Star
Peak

Pearl
Pass

31
FRIENDS
HUT

32
CEMENT
CREEK
YURT

Elk Mountains

See map key on page 7

© Brian Litz 1995

East River Drainage

Crested Butte
Ski Area

Mount Crested Butte

FR 738

135

FR 740

to Gunnison & US 50

33
GOTHIC
CABIN

FR 317

Gothic
Mountain

34
ELKTON
CABIN

Meridian
Lake

Washington Gulch
FR 811

Crested Butte

Keebler Pass
CR 12

Whetstone
Mountain

Purple
Mountain

Ruby
Peak

CRESTED BUTTE
HUTS

N

miles

0   1   2   3

31   FRIENDS HUT

A sign in the Friends Hut states that the hut is for serious skiers — and I agree! This hut offers expert skiers a total Rocky Mountain ski adventure. Located below the south faces of Star and Crystal peaks, the Friends Hut provides access to many acres of skiable alpine terrain as well as long, challenging routes to the hut.

The Friends Hut was constructed as a memorial to ten residents of Aspen and Crested Butte who died in a plane crash above East Maroon Pass. Volunteers provided the labor to build the hut, which opened during the winter of 1985-86. Today, the Friends Hut stands as a backcountry link between the mountain communities of Aspen and Crested Butte — a fitting tribute to a group of people who loved the Colorado Rockies.

The Friends Hut is recommended for advanced skiers who understand the severity of backcountry skiing and are capable of self-sufficient winter travel. Strong, intermediate-level skiers can also enjoy this trip if accompanied by experienced partners or guides. Due to the remoteness of this cabin, it is recommended that groups book the hut for a minimum of two nights, so skiers can enjoy a full day of rest or day touring. Extra time spent at the hut also provides good weather insurance should parties need to recross Pearl Pass.

Doug Johnson and Rich Waggener at the Friends Hut, near Crested Butte.

Located 1,000 feet below the summit of Pearl Pass, the Friends Hut completes the hut system across the Elk Mountains. Many skiers tour to the Friends Hut via Pearl Pass; the Braun system's Tagert and Green-Wilson huts work well as a jumping-off point for crossing the pass. Because skiers are dependent on windows of settled mountain weather to ensure a safe crossing, this itinerary is very committing.

Approaching the Friends Hut from Crested Butte, skiers are faced with a long trek up Brush Creek. This route is less spectacular than skiing from Ashcroft, but it is also considerably less alpine and exposed to far less avalanche danger.

The hut's rough-hewn timbers and wood paneling create a warm and restful winter oasis. The hut sleeps nine on beds in a sleeping loft and around the wood-burning stove on the main floor. Amenities include a photovoltaic lighting system, propane cook stove, cookware, a ski storage room, and an outhouse with a large window (to inspire contemplative thought). Water can be drawn from the creek for most of the winter; notices in the hut direct skiers to the most reliable water sources. Creek water should be treated or boiled before using.

The Friends Hut is open only during the winter, and additional groups may be booked into the hut if your group does not fully occupy it. Book reservations through the 10th Mountain Division Hut Association (see Appendix A).

TOUR 31A   EAST RIVER TRAILHEAD

Difficulty:	Advanced
Time:	7 to 10 hours
Distance:	11 miles
Elevations:	Trailhead 8,920', Hut 11,500', +2,580'
Avalanche Note:	Route crosses avalanche runout zones; can be dangerous during high-hazard periods.
Maps:	USGS 7.5': Gothic, 1961; Pearl Pass, 1961
	National Forest: Gunnison
	Trails Illustrated: Map #131 (Crested Butte/ Pearl Pass)
	Alfred A. Braun System: Star Peak
	See map pages 199 and 206-207

The route to the Friends Hut from Crested Butte is one of the longest and most arduous tours to any backcountry hut. Classic cross-country skiing follows Brush Creek Road and then East Brush Creek Road on a consistent climb from the East River near the Cold Spring Ranch to treeline below Star Peak. This route takes a lot of work but is worth the effort. Get an early start and be prepared for a long day if you expect to have to break trail.

The route passes near the runout zones of several large slide paths, especially in upper East Brush Creek. Skiers should be able to assess avalanche danger and to make necessary adjustments in route selection. Your group should also be prepared for severe winter conditions. Since the trail lies within deep valleys and is well marked, route finding is not too difficult. The trickiest task is locating the hut as you approach it through the woods.

To reach the parking area and the trailhead, drive from the town of Crested Butte for 2 miles south on CO 135 to the Skyland Country Club/Airport Road (CR 738). This turn is immediately southeast of the bridge across the Slate River. Follow the road as it curves past the entrance to Skyland Country Club on the left. Continue along the road as it skirts the southeast flank of Mount Crested Butte. After driving 2.5 miles, you'll arrive at a small, plowed parking area on the left. Park here. Do not drive past the Lazy F Bar Outfitters sign; there is no public parking beyond this point.

Ski on the road past this sign and contour north past the ranch on the left. Near the 1.5-mile mark, you'll reach the broad, treeless mouth of Brush Creek. Turn northeast and follow the summer four-wheel-drive road along the left side of the creek. Turn right at the marked intersection of the West Brush Creek Trail (FR 738.2A) and the Brush Creek/Middle Brush Creek Trail (FR 738).

Ski down and across the creek and begin a short ascent to a fork in the trail near the 4-mile mark. Take the left fork on a steep climb high above a narrow and precipitous constriction in the valley bottom. After making a traverse across the toe of lower Teocalli Ridge, drop back down into Brush Creek and ski up the drainage along the broad valley bottom.

The trail eventually crosses the creek via snow bridges in an area filled with willows. Near the end of the valley, ascend east onto East Brush Creek Road (FR 738.2B). Follow the road into thicker spruce forests and continue up the valley. The road in the upper valley is on the west side of the creek and leads directly under several avalanche runout zones. Many skiers cross to the east side of the creek and ski in the relative safety of the thicker trees on that bank. The actual point of creek crossing is left to the discretion of the group.

The Friends Hut sits above the confluence of the two highest, unnamed forks of East Brush Creek. By traversing upward above the northeast fork of the creek, near the upper limit of the forest, you ski directly to the hut, which sits atop a tiny knoll protected by tall spruce trees.

Alpine backcountry skiing near Conundrum
Pass, north of the town of Gothic

32 CEMENT CREEK YURT

The Cement Creek Yurt is the first backcountry shelter of the Elk Mountain Hut System, a new hut system based out of Crested Butte. Presently there is only one yurt, but the Elk Mountain Hut System also oversees the Elkton Cabin in upper Washington Gulch. In the future they plan on adding more huts along the southern end of the Elk Mountains.

Cement Creek, which lies to the east of Crested Butte, has pleasant ski touring. Interestingly enough, it was the site of one of Colorado's first downhill ski areas, although it consisted of only one run cut through the woods.

The Cement Creek Yurt sleeps six, has a cook stove, heater, dishes, and, of course, an outhouse. The yurt's water source is the creek, 250 feet from the yurt. This water should be boiled, filtered, or treated before drinking.

For day trips, skiers can continue up Cement Creek or explore a side valley. Exercise caution, for there are potential avalanche slopes in the higher valleys. All groups should carry avalanche safety equipment. For reservation information, please refer to Appendix A.

TOUR 32A   CEMENT CREEK TRAILHEAD

Difficulty:	Intermediate/Advanced
Time:	5 to 8 hours
Distance:	6.5 miles
Elevations:	Trailhead 9,260', Hut 10,160', +900'
Avalanche Note:	Route crosses avalanche runout zones; can be dangerous during high-hazard periods.
Maps:	USGS 7.5': Cement Mountain, 1970; Pearl Pass, 1980
	National Forest: Gunnison
	Trails Illustrated: Map #131 (Crested Butte/ Pearl Pass)
	See map pages 199 and 206-207

To reach the trailhead, take CO 135 to the Cement Creek Road (CR 740) turnoff, which is roughly 8 miles south of Crested Butte. Turn east onto this road, pass the Crested Butte South subdivision, and continue to the end of the plowed road. The ultimate length of this tour depends upon how far up-valley the road is plowed.

Basically this route is a straight shot along a valley floor, following a summer road (CR 740), which then becomes FR 740. Leave the parking area and begin skiing along the road. The first few miles are popular with local cross-country skiers and snowmobilers and are usually snow packed.

Near the 3-mile mark, the valley narrows considerably, exposing skiers to potential avalanche hazards on both sides for about a mile. Cross a bridge, then ski through several switchbacks on the eastern side of Cement Creek. Above the switchbacks the valley begins to widen again. Continue due north upstream for 2.5 miles to the yurt. Cement Creek Yurt sits right in the middle of the valley, due south of the base of the southern ridge of 12,618-foot Hunter's Hill.

Alan Keefe enjoying a hot combo — gravity and fresh powder snow.

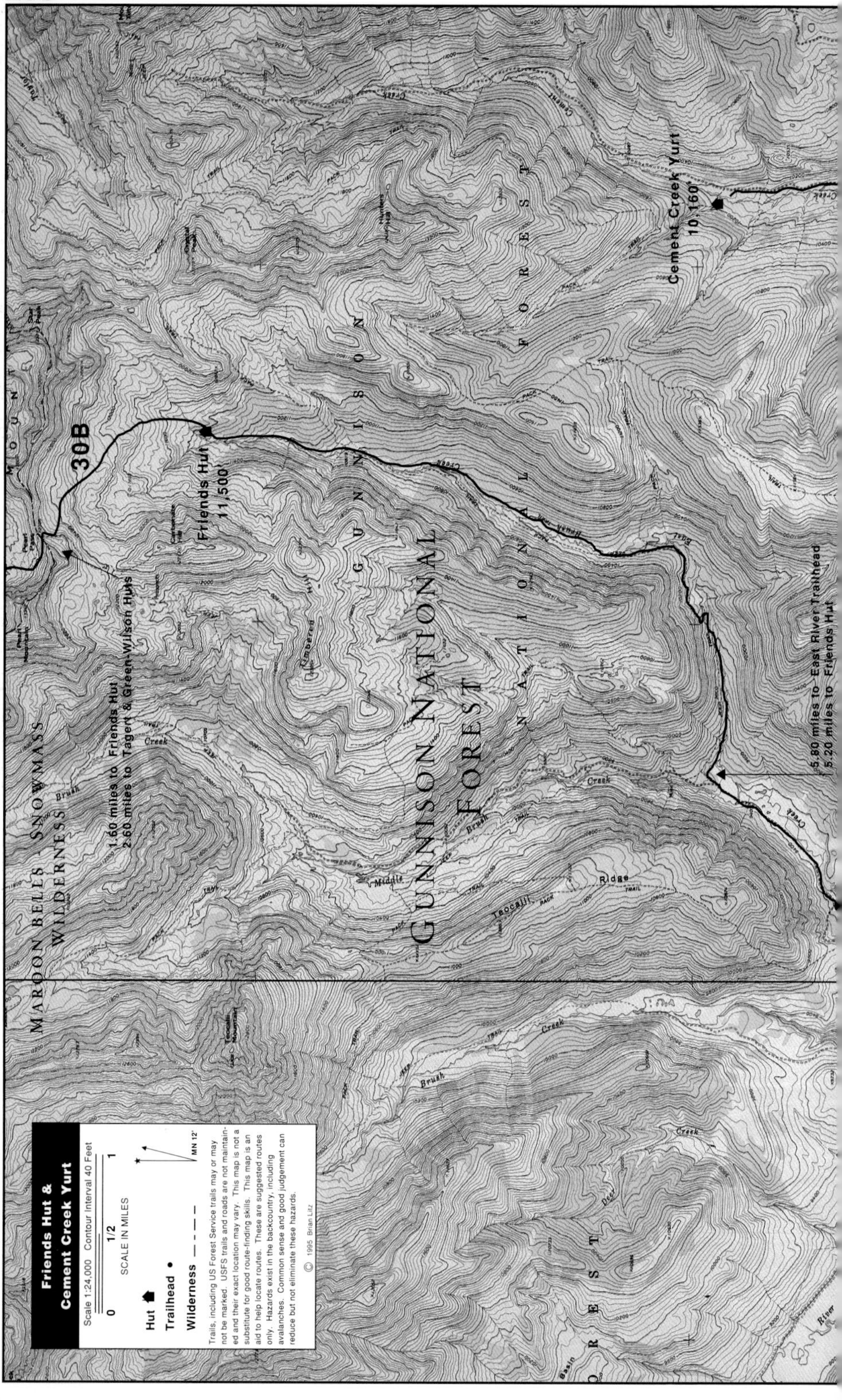

SOUTHERN ELK MOUNTAINS

32A

3.50 miles to Cement Creek Yurt
3.00 miles to Cement Creek Trailhead

Cement Creek Trailhead
9,260

GUNNISON

PEARL PASS
GOTHIC
CRESTED BUTTE
CEMENT MOUNTAIN

NATIONAL FOREST

East River Trailhead
8,920

33   GOTHIC CABIN

Tucked away in a valley below Gothic Peak, Schofield Pass, and Copper Creek is the community of Gothic. During the late 1800s, Gothic was a highly profitable gold and silver mining community, as well as a supply point for the surrounding mines and mining camps. According to Perry Eberhart's *Guide to the Colorado Ghost Towns and Mining Camps*, during its heyday Gothic boasted a population of around 8,000. In addition to being the wealthiest town in Gunnison County, Gothic was also one of the wildest towns in all of Colorado.

Today, Gothic is a haven for recreationalists and budding naturalists. The Rocky Mountain Biological Labs are the center of activity, offering a multitude of summer workshops and classes for college students and others interested in the ecology of the Rockies. Winter finds Gothic deserted except for caretakers, snowshoe hares, and the occasional nordic skier. It is a great place to escape to in the winter and makes an excellent base camp, allowing skiers many day explorations into the beautiful valleys surrounding the town.

Cabins used by summer students are available to cross-country skiers for a fee during the winter and are booked through the Crested Butte Nordic Center (see Appendix A). The exact number of cabins available for skiers may change from year to year, so call the nordic center for the latest information. The cabins are well equipped with stoves, cookware, beds, and outhouse facilities.

TOUR 33A   GOTHIC ROAD TRAILHEAD

Difficulty:	Novice/Intermediate
Time:	3 to 5 hours
Distance:	3.5 miles
Elevations:	Trailhead 9,580', Hut 9,480', +140'/-240'
Avalanche Note:	Route crosses avalanche runout zones; can be dangerous during high-hazard periods.
Maps:	USGS 7.5': Gothic, 1961
	National Forest: Gunnison
	Trails Illustrated: Map #131 (Crested Butte/ Pearl Pass)
	See map pages 199 and 210

The trail follows the snow-covered summer road that begins near the Crested Butte downhill ski area. To reach the trailhead from the town of Crested Butte, drive north on CR 317 (CO 135 turns into CR 317), go past the ski resort to the winter road closure and park. The total distance from old town Crested Butte to the public winter road closure is roughly 4.4 miles.

From the parking area, the road (FR 317) is obvious and easy to follow. Begin skiing along the exposed trail traversing above the East River. Ski around a sharp curve that overlooks the river and begin a gradual descent for 1.8 miles, until you cross the river. From the crossing, a very gentle climb takes you up to the center of Gothic.

Be aware of several potential slide paths that drop off the northeast aspect of Snodgrass Mountain. Stop in or call the Crested Butte Nordic Center to get the latest information on avalanche activity.

Gothic Cabin on a winter night.

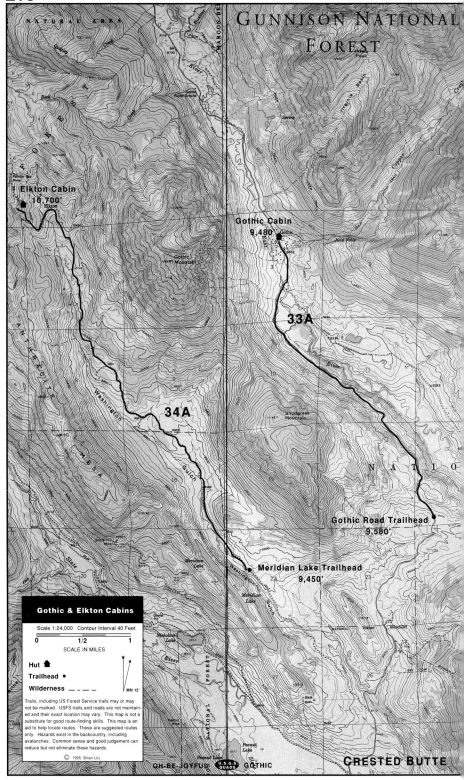

GUNNISON NATIONAL FOREST

Elkton Cabin
10,700'

Gothic Cabin
9,480'

33A

34A

Gothic Road Trailhead
9,580'

Meridian Lake Trailhead
9,450'

NATIO

Gothic & Elkton Cabins

Scale 1:24,000   Contour Interval 40 Feet

0   1/2   1

SCALE IN MILES

Hut 🏠

Trailhead •

Wilderness — — —

MN 12°

Trails, including US Forest Service trails may or may not be marked. USFS trails and roads are not maintained and their exact location may vary. This map is not a substitute for good route-finding skills. This map is an aid to help locate routes. These are suggested routes only. Hazards exist in the backcountry, including avalanches. Common sense and good judgement can reduce but not eliminate these hazards.

© 1995 Brian Litz

QH-BE-JOYFUL   GOTHIC

U.S.G.S.
QUADS

CRESTED BUTTE

34 ELKTON CABINS

The Elk Mountain Hut System is privately owned and operates several small cabins near the abandoned mining camp of Elkton. The trip to the cabins is just over 5 miles. The elevation gain is moderate, averaging a little over 200 feet per mile, making the route to these cabins appropriate for most skiers. This is a popular day tour in the area, so expect to see other skiers.

The trail traces the easy-to-follow Washington Gulch Road. There are two relatively steep climbs: The first is near the 3-mile mark, the second is the final approach to Elkton Cabin. The hut is a simple log cabin, but serves well as a backcountry shelter and base camp for skiers making day excursions to surrounding glades and peaks.

The three cabins include the Elkton Cabin, the Miner's Delight, which sleeps 12, and the Silver Jewel, which sleeps four. All three cabins have wood-burning stoves for heat, gas cook stoves, cookware, and an outhouse. The Silver Jewel hut serves as the hut master's quarters as well as a bed-and-breakfast for four guests. Make reservations through Elkton Cabins (see Appendix A). The Elkton Cabins are now open year round and provide great access to many miles of high country mountain biking and hiking.

Skiing across the roof of the Rockies on Mount Baldy, near Elkton, with Elk Mountains in the distance.

TOUR 34A   MERIDIAN LAKE TRAILHEAD

Difficulty:	Novice/Intermediate
Time:	3 to 5 hours
Distance:	5.2 miles
Elevations:	Trailhead 9,450', Hut 10,700', +1,250'
Avalanche Note:	Some avalanche terrain encountered; easily avoided
Maps:	USGS 7.5': Gothic, 1961; Oh-Be-Joyful, 1961
	National Forest: Gunnison
	Trails Illustrated: Map #131 (Crested Butte/ Pearl Pass); Map #133 (Kebler Pass/ Paonia Reservoir)
	See map pages 199 and 210

Not far from the town of Crested Butte, the trailhead for the Elkton Cabin is near the Meridian Lakes development and is easy to locate at the end of a well-marked and well-travelled county road. From the stop sign at the intersection of Elk Avenue and CR 317 in Crested Butte (CO 135 turns into CR 317), drive north for 1.7 miles to the turnoff to Washington Gulch and Meridian Lake. Turn left onto Washington Gulch Road (FR 811) and proceed along the main thoroughfare to the plowed parking area at the winter road closure.

From the parking area and the trailhead signs, ski up the valley over very moderate terrain. After several miles of touring along the snow-covered road, you'll come to a noticeable climb near the southwest corner of Gothic Mountain. Once past this ascent, the road climbs gradually, passing below the mountain's southwest face. From here, the terrain becomes increasingly steep as you cross the mouth of a drainage (to the northeast), then contour west and south across a creek and the head of Washington Gulch.

After crossing the creek, make the final ascent to Elkton by climbing around a switchback, heading northwest. When you arrive at Elkton, which sits on top of a flat bench, look for two cabins off to the right. The first cabin, the one closest to the road, is the Elkton Cabin. It is roughly 100 feet south of the other, larger cabin.

35   LOST WONDER HUT

Anyone driving over Monarch Pass under clear conditions can't help but notice the distinctive profile of Mount Aetna to the north. Lost Wonder Hut sits at the foot of this 13,745-foot mountain, in the Middle Fork of the South Arkansas River drainage. This drainage is very quiet during the winter and sees few skiers or snowmobilers, although the presence of the hut will undoubtedly encourage more people to visit this high-country valley.

Once at the hut, you can tour to the head of the valley or explore the surrounding glades and burns. Skiers need to watch out for hazardous avalanche terrain. You can head up the valley, over the pass at the northern end, and drop down to Saint Elmo, or you can hike down to Boss Lake.

Named after the Lost Wonder Mine, this new hut is an old mining cabin that has been "pop-topped." The original first floor is the kitchen, dining room, and community area. The new second floor has two bedrooms, a loft,

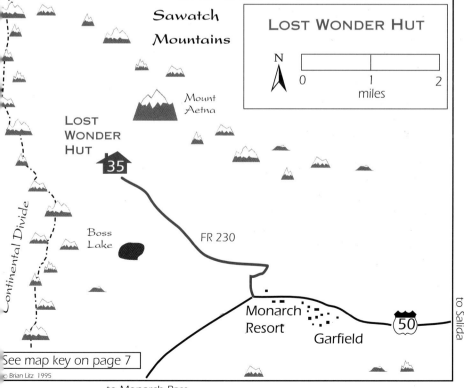

and a large community and sleeping area with tall, south-facing windows that gather copious amounts of solar energy, making this a great place to take a nap, read a book, or just enjoy the mountain panorama.

The Lost Wonder Hut is fully equipped with all the necessary amenities. It sleeps 8 to 10 comfortably. The hut is run by the Continental Divide Hut System, LLC. For reservation information, refer to Appendix A.

TOUR 35A   GARFIELD TRAILHEAD

Difficulty:	Intermediate	🚶 🚲 🚶‍♂️
Time:	2 to 4 hours	
Distance:	3 miles	
Elevations:	Trailhead 9,660', Hut 10,890', +1,230'	
Avalanche Note:	Route crosses avalanche runout zone; can be dangerous during high hazard periods	
Maps:	USGS 7.5': Garfield, 1982	
	National Forest: San Isabel	
	Trails Illustrated: Map #130 (Salida/ St. Elmo/Shavano Peak)	
	See map pages 213 and 215	

The route to the Lost Wonder Hut follows a summer four-wheel-drive road. Except for a few intersections and a crossing at the bottom of an avalanche runout zone, this route is straightforward and, for the most part, quite safe.

To reach the trailhead, drive on US 50 to the tiny town of Garfield, which is roughly 4 miles below the summit of Monarch Pass. Park across the street from the Monarch Lodge, just to the north at a plowed area for highway maintenance vehicles; make sure you don't block the post with electrical outlets. To find the trail, walk uphill along the northern shoulder of the highway, past the snowmobile rental business. Immediately on the western edge is a forked trailhead/road with a sign to Boss Lake.

Take the right fork, following the route to Boss Lake, and begin climbing a steep, south-facing road. Within minutes, the trail intersects a flat, low-angled, abandoned railroad grade that looks like a road. Do not turn here. Cross the grade and begin to climb again, then head to the right toward a switchback. Follow the switchback around to the left and start the climb up into the valley along a steep, open trail that is often sun-hardened.

The trail eventually enters a forest, and from here the route simply follows a road, bypassing small cabins, mines, the occasional side road, and the turnoff to Boss Lake Reservoir, near the 1.7-mile mark. Continue climbing until the road enters an obvious treeless area that marks the lower

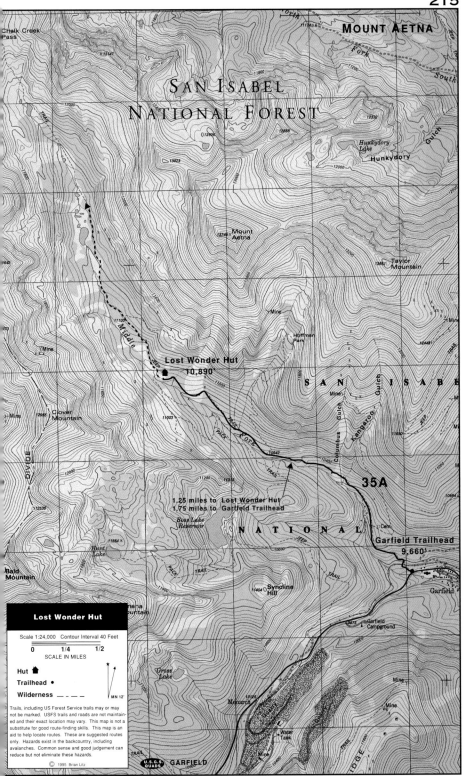

MOUNT AETNA

SAN ISABEL
NATIONAL FOREST

Chalk Creek
Pass

Hunkydory
Lake

Hunkydory

Mount
Aetna

Taylor
Mountain

Mine

Hoffman
Park

Lost Wonder Hut
10,890'

SAN ISABEL

Clover
Mountain

Mine

Columbus Gulch

Kangaroo Gulch

35A

DIVIDE

1.25 miles to Lost Wonder Hut
1.75 miles to Garfield Trailhead

Bass Lake
Reservoir

NATIONAL

Cem.

Garfield Trailhead
9,660'

Hunt
Lake

Bald
Mountain

PACK   TRAIL

Syncline
Hill

TRAIL

Garfield

Garfield
Campground

Grass
Lake

Menarch

Mine

Mine

Water
Tank

RIDGE

TRAIL

GARFIELD

Lost Wonder Hut

Scale 1:24,000   Contour Interval 40 Feet

0   1/4   1/2
SCALE IN MILES

Hut

Trailhead   •

Wilderness   — — —

MN 12°

Trails, including US Forest Service trails may or may
not be marked. USFS trails and roads are not maintained and their exact location may vary. This map is not a
substitute for good route-finding skills. This map is an
aid to help locate routes. These are suggested routes
only. Hazards exist in the backcountry, including
avalanches. Common sense and good judgement can
reduce but not eliminate these hazards.

© 1995 Brian Litz

U.S.G.S.
QUADS

reaches of a huge, avalanche-prone gully on the southern flank of Mount Aetna. Be careful, for you can easily start a snowslide. From here it is possible to to see the Sangre de Cristo Mountains to the southeast.

Once you enter the forest again the hut is not much farther. Travel past two ancient Forest Service cabins on the right, drop down slightly and cross a small creek, then follow the road up a slight incline to the two-story Lost Wonder Hut.

Mike O'Brien, master of the lost art
of flapjack flipping.

36 SUNLIGHT BACKCOUNTRY CABIN

The Sunlight Backcountry Cabin is truly a historic destination. Although moved from its original site, the cabin was built during the 1800s and is thought to have served as the payroll building for a coal mining company that operated in the area. The name Sunlight comes from the town that once supplied the mine. During the intervening years the cabin has served many purposes, including housing ski area employees and ranch hands. Now the cabin is part of the nordic center of the Sunlight Ski Area and is open for day use as a warming hut and as a backcountry overnight shelter by reservation. It is open for year-round use.

The route is certainly one of the easiest hut tours in this book, and, consequently, is a great hut for beginning hut skiers and for more experienced skiers who want a quick overnight jaunt or an introduction to the simplicity of the hut experience.

The hut sleeps up to eight people and is outfitted with bunks and foam pads, a wood cook stove, a wood stove for heat, and a supply of chopped wood. There is, however, no cookware or propane gear (i.e., lights or stoves). Visitors are allowed to bring their own backpacking-type stoves to supplement the wood-burning cook stove. For obvious safety reasons, these must be used outside of the hut. To make reservations call the Ski Sunlight Nordic Center (see Appendix A).

TOUR 36A   SUNLIGHT SKI AREA

Difficulty:	Novice
Time:	2 to 4 hours
Distance:	0.8 mile
Elevations:	Trailhead 8,130', Hut 8,440', +310'
Avalanche Note:	None
Maps:	USGS 7.5': Cattle Creek, 1988
	National Forest: White River
	See map pages 218 and 219

To reach the Sunlight Mountain Resort and the trailhead, follow signs from the south end of Glenwood Springs on CO 82 to the turnoff for CR 117. Follow CR 117 for ten miles. When you reach the turn into the parking area entrance, look for a small, plowed parking area on the right side of the road. The trail is marked by a gate and a sign saying "Old Four-Mile Road."

Pass through the gate and follow the road, marked by signs for 0.7 mile to the cabin, which sits on the south side of Four Mile Creek at the mouth of Babbish Gulch. Babbish Gulch is a nice day-tour destination.

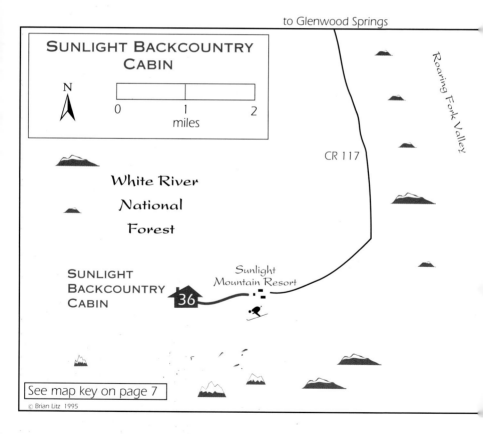

to Glenwood Springs

SUNLIGHT BACKCOUNTRY
CABIN

N

0   1   2
miles

Roaring Fork Valley

CR 117

White River

National

Forest

SUNLIGHT
BACKCOUNTRY
CABIN

Sunlight
Mountain Resort

36

See map key on page 7

© Brian Litz 1995

NATIONAL FOREST

SKI SUNLIGHT

Sunlight
Mine 1831
Gaging Sta
Footnote

Creek

Mule Gulch

8600

8200

8789

9400

Sunlight Ski Area

Ski Sunlight Trailhead
8,130'

8000

8600

SKI LIFT

SKI LIFT

SKI LIFT

9950

9200

37A

8400

Fourmile

32

Sunlight Backcountry Cabin
8,440'

Babbish Gulch

8800

WHITE RIVER
NATIONAL FOREST

31

9000

9400

9600

CATTLE CREEK

U.S.G.S. QUADS

9955

**Sunlight Backcountry
Cabin**

Scale 1:24,000   Contour Interval 40 Feet

0   1/8   1/4

SCALE IN MILES

MN 12°

Hut 🏠
Trailhead ●
Wilderness — — — —

© 1995 Brian Litz

Trails, including US Forest Service trails may or may
not be marked. USFS trails and roads are not maintained and their exact location may vary. This map is not a
substitute for good routefinding skills. This map is an
aid to help locate routes. These are suggested routes
only. Hazards exist in the backcountry, including
avalanches. Common sense and good judgement can
reduce but not eliminate these hazards.

Bernice Notenboom views Utah's canyon country on the San Juan Hut System,

SOUTHERN HUTS

SOUTHERN HUTS

Colorado is a state composed of three distinct regions. Delineated geologically and ecologically, these zones divide Colorado longitudinally into relatively equal areas. The Great Plains extend across the eastern third of the state, the Rocky Mountains form the middle, while plateaus and high desert carve out the western third of the state.

In the southwestern corner of Colorado, a mighty mountain range juts from the central Rockies into the desert lands of the Four Corners. These are the San Juan Mountains, one of the largest mountain ranges (covering roughly 10,000 square miles) in the lower 48 states. The former home of the grizzly bear and the birthplace of the San Juan and Rio Grande rivers, the San Juan Mountains are an alpine wilderness equalled in scenic beauty by few other North American ranges.

The San Juan Mountains are curious in that they were one of the most volcanically active ranges in prehistoric Colorado. Today's San Juans are the result of a complex mountain building process that began more than 500 million years ago and continues to this day. While the basement rocks of the San Juans are Precambrian granites and quartzites, the bulk of the high peaks, especially around Red Mountain Pass and the Sneffels Range, were formed from ancient upthrust sediments and geologically young (25 to 35 million years old) volcanic lavas, tuffs, and breccias. Nature put the finishing touches on the San Juans during the last three to five million years, as Pleistocene glaciers bulldozed the alpine uplands into deep, U-shaped valleys and cirques where we ski and ride today.

The irregular ridges, minarets, and peaks of the San Juans seem to tear at the azure Colorado skies, forming a spectacular backdrop for wilderness skiing. Because there are no metropolitan areas nearby, skiers encounter few crowds here. Those willing to strap on climbing skins will find copious amounts of untracked, backcountry terrain.

Near the Colorado/New Mexico border, atop Cumbres Pass, is the Southwest Nordic Center, a new addition to this book, although not a new hut system. In contrast to the severe topography of the central and northern San Juans, the terrain in this system is mostly gentle and avalanche free. And the snowpack is one of the deepest in the southern Rocky Mountains. This is a perfect destination for quiet touring or for people new to the backcountry hut-to-hut skiing experience. The Southwest Nordic Center also opens up mountains that are overlooked by most skiers.

In the central San Juans is the Hinsdale Haute Route. This system offers skiers excellent nordic and backcountry powder skiing in an environment relatively free of the dangerous avalanche slopes and gullies usually associated with skiing the San Juan backcountry. Situated between Lake City and

Creede, the Hinsdale Haute Route opens up vast areas of rolling, high-altitude terrain for free-heel skiing. This area is too far from most population areas to be used with any frequency. As the system continues to grow, it could become one of the state's safest and most scenic ski tours.

Between Ouray, the "Switzerland of America," and historic Silverton is Red Mountain Pass, also known as the Million Dollar Highway. Just off the summit of the pass is the Saint Paul Lodge, most likely the highest altitude bed and breakfast in the United States. Reached by a straightforward, one-mile ski tour, it is one of the closest backcountry huts to any trailhead that offers quick access to true off-trail ski mountaineering. Saint Paul Lodge is only open to guided trips and winter mountaineering courses.

There is another hut system, a new one, located east of the old mining community of Rico. This system has only one yurt now, though the owners have long-term plans that include several more huts. They are not in a hurry to grow too quickly, but rather want to expand in an organized, thoughtful manner. Their first hut is located atop a massive, forested ridge that separates the Dolores River drainage on the west and the Animas River drainage on the east. This yurt opens up superb terrain and stellar views of the San Juan Mountains and should prove to be a popular destination.

And finally on the western side of the San Juans, near Telluride and Ridgway, is the San Juan Hut System, the largest single hut system in the region. There are five winter huts strung out along the northern escarpment of the Sneffels Range, with terrain that features everything from classic nordic trail skiing to extreme telemark chute skiing. The 200-mile summer mountain bike San Juan Hut System from Telluride to Moab, Utah, crosses every ecozone in Colorado and is one of the first hut-to-hut bike tours in the country.

SOUTHWEST NORDIC CENTER

The Southwest Nordic Center is the newest hut system covered in this book, although it has been in existence for eight years. This system was not included in the first edition of *Colorado Hut to Hut* because its headquarters is in Taos, New Mexico, and there was some confusion on my part as to the exact location of the three yurts, which indeed reside in Colorado near Cumbres Pass.

The mountains around Cumbres Pass (CO 17) are a southern extension of Colorado's San Juans, although they are certainly less alpine than their mighty northern siblings. A long, linear mountain range that runs from Wolf Creek Pass south to the Colorado/New Mexico border, it forms the western boundary of the San Luis Valley and the extensive Rio Grande drainage.

The region's rolling topography is forested and laced with logging trails and roads, yet there are also many open vistas of the surrounding mountains. The snowpack here is legendary. What these ingredients add up to is a recipe for adventurous yet user-friendly touring and telemark skiing. The Southwest Nordic Center's yurts are ideal for all skiers, especially novice and intermediate skiers who like cross-country touring. The Neff Mountain Yurt is easy to reach, even after a long drive; the Flat Mountain and Trujillo Meadows yurts offer easy yet longer tours for those wishing to experience a bit more adventure.

Adding to the user-friendly nature of this system is owner/operator Doug MacLennan's unique and comprehensive trail-marking system. Doug hangs wooden diamonds from strategic tree limbs along the trails. These markers are easy to see and actually swing in the wind, making them even more visible. Also unique is the color-coded system for the markers: The routes to the Neff and Trujillo yurts are painted blue; the Continental Divide route to the Flat Mountain Yurt is orange; and the small sections of trail that connect to form the hut-to-hut routes are yellow. These markers make this one of the most easily navigable hut systems included in this book. Additionally, there is very little in the way of major avalanche hazards — in fact, the overall level of potential hazard along these trails is minimal at best.

All three are standard 16-foot yurts that ideally sleep four but will accommodate six in a pinch. They are insulated and warmer than single-walled yurts. The yurts are fully equipped with wood-burning stoves, propane cook stoves and lanterns, wood supply, and cookware.

Keep in mind that this system is a long way from any major towns. The closest towns are the small communities of Chama to the south and Antonito and Conejos to the north. Alamosa, a large town with gas and grocery stores, is roughly one hour to the north, and Taos is roughly two hours to the south. Be sure to fill up with gas and bring all of your food and other supplies. The entire region is flavored with a very strong Spanish/Mexican influence. Place names such as Chama, Antonito, Del Norte, Alamosa, Conejos, Culebra Peak, and Montezuma Peak conjure up images of explorers searching for gold and other riches in a land inhabited by Native Americans. In fact some of the oldest churches in North America can be found in here. This is a very historic and magical area!

37 Neff Mountain Yurt

The Neff Mountain Yurt has the shortest approach route of any of the yurts managed by the Southwest Nordic Center. For a reasonably strong party with an early start, it is possible to drive all the way from Denver and still have enough time to reach the yurt. The most popular of the three yurts, it possesses one of the best views and some of the most readily available telemark skiing in the area. Immediately behind the yurt to the south is Neff Mountain.

The mountain's broad northern flank is comprised of a large treeless meadow that is perfect for powder skiing; there is enough skiable acreage here to last a group for several days. The eastern side of the mountain also has some nice glades and open slopes and is a good route for skiing to the top of Neff Mountain, a recommended day trip.

For reservations, see the Southwest Nordic Center listing in Appendix A.

Tour 37A   Neff Mountain Trailhead

Difficulty:	Novice/Intermediate
Time:	2 to 4 hours
Distance:	2.9 miles
Elevations:	Trailhead 9,820', Hut 10,400', +580'
Avalanche Note:	None
Maps:	USGS 7.5': Cumbres Pass, 1975
	National Forest: Rio Grande
	See map pages 229 and 232

The northernmost trailhead in the system, the Neff Mountain trailhead is 3.9 miles south of La Manga Summit and 3.4 miles north of Cumbres Pass. It is immediately south of where CO 17 crosses Los Piños Creek (near a small cabin development and the yellow water tank for the Cumbres & Toltec Scenic Railroad line) and is marked by a large, blue disk on the west side of the road. Park on the east side of the road.

Cross the road and gain FR 116, an old, four-wheel-drive road. Pass the yurt sign and begin skiing north, slowly gaining elevation above Los Piños Creek. Follow this well-marked route for 1.9 miles until you reach a fork in the trail. The right fork is marked with yellow diamonds — the connecting trail to the Flat Mountain and Trujillo Meadows yurts — while blue diamonds lead up a steeper trail to the southwest.

Climb up this steeper trail for a few hundred feet, then switchback to the east. Follow the obvious road (a closed logging road) for roughly 0.8 mile as it traverses east, passing two treeless gullies and some steep terrain below and to the north. When you reach the large, flat shoulder on the northeastern flank of Neff Mountain, you will enter a meadow.

Continue east through a stand of trees, then angle to the southeast and follow blue diamonds through small, sparse evergreen trees to the yurt, which sits on the southern edge of the meadow directly below the steeper slopes of Neff Mountain.

37B   NEFF MOUNTAIN YURT TO TRUJILLO MEADOWS YURT

Difficulty:	Novice/Intermediate
Time:	4 to 7 hours
Distance:	6.4 miles
Elevations:	NM Yurt 10,400', TM Yurt 10,450', +680/-670'
Avalanche Note:	None
Maps:	USGS 7.5': Cumbres Pass, 1975
	National Forest: Rio Grande
	See map pages 229 and 232

This route is technically very easy skiing. However, it is more than 6 miles long, and if you have to break trail, it can be a strenuous outing. From the Neff Mountain Yurt, retrace your tracks back down to FR 116. Turn west (left) onto FR 116 and follow the yellow diamonds. The route is easy to follow and contours up and around Elevation Point 10,445' before it hooks to the west and descends slightly to FR 118, a major backcountry road that leads to Trujillo Meadows Reservoir. This road is also frequented by snowmobilers, so watch out! From here follow Tour 38A to the Trujillo Meadows Yurt.

TOUR 37C   NEFF MOUNTAIN YURT TO FLAT MOUNTAIN YURT

Difficulty:	Intermediate
Time:	4 to 6 hours
Distance:	6 miles
Elevations:	NM Yurt 10,400', FM Yurt 11,000, +1000'/-300'
Avalanche Note:	None
Maps:	USGS 7.5': Cumbres Pass, 1975
	National Forest: Rio Grande
	See map pages 229 and 232

This route is exactly the same as Tour 37B up to the point where you reach FR 118 and ski north 0.2 mile to the yellow diamonds marking the small Forest Service trail/road that connects FR 118 to the Cumbres Pass/Flat Mountain Route. From here, turn west onto this trail and ski 0.6 mile until you reach the Cumbres Pass/Flat Mountain Trail—marked by orange diamonds. Follow that route (Tour 39A) to the Flat Mountain Yurt.

The cozy Neff Mountain Yurt sits below beautiful, open slopes.

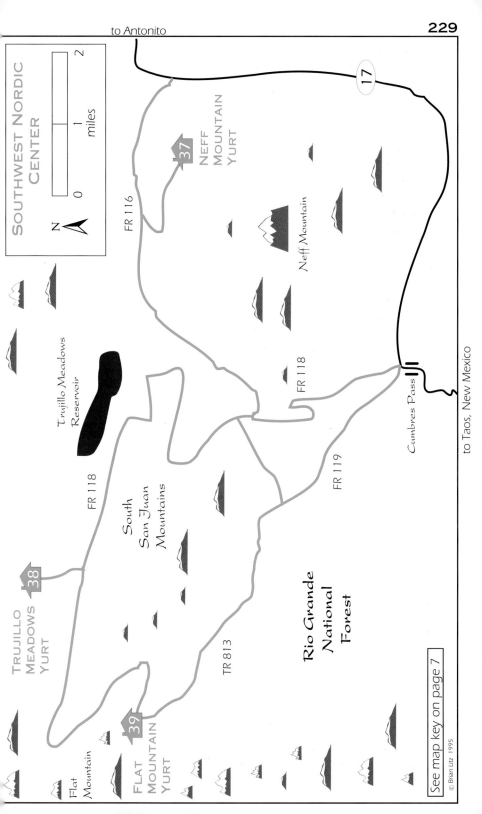

to Antonito

17

SOUTHWEST NORDIC CENTER

N

0   1   2
miles

NEFF MOUNTAIN YURT

37

FR 116

Neff Mountain

FR 118

Cumbres Pass

to Taos, New Mexico

Trujillo Meadows Reservoir

FR 118

South San Juan Mountains

FR 119

TRUJILLO MEADOWS YURT

38

TR 813

Rio Grande National Forest

Flat Mountain

FLAT MOUNTAIN YURT

39

See map key on page 7

© Brian Litz 1995

38 TRUJILLO MEADOWS YURT

The Trujillo Meadows Yurt sits in a sparsely timbered clearing overlooking Los Piños Creek and Trujillo Meadows. The main route to the yurt is a moderately long, moderately difficult tour. If you can put one foot in front of the other, you can reach this hut. The standard route simply follows a wide, summer four-wheel-drive road for its entire length. This road is often used — and packed — by snowmobilers, so you will rarely have to break trail. The terrain around the yurt is also gentle, well suited for short day tours. There are some steeper glades to the south, back across FR 118, where more proficient skiers can find some telemark terrain.

For reservations, see the Southwest Nordic Center listing in Appendix A.

Classic ski touring in Colorado's southern mountains.

TOUR 38A   CUMBRES PASS TRAILHEAD

Difficulty:	Novice/Intermediate
Time:	4 to 6 hours
Distance:	4.8 miles
Elevations:	Trailhead 9,987', Yurt 10,450', +773'/-350'
Avalanche Note:	None
Maps:	USGS 7.5': Cumbres Pass, 1975
	National Forest: Rio Grande
	See map pages 229 and 232

The trailhead for this route is immediately north of Cumbres Pass at the plowed pullout just before the well-marked turnoff to Trujillo Meadows Reservoir. This parking area is 14.2 miles north of the town of Cumbres and 7.3 miles south of La Manga Summit.

From the parking area, follow the Trujillo Meadows Reservoir Road (FR 118) as it climbs north/northwest along a road cut on the right, or eastern edge, of a large meadow. (You'll pass the Neff Mountain Yurt Trail/FR 116 turnoff to the right at mile 1.4, which is marked by yellow diamonds.) Cross a gentle pass at 1.5 miles, and after a brief 0.1 mile, descend past a left turn (marked by yellow diamonds) to the small forest road that connects to the Flat Mountain Yurt Trail.

Follow the marked road north and downhill through a large switchback and into a meadow until you reach a fork in the road. The right fork leads to Trujillo Meadows Campground. Take the left fork and, after 0.1 mile, take a sharp left turn onto another road. Climb southwest up this road for a few hundred feet until the road switchbacks north. Continue along this well-marked road for roughly 1 mile to the marked turnoff to the yurt. Turn here and follow the markers down to the Trujillo Meadows Yurt.

Trails connect just beyond edge of map

39B

Trujillo Meadows Yurt 10,450'

38A
37B

0.40 miles to Trujillo Meadows Yurt
3.50 miles to Flat Mountain Yurt
4.40 miles to Cumbres Pass Trailhead
6.00 miles to Neff Mountain Yurt

39B

Flat Mountain Yurt 11,000'

39A
37C

3.20 miles to Neff Mountain Yurt
1.60 miles to Cumbres PassTrailhead
2.80 miles to Flat Mountain Yurt
3.20 miles to Trujillo MeadowsYurt

37C

3.80 miles to Neff Mountain Yurt
1.60 miles to Cumbres PassTrailhead
2.20 miles to Flat Mountain Yurt

37A

1.90 miles to Neff Mountain Trailhead
1.00 miles to Neff Mountain Yurt
2.00 miles to Forest (Route 118

Neff Mountain Trailhead 9,820'

Neff Mountain Yurt 10,400'

37B
37C

2.20 miles to Trujillo Meadows Yurt
2.60 miles to Cumbres Pass Trailhead

3.00 miles to Neff Mountain Yurt
1.40 miles to Cumbres PassTrailhead
3.00 miles to Flat Mountain Yurt
3.40 miles to Trujillo MeadowsYurt

38A

39A

Cumbres Pass Trailhead 9,987'

RIO GRANDE NATIONAL FOREST

CUMBRES PASS

NATIONAL FOREST

Southwest Nordic Center

Scale 1:24,000   Contour Interval 40 Feet

SCALE IN MILES

Hut
Trailhead
Wilderness

© 1995 Brian Litz

Trails, including US Forest Service trails may or may not be marked. USFS trails and roads are not maintained and their exact location may vary. This map is not a substitute for good route-finding skills. This map is an aid to help locate routes. These are suggested routes only. Hazards exist in the backcountry, including avalanches. Common sense and good judgement can reduce but not eliminate these hazards.

39 FLAT MOUNTAIN YURT

The Flat Mountain Yurt is probably the most difficult yurt in this system to reach — and it is not that difficult. It sits just off the Continental Divide Trail in close proximity to a large, treeless ridge on the west — a good destination for a day trip. The reason this trip is slightly more demanding than the other routes is because the trail crosses a number of meadows, which are a little bit harder to navigate. Additionally, the trail gains slightly over 1,100 feet in roughly four miles.

The yurt is well hidden in a little, forested cove at the corner of a small, treeless clearing. There are nice views to the southeast. For reservations, see the Southwest Nordic Center listing in Appendix A.

39A   CUMBRES PASS TRAILHEAD

Difficulty:	Intermediate
Time:	3 to 5 hours
Distance:	3.8 miles
Elevations:	Trailhead 9,987', Yurt 11,000', +133'/-40'
Avalanche Note:	None
Maps:	USGS 7.5': Cumbres Pass, 1975;
	Archuleta Creek, 1984 (for day trips)
	National Forest: Rio Grande
	See map pages 229 and 232

The trailhead is the same one as for the Trujillo Meadows Yurt. The parking area is immediately north of Cumbres Pass at the plowed pullout just before the well-marked turnoff to Trujillo Meadows Reservoir. It is 14.2 miles north of the town of Cumbres and 7.3 miles south of La Manga Summit.

The trail begins at the same trailhead, but rather than following FR 118, it heads to the northwest, following FR 119/Trail 813, which is the Continental Divide Trail. The start is marked by a large orange disk on a post. Follow the orange diamonds as the trail climbs steadily through the woods past the turnoff to Neff Mountain Yurt and FR 118 at roughly 1.6 miles. Near mile 2, the trail enters a large, treeless meadow. Ski to the west/northwest, leaving Trail 813 at a junked car, which is usually buried in snow. Keep an eye out for the trail markers that lead to the left through the meadow.

Eventually the trail regains a more obvious road/trail that continues to the west/northwest into the upper reaches of Wolf Creek. The valley becomes noticeably steeper and narrower as you begin the final ascent to the yurt; a high, corniced ridge to the west also becomes visible. Finally, the trail approaches a treeless clearing which, from below looks like a natural site for a yurt, and it is. Once you enter the clearing, head to the northwest corner and find the yurt tucked into the edge of a grove of evergreen trees.

39B FLAT MOUNTAIN YURT TO TRUJILLO MEADOWS YURT

Difficulty:	Novice
Time:	2 to 4 hours
Distance:	3.8 miles
Elevations:	FM Yurt 11,020', TM Yurt 10,450', +60'/-580'
Avalanche Note:	None
Maps:	USGS 7.5': Cumbres Pass, 1975;
	Archuleta Creek, 1984
	National Forest: Rio Grande
	See map pages 229 and 232

The trail follows a road for the entire length and is straightforward. The route can be skied in either direction, although its difficulty is dependent on which direction you happen to be traveling. I skied it from south to north under "fast" conditions and it only took one hour. If you ski the route in reverse, from the Trujillo Meadows Yurt to the Flat Mountain Yurt, you will be climbing rather than descending for most of the trip, and it will take considerably longer.

From the front porch of Flat Mountain Yurt, head to the east/southeast through the clearing, remaining on the left (north) side of the meadow. Ski around a small ridge and make a slight descending traverse toward a tiny creek. On the far side of the creek, a road enters the forest. This is the marked route.

Simply follow the yellow diamonds as the road heads east, then north and, finally, takes a long descent to a spruce park, a large meadow that marks the end of the upper descent. Continue along the road as it switchbacks to the east/southeast and descends along a broad drainage. After roughly 1 mile, you reach a well-marked turn (blue diamonds) on the left. Turn and follow the road until you reach another sign, where you then leave the road and drop north into a clearing. There you'll find the Trujillo Meadows Yurt.

HINSDALE HAUTE ROUTE

Colorado's Hinsdale County is a beautiful, remote area protected by the towering San Juans, a region of rolling ranchlands and rich forests hemmed by some of Colorado's tallest mountains. A favorite summer vacation destination, Lake City (the county seat and only town) is nearly deserted during the winter months, except for a few hundred determined year-round residents. Hinsdale County is one of the least populated counties in the nation. It also contains the greatest percentage of alpine tundra of any county outside of Alaska and has the highest mean elevation of any county in the United States (10,000 feet). Forty-six percent of the county is federally protected wilderness lands.

Aside from the county's notoriety as a vastly profitable gold, silver, and lead mining district from 1874 until the turn of the century, perhaps its greatest claim to fame is Alferd Packer, the man eater. Packer had an appetite for adventure and living on the edge of the law. During the winter of 1874-75, Packer, an "experienced" mountain guide, collected a fee to lead prospectors through the rugged San Juan Mountains. The group encountered severe weather and suffered from lack of food. Packer was the only one to return to civilization several weeks later. He was tried for murder and cannibalism and sentenced to 40 years of hard labor.

Hinsdale County's hut system is one of the newest and most intriguing backcountry trail systems in Colorado. The most unusual feature of the Hinsdale Haute Route is, in fact, its route. Beginning near Cebolla Creek between Slumgullion Pass and Spring Creek Pass on CO 149, which connects Lake City to Creede and South Fork, the route follows the old La Garita stock trail along the Continental Divide where cowboys once drove herds of cattle.

Since the La Garita stock trail runs along a broad, gently rolling ridge, this route is almost completely free of serious avalanche danger, yet covers a great deal of true alpine terrain. Spectacular and rarely seen winter panoramas of the Big Blue Wilderness and five 14,000-foot peaks are visible along the way.

The first shelter, the Jon Wilson Memorial Yurt, opened during the winter of 1991-92. The Rambouillet Yurt opened during the winter of 1992-93, the Colorado Trail Friends Memorial Yurt in 1995, and the Fawn Lakes Yurt will open in 1996. The first two yurts are great for novice and intermediate skiers, while the two new huts add a real alpine flavor to the system.

All of the yurts are large and light filled. They are carpeted, designed to sleep six to eight people on bunks and cots, and are well stocked with wood-burning stoves, lanterns, propane cook stoves, pots, pans, utensils, dishes, etc. Of special interest are the "out-yurts" — outdoor toilets built like tiny versions of the main yurts. These out-yurts are some of the nicest backcountry commodes that I have had the pleasure to ruminate in.

The Hinsdale Haute Route should prove to be one of the safest, most spectacular, and most remote hut-to-hut trips in Colorado. Be sure to call the yurt system for up-to-date trail and reservation information (see Appendix A.

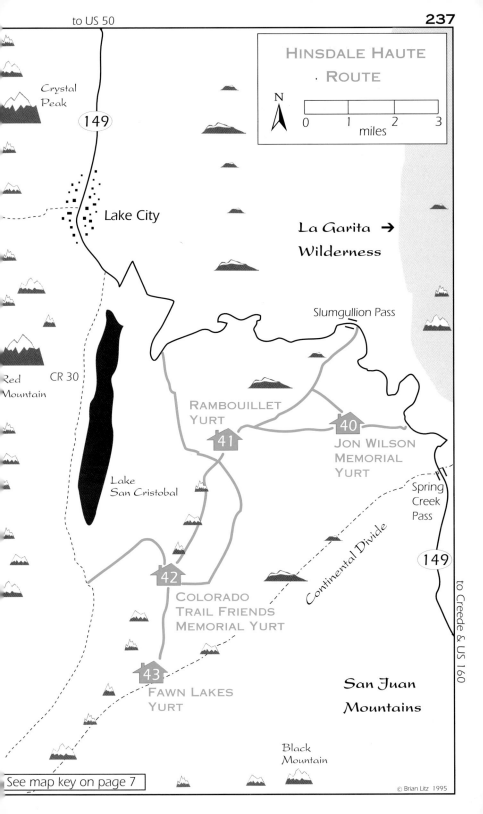

HINSDALE HAUTE
· ROUTE

N

| 0 | 1 | 2 | 3 |

miles

Crystal
Peak

149

Lake City

La Garita →
Wilderness

Slumgullion Pass

Red
Mountain

CR 30

Lake
San Cristobal

RAMBOUILLET
YURT

41

40

JON WILSON
MEMORIAL
YURT

Spring
Creek
Pass

Continental Divide

149

to Creede & US 160

42

COLORADO
TRAIL FRIENDS
MEMORIAL YURT

43

FAWN LAKES
YURT

San Juan
Mountains

Black
Mountain

© Brian Litz 1995

40 JON WILSON MEMORIAL YURT

The Jon Wilson Memorial Yurt was the first shelter to be erected along the Hinsdale Haute Route. It is one of the easiest huts to reach, for the distance is short and the route finding is about as simple as it gets.

Easily handled by nordic skiers of all abilities, the most popular trail to the yurt follows gentle Cebolla (Spanish for onion) Creek to just slightly beyond an obvious fork in the tributary at 10,780 feet. The trail to the yurt is basically free from avalanche danger, making this an ideal introductory overnight ski trip for novices and families. From the yurt, skiers can tour up the drainages to the higher ridges or explore the surrounding forests.

Constructed as a memorial to a young man killed in a tragic auto accident, the Jon Wilson Memorial Yurt is located near the junction of the West and Middle Forks of Cebolla Creek. It is a large yurt filled with sunlight, thanks to clear vinyl panels built into the ceiling and around the front door. It sleeps six to eight and can be reserved through the Hinsdale Haute Route (see Appendix A).

Jerry Gray at the Jon Wilson Memorial Yurt, Hinsdale Haute Route.

TOUR 40A   CEBOLLA CREEK TRAILHEAD

Difficulty:	Novice
Time:	1 to 3 hours
Distance:	1.8 miles
Elevations:	Trailhead 10,440', Hut 10,840', +400'
Avalanche Note:	None
Maps:	USGS 7.5': Slumgullion Pass, 1986
	National Forest: Gunnison
	Trails Illustrated: Map #141 (Silverton/
	Ouray/Telluride/Lake City)
	See map pages 237 and 250-251

To reach the trailhead, drive on CO 149 to its crossing of Cebolla Creek, approximately 15 miles south from Lake City, or 57 miles north from the town of South Fork. There is a plowed parking area near mile marker 57 on the South Fork/Creede side of the creek. The trailhead is on the south side of the creek at a yurt system map.

The trail is blazed with wands with colored circles on top. These markers are mounted on white stakes and are used on a number of trails in the Hinsdale Haute Route.

Directions are simple: Follow the marked trail along the creek. There are no side canyons to turn into until you reach Cebolla Creek's main fork at the 1.5-mile mark. Take the left fork, skiing to the southwest toward the yurt, which sits on the northwest side of the creek in a small clearing. (The right fork is the alternate route to the Rambouillet Yurt, 41B, and the route to the Slumgullion Pass Trailhead, 40B.)

TOUR 40B   SLUMGULLION PASS TRAILHEAD

Difficulty:	Intermediate
Time:	3 to 5 hours
Distance:	4.5 miles
Elevations:	Trailhead 11,540', Yurt 10,840', +500'/-1,200'
Avalanche Note:	Some avalanche terrain encountered; easily avoided
Maps:	USGS 7.5': Slumgullion Pass, 1986
	National Forest: Gunnison
	Trails Illustrated: Map #141 (Silverton/
	Ouray/Telluride/Lake City)
	See map pages 237 and 250-251

Oops! Rick Sayre cleared for landing.

The first half, an unmarked, ski-only route, is fairly obvious because it follows a broad and thinly forested ridge before dropping to the Middle Fork of Cebolla Creek. While not the most direct path to the Jon Wilson Memorial Yurt, this route provides an alternative to the Cebolla Creek Trail. The middle section of the route follows a portion of the Lake City Continental Divide Snowmobile Club Trail (LCCDSC Trail). Please be patient and courteous and try not to let errant snowmobile tracks lead you off course.

This trail begins on CO 149, on the summit of Slumgullion Pass near the snow measuring station, which is roughly 4 miles west of Cebolla Creek. Park on the north side of the road in the small, plowed parking area. From the parking area, cross the road, pass the Slumgullion Snow Measuring Station stake and follow blue diamonds as they ascend into thick timber, heading southwest. This trail is intermittently marked with blue diamonds.

Continue directly up the ridge through thinning trees, gaining 500 feet of elevation. Cross over the top of Elevation Point 12,047'. Follow the broad ridge for 0.5 mile to the small rise on its southwest corner, then begin a descent off the top of the ridge heading south. Intercept and follow the Powderhorn Gulch snowmobile trail to the south. Continue traversing above the creek drainage, then contour to the west around a subtle ridge that is sparsely covered with evergreen trees.

Drop into the head of the Middle Fork of Cebolla Creek drainage and descend along the creek to the junction with the main West Fork. Turn upstream along the West Fork and proceed several hundred feet to the yurt, which is on the west side of the creek.

The Middle Fork of Cebolla Creek is an alternate route connecting the Jon Wilson Memorial Yurt and the Rambouillet Yurt (see Tour 41B).

41 RAMBOUILLET YURT

The Rambouillet Yurt (pronounced Rambo-lay), the second shelter in the Hinsdale Haute Route system, provides skiers with access to safe, classic backcountry touring terrain and provides an intermediate stop for longer, more advanced trips to yurts farther along the Continental Divide. Tucked into the trees below Hill 71, this yurt is surrounded by acres of moderate-to-advanced ski terrain. The short tour to the summit of Hill 71 — a 12,067-foot "hill" — affords an unbelievable panorama of the rugged San Juan Mountains to the west. Strong beginning skiers traveling with experienced partners should be able to reach this yurt despite its intermediate rating.

The first route begins at the Jon Wilson Memorial Yurt, although strong skiers could easily ski directly from the parking area at Cebolla Creek to the Rambouillet Yurt. Make reservations for the Rambouillet Yurt, which sleeps six to eight, through the Hinsdale Haute Route office (see Appendix A).

TOUR 41A JON WILSON MEMORIAL YURT TO RAMBOUILLET YURT VIA WEST FORK OF CEBOLLA CREEK

Difficulty:	Intermediate
Time:	3 to 4 hours
Distance:	3.2 miles
Elevations:	JWM Yurt 10,840', R Yurt 11,680', +840'
Avalanche Note:	Route crosses avalanche slopes; prone to skier-triggered avalanches during high-hazard periods
Maps:	USGS 7.5': Lake San Cristobal, 1973; Slumgullion Pass, 1986
	National Forest: Gunnison
	Trails Illustrated: Map #141 (Silverton/Ouray/Telluride/Lake City)
	See map pages 237 and 250-251

There are two routes from the Jon Wilson Memorial Yurt to the Rambouillet Yurt. The West Fork of Cebolla Creek is easier and shorter. This route passes under many avalanche runout zones that are potentially dangerous, however, and should only be used when conditions are very safe. Additionally, skiers should use avalanche terrain travel procedures and equipment, including transceivers and shovels. If conditions are questionable, use the Middle Fork route (Tour 41B). This route is recommended during periods of avalanche hazard because the creek is protected by trees throughout the ascent to Rambouillet Park. Both tours are straightforward, take a half day or less, and should present very few problems.

For the West Fork route from the Jon Wilson Memorial Yurt, follow the creek upstream for 2 miles until you pass a constriction in the valley between a knob on the south and steeper slopes on the north. Continue due west, past a tributary coming in from the north, to a fork in the creek where a large meadow contours south. Begin climbing out of the drainage on a northwest heading, aiming for the east side of the south ridge of Hill 71. The Rambouillet Yurt is at 11,680 feet in a tiny meadow, just below a small, flat shoulder and rock outcrops on the south ridge of Hill 71.

TOUR 41B   JON WILSON MEMORIAL YURT TO RAMBOUILLET YURT VIA MIDDLE FORK

Difficulty:	Intermediate
Time:	3 to 5 hours
Distance:	3.7 miles
Elevations:	JWM Yurt 10,800', R Yurt 11,680', +840'
Avalanche Note:	Some avalanche terrain encountered; easily avoided
Maps:	USGS 7.5': Lake San Cristobal, 1973; Slumgullion Pass, 1986
	National Forest: Gunnison
	Trails Illustrated: Map #141 (Silverton/ Ouray/Telluride/Lake City)
	See map pages 237 and 250-251

This route is a safer path to the Rambouillet Yurt from the Jon Wilson Yurt when compared to the West Fork route (Tour 41A). Use this route if avalanche conditions are questionable.

From the Jon Wilson Memorial Yurt, return downstream to a junction of the West Fork and the Middle Fork of Cebolla Creek. From this point, turn and proceed upstream through the Middle Fork drainage (which is on the left). Heading due west, climb out of the drainage and enter Rambouillet Park. Intercept the LCCDSC snowmobile trail and follow it as it contours south around the small basin between Slumgullion Point and Hill 71. Rambouillet Yurt is at 11,680 feet, situated on the south ridge of Hill 71.

TOUR 41C   SLUMGULLION PASS TRAILHEAD

Difficulty:	Intermediate
Time:	4 to 6 hours
Distance:	4.0 miles
Elevations:	Trailhead 11,540', Yurt 11,680', +500'/-320'
Avalanche Note:	Some avalanche terrain encountered; easily avoided
Maps:	USGS 7.5': Lake San Cristobal, 1973; Slumgullion Pass, 1986
	National Forest: Gunnison
	Trails Illustrated: Map #141 (Silverton/ Ouray/Telluride/Lake City)
	See map pages 237 and 250-251

As long as the weather is stable and clear, this high-altitude traverse is quite moderate. By combining the first half of the Slumgullion Pass route to the Jon Wilson Memorial Yurt (Tour 40B) and the second half of the Middle Fork of Cebolla Creek/Rambouillet Yurt route (Tour 41B), you can create a very scenic tour. This trail is not marked though, so skiers should be experienced in basic backcountry route finding, navigation, and avalanche awareness.

John Fielder heads back to the Rambouillet Yurt after a morning photo shoot.

For detailed directions to the trailhead, refer to Tour 40B. From the trailhead at the Slumgullion Snow Measuring Site, the route ascends to the top of Elevation Point 12,047', the most difficult section of the trail.

From here, skiers can stay on top of the ridge and ski over Slumgullion Point and Hill 71 for a slightly higher elevation gain and a view of the incredible scenery. Or, they can take another route that descends onto an 11,800-foot shelf and follows the snowmobile trail south to the yurt. This route is more protected from the elements. During periods of severe weather and wind, skiers are advised to choose a route via Cebolla Creek and the Jon Wilson Memorial Yurt rather than the route from Slumgullion Pass.

TOUR 41D   SAWMILL PARK TRAILHEAD

Difficulty:	Intermediate/Advanced
Time:	4 to 6 hours
Distance:	4 miles
Elevations:	Trailhead 9,940', Yurt 11,680', +1,740'
Avalanche Note:	None
Maps:	USGS 7.5': Slumgullion Pass, 1986;
	Lake San Cristobal, 1973
	National Forest: Gunnison
	Trails Illustrated: Map #141 (Silverton/
	Ouray/Telluride/Lake City)
	See map pages 237 and 250-251

This trail, while not new, was not included in previous editions of this book because it is part of the Lake City Continental Divide Snowmobile Club (LCCDSC) trail system. Despite the presence of the snowmobilers, Jerry Gray, director of the Hinsdale Haute Route system, likes the trail because it is the shortest route to the Rambouillet Yurt. The route finding is easy, since the trail is protected by trees most of the way. On the other hand, it does climb steeply and is more strenuous than other routes to this yurt.

This trailhead is on the south side of the road just past the Lake San Cristobal overlook, which is the first sharp switchback above Lake City on the way up to Slumgullion Pass. From the point where CO 149 crosses the Lake Fork of the Gunnison, go 2.9 miles to the turnoff. You will see a steep road, marked with a sign, ascending straight uphill into the forest to the south. Park along the south side of the road on the shoulder. If coming from Creede, the turnoff is 5.3 miles west of Slumgullion Pass.

Climb directly up the road and follow it past a left turn, which is marked with snowmobile signs. (If you are descending, this trail bypass will appear as a right fork; it leads to another, more major snowmobile parking area farther up the pass from the trailhead).

Follow the road for roughly 1.3 miles until you reach the meadow of Sawmill Park, which presents about the only route finding complications on this tour. First of all, be careful not to be misdirected by the confusion of tracks in Sawmill Park. Snowmobilers like to tour around this meadow, which can obscure the main trail. To keep on the main route, ski along the very eastern edge of the park, near the trees. Keep an eye out for where the trail leaves the park and re-enters the woods, along a tiny creek. This stretch of trail is normally marked with wands.

Once back in the woods, the trail climbs even more steeply up to the pass on the western edge of Rambouillet Park. This ascent doesn't let up until gaining roughly 1,000 feet. As you enter Rambouillet Park, the snowmobile trail markers lead off to the southeast, directly into the heart of this vast, open meadow. Look to the left (northeast) for the hut system wands that lead past the edge of the trees another 0.7 mile to the Rambouillet Yurt.

42 COLORADO TRAIL FRIENDS MEMORIAL YURT

The Colorado Trail Friends Memorial Yurt was built with donations from the Colorado Trail Foundation and came on-line during the spring of 1995. It opened up adventurous terrain that truly puts the haute in the Hinsdale Haute Route. This yurt sits directly atop a saddle that straddles both the Continental Divide and the Colorado Trail and has the best views of all of the shelters in this system. All one has to do is walk out the front door to delight in a panorama of the the Lake City group of the San Juan Mountains, including 14,309-foot Uncompahgre Peak to the northwest, with 14,001-foot Sunshine Peak and 14,034-foot Redcloud Peak to the west/southwest. Out to the east is the peculiar sphinx-like summit of Bristol Head.

From the Slumgullion Pass and Spring Creek side of the system, skiers must travel hut-to-hut from the Rambouillet Yurt or the Wilson Yurt to reach the Colorado Trail Friends Memorial Yurt. The trails are more challenging and more committing than the routes to the Rambouillet and Wilson yurts, but then the destination may also be more rewarding.

The standard route follows a high, treeless ridge separating the Rambouillet and Colorado Trail Friends Memorial yurts and overlooking the multi-thousand-foot escarpment above Lake San Cristobal. It is about as

Atop the Continental Divide (11,800'), the Colorado Trail Friends Memorial Yurt provides an inviting shelter for backcountry skiers.

exposed as a trail could be to weather, and it also travels through avalanche-prone terrain. There is a longer, alternate route to the Colorado Trail Friends Memorial Yurt from the Rambouillet Yurt that follows Big Buck Creek; this is a better choice in foul weather.

Finally, there is another trail that climbs directly to the yurt out of the Lake Fork valley, gaining over 2,500 feet en route. Called the Camp Trail, it is a newer Forest Service trail that does not appear on any maps, although it has a parking lot and official trailhead up-valley from Lake San Cristobal.

What all of this means is that a ski trip to this hut is less suitable for beginning hut skiers, although strong beginners can certainly make the journey under optimal conditions, or with the help of a guide.

Spring is a great time to visit this hut, for skiers have longer days and great touring on the stable snowpack. Also of interest to skiers are the forested slopes high above the hut to the south, where short powder runs abound.

NOTE: **The Colorado Trail Friends Memorial Yurt has been moved slightly to the west and now sits protected on the eastern side of a small stand of evergreen trees.** This new location is a short walk from the old one and does not affect route access information.

42A RAMBOUILLET YURT TO THE COLORADO TRAIL FRIENDS MEMORIAL YURT VIA CONTINENTAL DIVIDE

Difficulty:	Intermediate/Advanced
Time:	4 to 6 hours
Distance:	4.25 miles
Elevations:	Yurt 11,680', CTFM Yurt 11,800', + 800'/-1,000'
Avalanche Note:	Route crosses avalanche runout zones; can be dangerous in high-hazard periods
Maps:	USGS 7.5': Slumgullion Pass, 1986; Lake San Cristobal, 1973
	National Forest: Gunnison
	Trails Illustrated: Map #141 (Silverton/ Ouray/Telluride/Lake City)
	See map pages 237 and 250-251

This is the standard route to the Colorado Trail Friends Memorial Yurt. It is an exciting, high-elevation tour that in clear weather presents skiers with some of the most scenic ski touring in the state. Navigation is easy, and, for the most part, moderately capable skiers should be able to traverse it under good conditions. Avoid it like the plague if weather threatens; take the Big Buck Creek route instead.

Avalanche hazards here are minimal under normal conditions, and, because of the wide-open nature of the terrain, most potential hazards are visible. Probably the most dangerous stretch is a short slope that must be negotiated to gain a narrow ridge near the 3 mile mark just before the final descent to the hut.

Leave the Rambouillet Yurt and traverse southwest to the saddle at 11,600 feet. Cross the marked snowmobile route and continue on a westerly course up and onto a ridge, where you can overlook the Lake Fork Valley below to the west.

Follow the ridge crest up through a thinning stand of trees until you reach treeline. From here the goal is to reach the summit of Elevation Point 12,305' by choosing the path of least resistance directly up the ridge. Exercise caution by trying the safest route up this slope, which is usually the windblown sastrugi that forms the transition from the windward and leeward aspects of the ridge.

Continue over the summit of Elevation Point 12,305', past a radio tower. Descend roughly 240 feet to a saddle and then climb 160 feet up towards Elevation Point 12,282'. You can ski directly over this summit, or traverse around its eastern flank. Continue on this rollercoaster ride by descending to another, less obvious saddle.

From here, the route continues south along a narrow ridge before descending directly to the yurt. The short climb on this ridge, near Elevation Point 12,105', places skiers in close proximity to some wind-loaded slopes, so once again exercise extreme caution. If this slope causes anxiety, it is possible to avoid it by descending due south from the "less obvious" saddle toward Big Buck Creek for about 400 feet, then traversing around to a tributary that leads up to the saddle and the yurt.

In fact, it is possible to abandon the route at many points for the safety of the Big Buck Creek drainage if the weather begins to deteriorate or if the level of avalanche hazard is deemed too great.

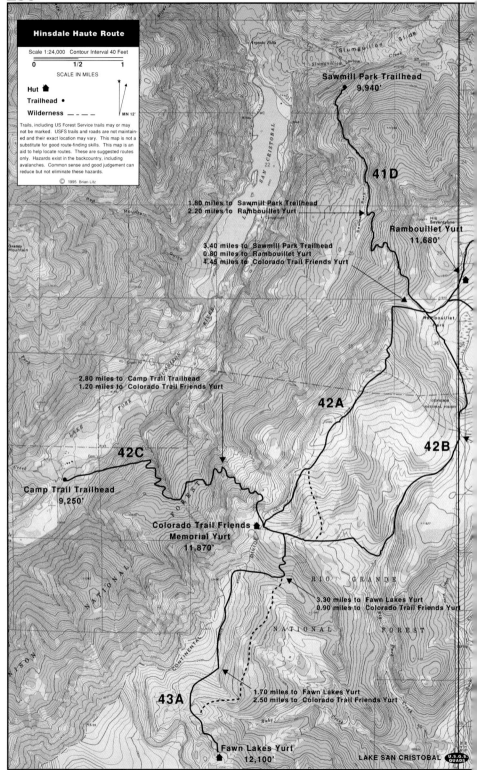

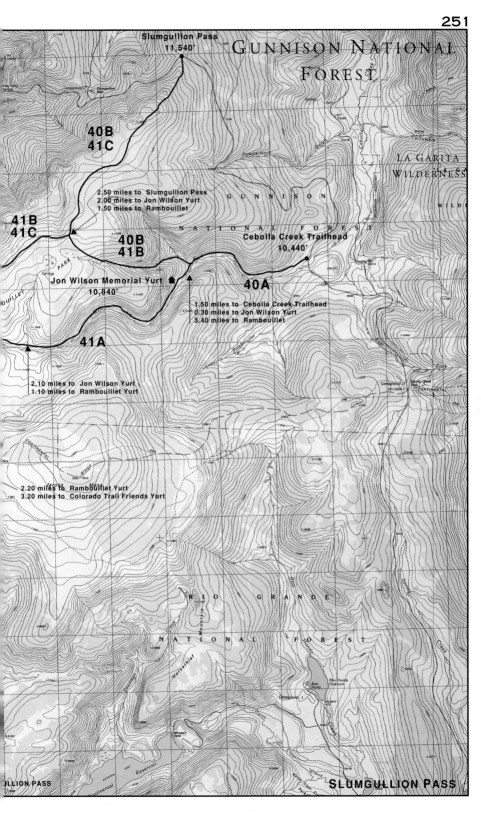

GUNNISON NATIONAL FOREST

Slumgullion Pass
11,540'

LA GARITA
WILDERNESS

40B
41C

2.50 miles to Slumgullion Pass
2.00 miles to Jon Wilson Yurt
1.50 miles to Rambouillet

GUNNISON

41B
41C

NATIONAL FOREST

40B
41B

Cebolla Creek Trailhead
10,440'

Jon Wilson Memorial Yurt
10,840'

40A

1.50 miles to Cebolla Creek Trailhead
0.30 miles to Jon Wilson Yurt
3.40 miles to Rambouillet

41A

2.10 miles to Jon Wilson Yurt
1.10 miles to Rambouillet Yurt

2.20 miles to Rambouillet Yurt
3.20 miles to Colorado Trail Friends Yurt

RIO GRANDE

NATIONAL FOREST

42B RAMBOUILLET YURT TO COLORADO TRAIL FRIENDS MEMORIAL YURT VIA BIG BUCK CREEK

Difficulty:	Intermediate
Time:	5 to 7 hours
Distance:	5.4 miles
Elevations:	Yurt 11,680', CTFM Yurt 11,870', +800'/-760'
Avalanche Note:	Route crosses avalanche runout zones; can be dangerous in high-hazard periods
Maps:	USGS 7.5': Slumgullion Pass, 1986; Lake San Cristobal, 1973
	National Forest: Gunnison
	Trails Illustrated: Map #141 (Silverton/ Ouray/Telluride/Lake City)
	See map pages 237 and 250-251

Big Buck Creek is the foul-weather tour to the Colorado Trail Friends Memorial Yurt. It remains well below the Continental Divide in the shelter of forests. Skiers still must cross several large, windswept meadows en route, and there are some small yet potential avalanche slopes during high-hazard periods.

From the Rambouillet Yurt, ski south to the marked snowmobile route that comes up from Sawmill Park. Turn to the southeast and follow the wands of the snowmobile route 1 mile across Rambouillet Park to a point where the route heads south up a draw, still following the snowmobile route. Not much trail breaking is required here under normal conditions!

From the top of the draw at the trail junction sign, cross the snowmobile trail and begin a gentle descent down the right side of Big Buck Creek. After descending 2 miles and roughly 500 feet in elevation, a side tributary to the west becomes apparent where the forest begins to thin out. Contour out of main Big Buck and head directly west up a large tributary, gaining roughly 600 feet to a saddle and the Colorado Trail Friends Memorial Yurt.

42C   CAMP TRAIL TRAILHEAD

Difficulty:	Advanced	🚶
Time:	2 to 7 hours (depending on direction)	
Distance:	5.5 miles	
Elevations:	Trailhead 9,250', CTFM Yurt 11,870', +2,530'	
Avalanche Note:	Some avalanche terrain encountered; easily avoided.	
Maps:	USGS 7.5': Slumgullion Pass, 1986; Lake San Cristobal, 1973	
	National Forest: Gunnison	
	Trails Illustrated: Map #141 (Silverton/ Ouray/Telluride/Lake City)	
	See map pages 237 and 250-251	

This relatively new trail is not used with any frequency during the winter months. This is because there are not very many day skiers in the Lake City area, the trail is steep — gaining over 2,500 feet in 5.5 miles — and it includes many treacherous, switchbacky stretches. This is a challenging ski, whether you are skiing up to or down from the yurt.

And if that is not enough, navigation is tricky throughout, especially on the lower sections where the trail weaves through confusing aspen forests. The trail is so new that it has not been marked, although the upper section is marked with blue spray paint on trees. The route indicated on the topo map in this book is a close approximation, as the trail does not yet appear on the latest USGS map.

This is unfortunate for hut skiers because it is the shortest, most direct route to the Colorado Trail Friends Memorial Yurt (all other routes go via the Rambouillet and Jon Wilson Memorial yurts). Consequently, I only recommend this trail for strong, competent skiers who are good backcountry route finders.

A final note: Although described as an ingress route, for most people this trail works better as an egress, or descent, route from the Colorado Trail Friends Memorial Yurt. Skiers can park on Slumgullion Pass, ski to either the Rambouillet or Jon Wilson Memorial Yurt, then to this yurt, and finally exit via the Camp Trail to an awaiting shuttle car.

To reach the trailhead, drive south of Lake City to the turnoff to Lake San Cristobal (CR 30). Drive up this road first on pavement, then on gravel for 8 miles to the trailhead parking area on the left. The parking area is marked. Ski or walk past the sign and begin traveling on the obvious trail. The first section is easy to follow, although it is sometimes free of snow due to its southern exposure and low elevation. From here the trail ascends on a traverse to the north/northeast and eventually enters an aspen forest. Keep an eye out for the trail, especially if no one has skied in the area lately. The trail continues upward through the forest, both aspen and evergreen, until it begins to climb onto a distinct ridge that runs east/west and connects with the Continental Divide high above to the east. The trail continues up the sunbaked south-face of this ridge through more aspen forests; an area where the trail, now more obvious, is often free of snow. Near the top of the ridge, the trail switchbacks up to the east/northeast and then gains the narrow top of the ridge. There are great views here of the surrounding mountains.

Now turn east and ski directly along the top of the ridge for a few hundred feet through more aspen trees. Follow the ridge until it becomes a flat shoulder, just below very steep terrain. From here the trail veers off to the north and begins to climb along a creek that parallels the upper ridge. This is where the blue spray paint markers begin to appear.

Once in the shaded forest on the north side of the ridge, keep an eye out for blue markers and climb east up toward the higher terrain above. The trail runs along a creek for a short while, then begins to ascend dramatically up a smaller, parallel ridge connected to the main one. To the north is a large, treeless talus slope that comes down from the Continental Divide. Never enter this feature; remain in the safety of the trees.

The trail just barely enters the high, southeastern corner of the talus slopes, below a large rock face. Keep an eye out for a faint trail and markers that indicate where the trail traverses due south toward the yurt, up and away from the talus slope. The trail continues traversing until it reaches the edge of another expansive, treeless gullylike feature. Once you enter this, turn uphill to the east/southeast, past two trail markers up to a saddle and the Colorado Trail Friends Memorial Yurt.

For those heading out his route: To find the trail, leave the yurt and ski north across a meadow. Due west of the yurt is the large, treeless gullylike feature. Head for the trees along this feature's northern edge. Go past a post, then veer more to the west and drop past another postlike trail marker. Just past this the terrain begins to steepen. Drop down another 10 to 15 feet past two dead tree stumps and a few trees, then stop. The trail now veers due north and traverses down and around to the edge of the talus slope. Refer to the above trail descriptions from here on out.

43   FAWN LAKES YURT

At the time this book went to print, the Fawn Lakes Yurt was in the planning stage and slated for construction during the summer of 1995. It will be built on a secluded, forested knoll surrounded by snow-covered lakes at 12,100 feet, making it the most remote and highest of all the Hinsdale Haute Route shelters. The elevated knoll affords nice vistas to the north and east. Towering above the site to the south and west are heavily corniced cirque walls, which can be potential avalanche threats for anyone who meanders too closely.

The clear panels of the Hinsdale Haute Route yurts provide sunlight and warmth.

True backcountry telemark skiing here is probably the most unlimited of any in the Hinsdale Haute Route system. Directly north of the Fawn Lakes Yurt there are many gladed slopes for powder skiing and a huge basin and gentle peaks to the north and west that offer moderate, above-treeline skiing. Call the Hinsdale Haute Route system to find out the status of this yurt (see Appendix A).

43A COLORADO TRAIL FRIENDS MEMORIAL YURT TO THE FAWN LAKES YURT VIA THE CONTINENTAL DIVIDE

Difficulty:	Intermediate/Advanced
Time:	4 to 6 hours
Distance:	4.2 miles
Elevations:	CTFM Yurt 11,840', FL Yurt 12,100', +980'/-680'
Avalanche Note:	Route crosses avalanche runout zones; can be dangerous during high-hazard periods.
Maps:	USGS 7.5': Slumgullion Pass, 1986; Lake San Cristobal, 1973
	National Forest: Gunnison
	Trails Illustrated: Map #141 (Silverton/ Ouray/Telluride/Lake City)
	See map pages 237 and 250-251

This route is very similar in character to the Rambouillet/Colorado Trail Friends Memorial Yurt route (Tour 42A). Although this tour is shorter, exposed to less potential avalanche hazards, and, overall, just seems less strenuous. Under clear skies and on a solid snowpack, quick progress can be made across the ridge. Probably the most difficult stretch is navigating the hummocky terrain on the final half mile.

There is an alternate foul-weather route that traverses roughly 500 feet below to the east. About as difficult and approximately the same length as this tour, the route is obvious and will not be described separately.

Begin the tour by leaving the Colorado Trail Friends Memorial Yurt and descending down valley to the east over gentle terrain. After only about 100 feet of elevation, look for a narrow finger of meadow (which is visible from the yurt) that cuts directly into the forest on the south. Head into this clearing and ski to the very left corner. From here, markers and a trail cut (the Colorado Trail) lead due south through the forest and up onto the top of a wide open ridge. From this vantage point, the rest of the route is visible to the west and south.

Turn due west and begin the slow, gradual ascent toward Elevation Point 12,490'. It not necessary to climb directly to the top of this point, although on clear days the views make it worthwhile. From here, either travel south directly along the crest of the Continental Divide or traverse lower down along the eastern flank. This second option may provide more protection from the elements. (Note: The foul-weather route descends off the point for about 200 feet and then makes a long traverse south toward Fawn Lakes.)

Continue south until the ridge begins to fade into a large basin. Contour slightly to the west and descend across this feature. Aim for the left (eastern) side of the highest forested knoll, which is framed against the cirque walls to the south/southeast. Navigation tools are handy here for choosing the most direct route to the yurt. Just remember to stay around 12,000 feet as you ski back into the woods and traverse east toward the southeastern boundary of the basin. Also be sure to traverse below the short, steep forested slopes that protect the northern aspects of the knoll.

Once around on the east side of the knoll, climb up through an indistinct creek drainage to the edge of the trees and a small lake just below the knoll. The Fawn Lakes Yurt is located directly on top of a small, flat, benchlike knoll on the northern edge of the largest lake. The southeastern-most of the Fawn Lakes, it is marked 12,062 feet on the USGS topo map. Bear in mind that all of these small lakes are often covered with a deep layer of snow and the area may look more like a meadow.

INDEPENDENT HUTS

To the west of the Hinsdale Haute Route, across the Continental Divide on Red Mountain Pass, is the Saint Paul Lodge. Red Mountain Pass was the center of extensive mining during the late 1800s and early 1900s. While the age of the lodge is not known, the small cabin nearby was built in 1887. Owner and operator Christopher George works as an avalanche forecaster in the area and is involved with San Juan Search and Rescue. He is also the founder of the Colorado Institute for Snow Science and Avalanche Research. The International Alpine School (IAS) hut, which was included in the first edition of this book, has, sadly, burned down. The old mining cabin at the foot of majestic Gilpin Peak in Yankee Boy Basin was probably the most alpine location of any hut in this book. It will be missed. Taking its place, however, is a new hut owned and operated by Rico Snowcountry Tours. This exciting new hut, which may be the first in a future hut system, opens up a backcountry ski area of considerable size and diversity. It would be quite possible to spend several days exploring the various ridges that spiral outward from this hut. Dubbed the Scotch Creek Yurt (officially without a name, I refer to it as the Scotch Creek Yurt for clarity), it continues the superb tradition of adventurous skiing, superb snow, and unparalleled scenery of Colorado's southern huts.

44 SAINT PAUL LODGE

The Saint Paul Lodge is located less than a mile from the summit of Red Mountain Pass on US 550, between Ouray and Silverton. The route into this old mining structure is short, steep, and manageable by most skiers.

From the lodge, guests can ski into U. S. Basin and McMillan Basin for scenic and challenging day trips. Because this trailhead and the lodge are at such a high altitude, it offers less experienced skiers true alpine backcountry skiing usually available only to more advanced skiers. This is not a beginner's area; skiers should be in good shape and possess solid touring abilities.

Saint Paul Lodge is on Red Mountain, which was the center of prolific mining during the late 1800s and early 1900s. Historically, the lodge served as the tipple house, where buckets of ore were raised and tipped to unload their cargo. The 800-foot shaft still exists — directly below the dining table!

The Saint Paul Lodge offers a variety of packages for guests, including board and lodging, guide services and instruction, as well as medical and

Saint Paul Lodge, near Red Mountain Pass, is a historic structure from the late 1800s.

avalanche seminars. The lodge sleeps 22 and is well suited for large groups. There is an old cabin on the property that can be rented on a weekly basis. The cabin sleeps six to eight and is open all year; in summer it is car accessible. Owner and operator Christopher George, a colorful English gent, bakes a mean apple pie and has stories to fill many a winter night.

The Saint Paul Lodge opens for the season around Thanksgiving and stays open through April, when skiers may enjoy superb springtime snow. Contact the lodge to make reservations (see Appendix A).

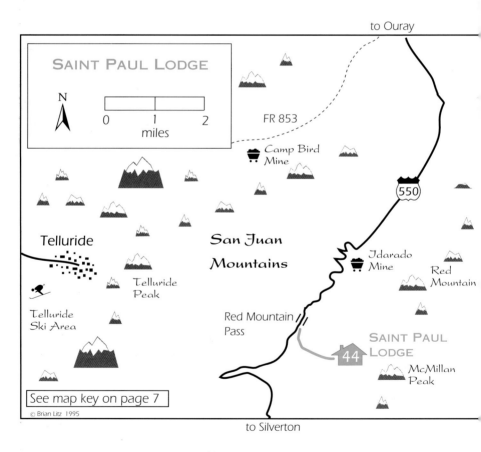

to Ouray

SAINT PAUL LODGE

N

0   1   2
miles

FR 853

Camp Bird
Mine

550

Telluride

San Juan
Mountains

Idarado
Mine

Red
Mountain

Telluride
Peak

Telluride
Ski Area

Red Mountain
Pass

SAINT PAUL
LODGE

44

McMillan
Peak

See map key on page 7

© Brian Litz 1995

to Silverton

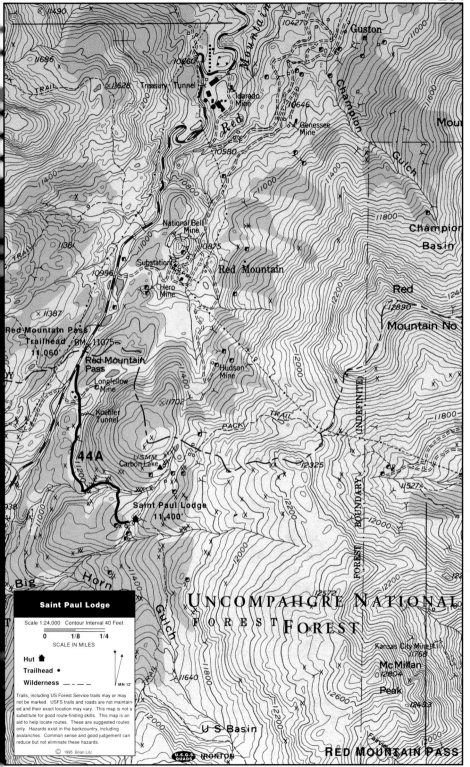

Saint Paul Lodge

Scale 1:24,000   Contour Interval 40 Feet

0   1/8   1/4

SCALE IN MILES

Hut

Trailhead •

Wilderness — – – –

MN 12°

Trails, including US Forest Service trails may or may not be marked. USFS trails and roads are not maintained and their exact location may vary. This map is not a substitute for good route-finding skills. This map is an aid to help locate routes. These are suggested routes only. Hazards exist in the backcountry, including avalanches. Common sense and good judgement can reduce but not eliminate these hazards.

© 1995 Brian Litz

TOUR 44A   RED MOUNTAIN PASS TRAILHEAD

Difficulty:	Intermediate/Advanced 🏃
Time:	1 to 2 hours
Distance:	1 mile
Elevations:	Trailhead 11,060', Hut 11,400', +340'
Avalanche Note:	Some avalanche terrain encountered; easily avoided
Maps:	USGS 7.5': Ironton, 1972
	National Forest: San Juan
	Trails Illustrated: Map #141 (Silverton/ Ouray/Telluride/Lake City)
	See map pages 260 and 261

To reach the trailhead, drive to the summit of Red Mountain Pass on US 550. Immediately to the south of the summit is a small, plowed parking area on the east side of the highway. Park there and ski south/southeast along a snow-covered road, passing several old mining buildings. Ski around a steep knob and up into a small drainage.

Continue up the north side of the creek along a steep road. After gaining about 160 feet of elevation, the road abruptly crosses a creek and begins a traversing ascent out of the creek bed to the Saint Paul Lodge. Be careful that you do not remain in the creek bed, or you will miss the turn and end up heading north onto a small bench.

45 SCOTCH CREEK YURT

This yurt is the result of the efforts of long-time Rico resident Gary Gass. He has been skiing the backcountry around this mining town for the past 18 years with very little in the way of competition for the superb terrain and fresh snow found in these often overlooked mountains.

Scotch Creek Yurt sits high up on the forested ridge that separates the Dolores River drainage from the Hermosa Creek drainage. From atop a knoll east of the yurt, skiers are treated to a 360-degree vista of the summits of southwestern Colorado: To the north is Hermosa Peak and the Silverton West Group of the San Juan Mountains; to the northeast are the mighty Twilight and Needle mountains and Weminuche Wilderness; Purgatory Ski Area is to the east; the La Plata Mountains are located to the south, and to the west you can see 12,095-foot Storm Peak. Truly some of the most beautiful country in Colorado!

The skiing equals or even exceeds the standards set by the scenery. The terrain reminds me of the backcountry skiing near Wolf Creek Pass, with forested ridges radiating from a central ridge. There are so many different

Eric Fagrelius surveys the superb terrain from the "front porch" of the Scotch Creek Yurt.

aspects to these ridges that skiers should be able to find great skiing most of the season. The slope angles are varied, with everything from gentle, open slopes suitable for the less-experienced skier to radical, backcountry tree skiing for the expert. And because the area has been logged repeatedly over the years, there are plenty of clearings and thinned glades. A group of experienced skiers could spend many days exploring these lonesome slopes. Get ready to shred!

This yurt has standard hut amenities, including a wood-burning stove for heat, propane lights and cook stove, pots, pans, etc. For more information and reservations, call Rico Snowcountry Tours (see Appendix A).

TOUR 45A   SCOTCH CREEK TRAILHEAD

Difficulty:	Intermediate/Advanced
Time:	4 to 7 hours hours
Distance:	6.7 miles
Elevations:	Trailhead 8,560', Hut 10,460', +1900'
Avalanche Note:	Some avalanche terrain encountered; easily avoided.
Maps:	USGS 7.5': Hermosa Peak, 1975; Rico, 1975
	National Forest: San Juan
	Trails Illustrated: Map #504 (Durango Area Mountain Bike Map)
	See map pages 265 and 266

This scenic, secluded route is presently the only one to the Scotch Creek Yurt and it makes for a fairly stout day of skiing (get an early start), even though the first 3 miles consist of very easy ski touring on a nearly flat road. Once the trail leaves Scotch Creek, the route begins to climb steadily along jeep trails and small logging roads, packing in most of its nearly 2,000 feet of elevation gain. Navigation and route finding are not difficult, although during the last third of the route skiers will need to pay close attention to their surroundings and the map, as the trail passes several old logging roads and large clear cuts that do not appear on the latest USGS Rico map.

The Scotch Creek Trailhead is located at a small pullout right next to an obvious creek — Scotch Creek — 3 miles southwest of Rico on CO 145. The pullout is on the east side of the road and is not very big, so park with care.

The trail begins just off the road, near a sign telling the history of the old Scotch Creek Toll Road. The first part of the route follows this obvious roadbed east up through a distinct valley for 3 miles, meandering gently along Scotch Creek. Near the 3-mile mark, the ski route abandons the

Scotch Creek Yurt

Scale 1:24,000 Contour Interval 40 Feet

0   1/2   1
SCALE IN MILES

MN 12

Hut
Trailhead •
Wilderness – – – –

© 1995 Brian Litz

Trails, including US Forest Service trails may or may not be marked. USFS trails and roads are not maintained and their exact location may vary. This map is not a substitute for good route-finding skills. This map is an aid to help locate routes. These are suggested routes only. Hazards exist in the backcountry including avalanches. Common sense and good judgement can reduce but not eliminate these hazards.

SAN JUAN NATIONAL FOREST

RICO MOUNTAINS

NATIONAL FOREST

BLACKHAWK MOUNTAIN

Blackhawk Mountain

Hermosa Creek

Corral Creek

Straight Creek

Aspen Creek

Hotel Draw

Scotch Creek Yurt
10,460'

San Juan Co.
Dolores Co.

San Juan Co.
La Plata Co.

0.60 miles to Rico Snowcountry Yurt
6.10 miles to Scotch Creek Trailhead

3.70 miles to Scotch Creek Yurt
3.00 miles to Scotch Creek Trailhead

Dolores Co.
Montezuma Co.

RICO USGS HERMOSA PEAK

45 A

Scotch Creek Trailhead
8,560'

Scotch Creek

Dolores River

Dolores Mountain

Whitecap Mtn

Hermes Peak

Rico

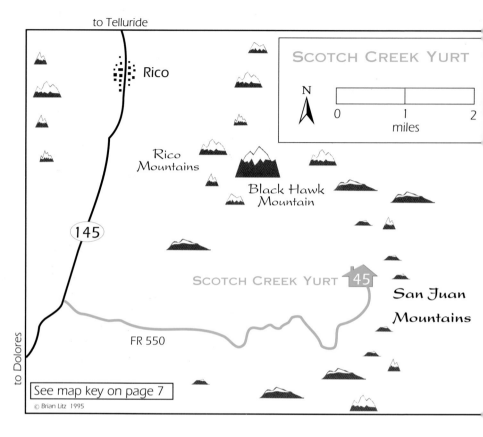

Scotch Creek Toll Road, taking a right turn to the southeast over the creek
via a small, earthen bridge.

Once across the creek, follow another, smaller road under a reddish rock
outcrop and up into a narrow, steep-sided valley to the southeast. Once in this
side drainage of Scotch Creek, watch for potential small snowslides along the
northeast (left) side of the valley. The exposure to this slight hazard is brief,
as the route then switchbacks out of the valley and begins to climb north, traversing heavily forested, north-facing slopes above Scotch Creek.

Along this traverse the route switchbacks in and out of three minor tributaries of Scotch Creek. The third switchback, directly northeast of Elevation
Point 10,391' enters the first clear cut, which does not appear on the USGS
map. As you leave this clear cut and begin to head back into the forest, you
contour to the southeast, bypassing a right turn to a logging road.

The trail traverses, rather than climbs, on the final ascent. Continue above another, larger clear cut to the north. You have great views of the Rico Mountains and the San Juans from here. You will pass orange flagging as the road reaches the top of the ridge at a pass. There are several roads crossings on the summit, so pay attention to the map and directions. Ski past a "One Lane Road" sign, a FR 550 sign, and several small Colorado Trail signs. Continue along the crest of the ridge, crossing a larger summer road and past a "Motorized Restriction" sign. Remain on the ridge, enter the forest, pass another Colorado Trail sign and then drop off the ridge. Traverse due north along another logging road (not on the USGS map) across the western, forested flank of Elevation Point 10,637'. Keep heading north and climb a tiny ridge to the Scotch Creek Yurt, which is on the north side of Elevation Point 10,637'.

RECOMMENDED DAY TOURS: Great skiing is found in every direction. Immediately below Scotch Creek Yurt to the north is a low-angled clearing that is perfect for novice and intermediate free-heel skiers. Elevation Point 10,637' is a quick jaunt for all levels of skiers, providing panoramic views of southwestern Colorado. Steep drops into Hotel Draw will be of interest to expert skiers. All skiers can also retrace their tracks southwest and past the turnoff back down in Scotch Creek and follow the ridgeline out towards Elevation Point 10,933' for a great day trip. Again, great views and runs drop off these ridges in every directions. Feel free to improvise — just be careful!

SAN JUAN HUT SYSTEM — SKI (TELLURIDE/RIDGWAY/OURAY)

During the mid-1980s, two Telluride-area residents, Mike Turrin and Joe Ryan, concluded that the San Juan Mountains of southwestern Colorado would be an ideal spot for a winter and summer hut system. While there were several independent backcountry lodges catering to telemark skiers, no true hut-to-hut routes existed.

The San Juan Mountains, Colorado's largest range, have long been a favorite arena for summer mountaineers, rock climbers, and winter ice climbers, as well as both downhill and backcountry skiers. However, the vertical relief is enormous, and the topography presented unique challenges to backcountry skiers and hut planners alike.

The ridgelike San Juans tower above treeline, with few skiable passes. There are also numerous avalanche paths throughout the area. Consequently, natural hut routes are not common. After considerable exploration, Turrin and Ryan were able to piece together a 38-plus-mile linear route from Telluride to Ouray. By judiciously situating the shelters along a network of trails and old logging roads, they were able to provide access to some of the most incredible wilderness skiing in the West.

The hut system lies in the shadow of the Sneffels Range, a unique sub range of the San Juans that runs east to west. The castellated summits and ridges present a formidable wall to the north. Below the steep, alpine towers, thick spruce and aspen forests sweep down to piñon- and juniper-covered foothills and some of North America's most scenic ranches. This is one of the most beautiful backcountry skiing areas not only in Colorado, but North America.

San Juan Hut System skiing is always adventurous, and at times extremely challenging. Some trails are easy-to-follow roads while others are old summer trails obscured by winter snow. Trails are not consistently marked, although a new blue diamond-marker system is gradually being introduced. Navigating on these trails can be the greatest challenge, often requiring astute route finding through thick forests or across open meadows. Trail breaking on the less-frequently traveled routes can be physically taxing. The entire region is laced with secondary trails and roads that do not appear on the most recent USGS topo maps; consequently, competent navigation and route-finding skills are essential for safe, efficient travel.

Skiers should be relatively fit, for many of the trails are long and strenuous. As a general rule, skiing to the Blue Lakes and Burn huts is suitable for strong novice skiers, the routes to the Ridgway and Last Dollar huts are suitable for strong intermediate skiers, while the West Dallas Creek trail to the North Pole Hut should be left to advanced skiers with good route find-

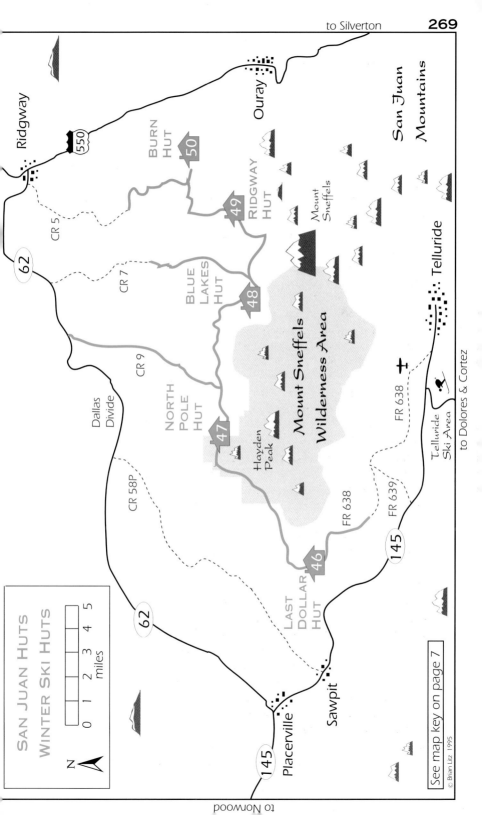

to Silverton

Ridgway

Ouray

San Juan Mountains

550

62

BURN HUT 50

CR 5

RIDGWAY HUT 49

CR 7

Mount Sneffels

Telluride

BLUE LAKES HUT 48

CR 9

Mount Sneffels Wilderness Area

Dallas Divide

NORTH POLE HUT 47

Hayden Peak

FR 638

Telluride Ski Area

CR 58P

FR 638

FR 639

to Dolores & Cortez

62

46 LAST DOLLAR HUT

145

145

Placerville

Sawpit

SAN JUAN HUTS
WINTER SKI HUTS

miles
0 1 2 3 4 5

N

See map key on page 7

© Brian Litz 1995

to Norwood

ing skills. The inter-hut trails, with the exception of the Ridgway-Burn route, are only appropriate for strong intermediate and advanced skiers.

The vast, rarely skied slopes around these high alpine huts will provide endless hours of recreation for experienced skiers. Day telemark skiing is usually exceptional, but does require knowledge of backcountry snow conditions, an understanding of avalanche terrain, and the use of avalanche safety equipment. Less experienced groups should consider guided trips.

Five shelters make up the San Juan Hut System. Each hut is supplied with wood and a wood-burning stove, propane lights, a cook stove, utensils and cookware, bunks, foam pads, axes, snow scoops, and simple outdoor toilets. These huts are cozy and uncomplicated, and they provide skiers with all that is necessary to live comfortably in the backcountry. Each hut sleeps about eight people, with the optimum group size being five to seven. Skiers pay a per-person rate. Presently, the huts are only open in winter for skiing.

The huts and trails are described from Telluride to Ridgway. Each hut can be reached from its own trailhead or via the hut-to-hut trails. To make reservations or to arrange for a guided trip, call the San Juan Hut System (see Appendix A).

46   LAST DOLLAR HUT

The Last Dollar Hut, which sleeps eight, was one of the first two huts built in the San Juan Hut System. This hut has one of the most spectacular panoramic vistas in the state — the view overlooking the Silverton West Group of the San Juans, the Wilson Peaks, and the La Sal Mountains in Utah.

For experienced backcountry skiers, there is an abundance of day telemark skiing beyond the hut to the east. The north-facing slopes and glades on the ridge behind the hut boast acres of skiable terrain best suited to strong skiers with good downhill backcountry technique. There are a series of avalanche gullies in this area, too. They do not appear on the USGS topo maps, but they are there, they are obvious, and, under the right conditions, they are dangerous. Under safe conditions (i.e., spring) these gullies provide superb skiing, especially on their lower stretches.

An ascent to the ridge at treeline to the east makes a nice day trip for an even better view of southwestern Colorado. In addition, the hut has plenty of "front yard" for just sunning and enjoying the view.

Jordan Campbell, "Harmonica" Dan Mosle, Ace Kvale, and Joe Ryan sing the eight-men-in-a-small-hut blues.

This is the closest hut to Telluride and is a fine destination for an overnight or a long weekend trip. Consequently, this is one of the most popular San Juan huts, and it is often booked by more than one group. Less experienced skiers can simply take in the beautiful surroundings or they can ski the more limited moderate terrain; hiring a guide may be helpful to find some of the less taxing skiing in the area. To make reservations, call the San Juan Hut System (see Appendix A).

TOUR 46A   DEEP CREEK MESA TRAILHEAD

Difficulty:	Intermediate
Time:	4 to 7 hours
Distance:	4.6 miles
Elevations:	Trailhead 9,040', Hut 10,980', +2,020'/-80'
Avalanche Note:	Route crosses avalanche runout zones; can be dangerous during high-hazard periods
Maps:	USGS 7.5': Grayhead, 1953; SAMS, 1982
	National Forest: Uncompahgre
	Trails Illustrated: Map #141 (Silverton/ Ouray/Telluride/Lake City)
	See map pages 269 and 282-283

In summer, Last Dollar Road is a favorite of mountain bikers and wildflower photographers. Unplowed and closed in winter, it is the shortest route to the Last Dollar Hut. Route finding is easy, though the trail climbs 2,000 feet in 4.6 miles. The steepest part of the climb is onto Last Dollar Pass near the end of the tour. Less experienced skiers can also enjoy this trail; just leave early and take your time.

To reach the trailhead, drive on CO 145 to the Deep Creek turnoff, marked "Lime" on the USGS maps. This turn is near mile marker 75, which is 9.4 miles east of Placerville, or 7.2 miles west of the San Juan Hut System office in Telluride. Turn northeast into the narrow Deep Creek canyon. Drive up along Deep Creek until you intersect Last Dollar Road. Making a sharp left onto Last Dollar Road, drive through a group of barns, cabins, and fences to the parking area at the end of the plowed public road, near the edge of the national forest. Total distance from CO 145 is roughly 3.5 miles. In the spring, this road can be slick and muddy.

From the parking area, ski along the snow-covered road up to the summit of Last Dollar Pass, on the northeast corner of Last Dollar Mountain near Elevation Point 10,663' on USGS topo maps. Most of the ascent is through meadows and stands of aspen trees on moderate and steep hills.

The grueling part of the climb begins after crossing Summit Creek, where the road switchbacks up a very steep, treeless slope.

From the pass, near a brown Forest Service sign (Alder Creek/Trail No. 510), the hut is 0.25 mile and 300 vertical feet north/northeast up the ridge. Either ascend directly up the ridge next to the trees on the slope to the south, or follow the indistinct Whipple Mountain Trail (No. 419) that climbs through trees along the forested, northern aspect of the ridge. This trail is 50 to 100 feet north of the apex of the ridge and switchbacks just prior to reaching the hut. The Last Dollar Hut is at the edge of a huge, treeless, south-facing slope, hidden in a group of spruce trees.

The route crosses below several avalanche paths just prior to Summit Creek. These hazards are easily seen and avoided by dropping down off the road to the southwest and rejoining the road after several hundred feet.

TOUR 46B   LAST DOLLAR HUT TO NORTH POLE HUT

Difficulty:	Advanced
Time:	7 to 11 hours
Distance:	8.5 miles
Elevations:	LD Hut 10,980', NP Hut 9,960', +500'/-1,700'
Avalanche Note:	Route crosses avalanche slopes; prone to skier-triggered avalanches during high-hazard periods
Maps:	USGS 7.5': SAMS, 1982
	National Forest: Uncompahgre
	Trails Illustrated: Map #141 (Silverton/Ouray/Telluride/Lake City)
	See map pages 269 and 282-283

The ski route from the Last Dollar Hut to the North Pole Hut is one of the most difficult and potentially dangerous trails covered in this guidebook. The route follows the Alder Creek Trail, which is a well-worn summer path marked with occasional tree blazes, that crosses a small section of the Mount Sneffels Wilderness. The trail is very long, strenuous, is not skied regularly, and does not appear on the most recent USGS 7.5-minute topo map. There is an Alder Creek Trail on the Trails Illustrated map, but it is just a rough approximation of the route. A good sense for route finding, a willingness to ski off-trail, and map, compass, and altimeter skills are essential for this tour.

Another important note is that several large gullies and avalanche slide paths, which are easy to cross in summer, do not appear on the USGS topo map. These are very dangerous in winter. Because of this unfortunate fact, portions of the route near these slides vary throughout the ski season in an effort to avoid avalanche hazards. Skiers planning to travel from the Last Dollar to the North Pole Hut should call the San Juan Hut System to verify the route and conditions. Skiers who are not experienced in backcountry travel are advised to hire a guide.

From the Last Dollar Hut, return down to Last Dollar Pass and the brown Forest Service sign. Once you are back on the road, head north and west as you begin descending. Avoid the new Alder Creek Trailhead. (It is off to the right and marked by a large trailhead sign.) Cruise along the road on a fun drop until the road bends. Here, near a small clump of aspen trees and willow bushes, is a right fork. Take this fork and continue dropping down this road/trail until it cranks noticeably around a corner to the right (east/northeast).

As soon as you round the corner, slow down and look for a rusty, white metal stake on the right. This is the turnoff to the Alder Creek Trail and is marked with a blue diamond. From here, the road drops precipitously while the trail launches off into the forest and heads east/northeast on a 1.5-mile traverse across a steep, forested slope, remaining at roughly 10,600 feet. En route, the trail climbs over a small ridge before making a steep descent into a large, scenic basin southwest of Hayden Peak.

The trail enters a small clearing at about 10,640 feet on the floor of this basin, just northwest of a creek with flowing water. This clearing is a good lunch spot, with views of high ridges to the east and south. Consequently, with these unobstructed views, it is also a good spot for orienteering. The trail exits the northeastern corner of this small meadow, near a tiny creek, and begins a long traverse north. This stretch contains the hardest route finding of the journey. In fact, the stretch from here to the north side of North Pole Peak is difficult to follow at times.

Continue forging ahead and try to remain at roughly 10,800 feet. Cross obvious avalanche gullies at 3.4 miles, 3.6 miles, and 3.8 miles. These are the lower extensions of avalanche gullies marked on the USGS topo maps; the portions that the trail crosses do not appear on the map. They are, however, obvious, and make useful navigation points. To the trained map and compass person they can be identified using triangulation off the ridges and peaks above. The third gully, which is directly west of the summit of Hayden Peak, is very deep and has a creek running through it. The trail crosses right below a cliff band in the gully where there is a small waterfall (or frozen waterfall, as the case may be). Extreme caution must be exercised whenever crossing these gullies. Be sure to cross one person at a time, have your transceivers turned on, etc. If there is any hint of potential slide activity, drop way down and cross under the end of the runout zones, regaining the trail after safe passage. Under normal conditions the trail should cross these gullies at roughly 10,800 feet.

After crossing the third gully, the trail heads west/northwest up onto a distinct benchlike shoulder west of Hayden Peak. The trail then drops off the west side and down several switchbacks before it heads north on a traverse. This is where the trail becomes difficult to follow, as the forest is very homogeneous. If you can't follow the trail, don't fret. In fact, instead of wasting time and energy searching for it, it may be easier to use an altimeter and pick a traversing route north at about 10,600 to 10,700 feet.

Eventually the route begins to turn to the east at a point where a commanding vista to the north comes into view. If you have maintained the proper elevation, you will intercept a long, narrow, prominent avalanche gully that drops from the northwest corner of North Pole Peak down to about 10,400 feet. It is necessary to begin losing altitude here to cross this gully at the bottom, where the gradient is moderate. Again, exercise extreme caution when crossing this gully.

Once past the gully, traverse east across another gully and begin a descent north to a flat shoulder at 10,280 feet, north of North Pole Peak. If all goes according to plan, you should reach a four-way trail intersection, marked with an old trail sign, in the middle of a stand of huge aspen trees. To the north an obvious trail/road descends steeply, eventually into the San Juan Vistas Estates (not on the USGS topo); the same road heads uphill to the south/southeast (also not on USGS topo); while the Dallas Trail heads off into the woods to the east.

[Note: If you drop too far down, especially off the western side of the shoulder, you will soon encounter open meadows, fences, and ranches. If you do, try to gain the road on the crest of the ridge to the east, below the flat knob at 10,280 feet. Once you have gained the road, follow it uphill directly south to the intersection mentioned above.]

From the intersection, ski east, following the now relatively easy-to-follow trail, which is marked by occasional blazes. The trail rolls in and out of several drainages, passing a wilderness boundary sign en route, before making a descent into a large, wetland meadow at 10,000 feet. Immediately after the trail reaches the valley floor and a clearing, you come to a fork. Turn north and tour along the western perimeter of the meadow, passing under several large spruce trees. Once past these trees, there is a smaller, distinct clearing bounded by tall aspen trees on the west and north. The North Pole Hut sits in this clearing.

47   NORTH POLE HUT

The North Pole Hut is a very remote shelter, so you will not see day skiers here. The cabin rests in a small, aspen-lined clearing on the western edge of larger meadow. This location, with views of the peaks to the south, is one of the most breathtaking hut sites in all of the San Juans.

Ski mountaineers can tackle the north ridge of Hayden Peak (under appropriate conditions), while powder hounds can explore the many ridges and slopes found below treeline. Intermediate cross-country skiers will find nice touring on the old roads and trails south of the hut.

There was a canvas-topped yurt here, but it has been replaced by a sturdier wooden structure. The new hut is on par with the other winter shelters in the system and provides a rustic, warm, and cozy base camp for exploring the backcountry. Make reservations through the San Juan Hut System (see Appendix A).

Previously, this backcountry shelter was reached via a direct 5.5-mile tour from a trailhead on Hastings Mesa; however, this route is no longer available due to private-property closures. Consequently, skiers must now approach the hut from the northeast, via a very long and complicated route up the West Dallas Creek Road (CR 9) and the Dallas Trail. This has doubled the distance and drastically increased the commitment necessary, which is unfortunate, because the new route will certainly discourage some

The old North Pole Peak Yurt (above) has now been upgraded to a wood structure.

skiers from visiting The North Pole Hut and consequently miss the superb skiing above it on Hayden Peak.

TOUR 47A   WEST DALLAS CREEK TRAILHEAD

Difficulty:	Advanced +
Time:	6 to 10 hours
Distance:	11 miles
Elevations:	Trailhead 7,640', Hut 9,960', +900'
Avalanche Note:	Some avalanche terrain encountered; easily avoided.
Maps:	USGS 7.5': Mount Sneffels, 1987; SAMS, 1982
	National Forest: Uncompahgre
	Trails Illustrated: Map #141 (Silverton/ Ouray/Telluride/Lake City)
	See map pages 269 and 282-283

This tour begins at the intersection of CO 62 and CR 9 (West Dallas Creek Road), and travels up through ranches and oak shrublands to Box Factory Park. From the park, the trail heads west to the hut via an old summer trail (the Dallas Trail), which can be very difficult to follow when buried under snow.

The Dallas Trail is posted with a variety of markers, including blue diamonds, old silver diamonds, tree blazes, and small, red metal flags nailed to trees. Skiers will need to pay attention to these markers. Maps, compasses, and particularly altimeters are useful in navigating the last several miles to the hut.

This tour is only recommended for physically strong groups of expert backcountry navigators. The San Juan Hut System recommends that this route only be attempted by large groups of skiers who can share trail breaking duties, that groups be on the trail by no later than 8:00 AM, and that each group carry bivouac gear and flashlights or headlamps. Despite all of this ominous talk, this is a stunningly scenic tour throughout, especially along the lower road, where you ski along a valley rimmed with sandstone cliffs on a trail that glides through silent aspen forests in the shadow of high peaks. Make sure you plan enough time to fully enjoy this tour. Less-experienced groups should hire one of the herculean San Juan Hut guys as a guide/trail breaker. There is nothing these mountain goats would love more!

A word of warning about the trailhead: Because winter snowstorms or spring mud can entrap automobiles, it is recommended that you exercise caution after turning off CO 62. It is possible to shuttle loads a mile or two up the road, but don't park there because conditions can change quickly and you may get stuck. To be safe, you should park just off CO 62, beyond the "Double RL" ranch sign. The sign marks a private road into Ralph Lauren's ranch, but CR 9 is a public road, so don't worry about parking here. Also, don't confuse the East Dallas Creek Road (CR 7, marked as Dallas Creek) for West Dallas Creek Road (CR 9). Finally, do not leave valuables in your car at this parking spot.

To reach the trailhead, drive on CO 62 to the turnoff, which is 6 miles west of Ridgway and 13.5 miles east of Placerville. Begin skiing or walking south on CR 9 and follow it over West Dallas Creek, then up and around the eastern side of a hill. Pass through a flat clearing and begin climbing southwest up into shrubland. (The clearing works well as gear drop-off point when road conditions permit a car shuttle.) Keep climbing for about a mile as you gradually approach one of the most spectacular portions of the lower road — the sandstone canyon overlook. At 3 miles the road runs right along the cliffs. Pass an "Entering Public Lands" sign at 3.2 miles.

The road follows the canyon then veers slightly away from it, heading due south. At 4.5 miles, the road goes over a little rise as it bends east, passing a quaint log cabin and a sulfur spring on the left, then it contours sharply around a switchback to the southwest. Continue uphill on the road toward spruce/fir forests; the landscape gradually narrows along a ridge. Ski past a road on the left (behind a metal gate) at 5.2 miles, a cattle guard, a gate at 5.3 miles, and a national forest boundary sign at 6.5 miles.

You will know you are within a half mile of the Dallas Trail intersection when the road enters deeper woods and traverses across steep eastern slopes above the West Fork of Dallas Creek. Then, as you make the final approach, the road reaches flatter, more open terrain with views of the high cirque above Box Factory Park. Keep an eye out for a "Dallas Trail #200" sign just off the road to the left (east), near aspen trees at the base of a low north/south ridge. Continue to the south/southwest on the road (now the Dallas Trail), passing the trail sign, and descend roughly 150 yards down to the creek.

Cross the creek (usually with your skis off), climb up the west bank, then turn south into Box Factory Park. There is a barbwire fence running north/south through the park; pass through a red gate and head west toward a hillside, aiming for the trail, which climbs north through aspen trees. The spot where the trail enters the aspen trees is about 200 feet away from the fence and is marked with blue diamonds. From here, the trail diagonals up toward the north and then contours around a forested ridge, following a trail marked with occasional blue diamonds. The trail descends to the southwest off the ridge and enters the eastern edge of a large clearing (marked by diamonds for skiers heading back to the trailhead or to the Blue Lakes Hut) in a broad, basinlike creek drainage.

Head west along the drainage, then northwest across the creek and climb up the large treeless south/southeast-facing slope, which has aspen trees on top. Although there are number of red-flag trail markers, the exact route for your ascent is not critical here — in fact, the recommended route deviates from the Dallas Trail printed on the USGS topo map. As you near the crest of the ridge at 9,600 feet, turn west, then southwest, and pick up a road (shown on the topo map) that runs uphill along the southeast edge of the ridge. Pass a wooden sign on the left en route as you ski through aspen trees and up into spruce trees.

At a fork in the road, take the right fork (blue diamond) and follow the trail to a creek that is normally running. Cross the creek and continue on the trail as it veers north. Climb through aspen trees until the trail breaks into a large clearing on a steep slope with unobstructed views to the north and east, including 14,150-foot Mount Sneffels, which provides an opportunity for map and compass orientation. As you traverse this clearing, keep an eye out for small red, metal flags on aspen trees and one that marks the entrance back into the forest. After re-entering the woods, the trail continues west on a gently ascending traverse across steep, heavily forested north-facing slopes until it reaches a north/south-running road.

The 1.2 miles of trail between the two roads are probably the most difficult section of trail in terms of route finding. The key is to routinely take the time to stop, look around for trail markers, and get your bearings. An altimeter can be helpful here to keep you on a slightly rising traverse from roughly 9,800 feet at the trail intersection to just under 10,000 feet at the second road. Occasional blue diamonds, tree blazes, and red, metal flags mark the route here. This is not a good stretch of trail to be skiing at night!

Once you have reached the second road, cross to the trail on west side, which is now a summer logging road. This intersection is marked with blue diamonds. Contour west then southwest until you reach another logging road intersection along the eastern edge of a wetland meadow. There is another north/south-running road here and a number of silver trail markers. Cross this road and follow it west as it begins to contour around the southern edge of the meadow, through stands of evergreen trees with the occasional blaze. After crossing a creek, the trail contours slightly to the west/northwest and climbs a steep but short hill (about 15 feet high) to a clearing on the southwestern perimeter of the meadow. To the south and west are thicker woods and steeper slopes, and high above the forest stands Hayden Peak and other lofty ridges. The meadow rolls away to the north.

The North Pole Hut sits on the western edge of the meadow, hidden in a little clearing lined with aspen trees on the west and north. The turnoff to the hut is where the Last Dollar Hut Trail begins to climb noticeably to the west, up and over the forested north ridge of Hayden Peak. Turn to the north/northwest and ski along the edge of the forest, passing under large, isolated stands of spruce trees, and continue another couple hundred yards to the hut.

TOUR 47B NORTH POLE HUT TO BLUE LAKES HUT

Difficulty:	Advanced
Time:	6 to 10 hours
Distance:	7.2 miles
Elevations:	NP Hut 9,960', BL Hut 9,380', +1,020'/-1,410'
Avalanche Note:	Some avalanche terrain encountered; easily avoided
Maps:	USGS 7.5': Mount Sneffels, 1987; SAMS, 1982 National Forest: Uncompahgre Trails Illustrated: Map #141 (Silverton/ Ouray/Telluride/Lake City) See map pages 269 and 282-283

The trail between these two huts follows the Dallas Trail, an old pack trail that is now a well-traveled summer hiking route traversing the aspen- and evergreen-blanketed foothills of the Sneffels Range. Skiers on this route enjoy close-up views of Hayden Peak, Mears Peak, Wolcott Mountain, and, of course, Mount Sneffels. (The name Mount Sneffels, by the way, was used in the classic tale *Journey to the Center of the Earth*, by Jules Verne.)

This long tour requires good route-finding skills, for the trail is sinuous, often winding through nondescript woods, and it is marked with a variety of trail markers, including old overgrown trail blazes, wooden signs, blue diamonds, posts, and silver metal strips tipped with red paint and nailed to trees. Skiers should study the map before departing and always keep an eye out for trail markers.

The route follows the Dallas Trail very closely and is for the most part free of avalanche danger. However, you will encounter several small slide paths on the final road to the hut. These should be crossed carefully or bypassed if conditions warrant. Get an early start, especially if you are going to be breaking trail!

From the North Pole Hut, return south for several hundred yards to the main trail intersection, then turn east onto the trail marked by a diamond. Immediately climb onto a small hill, cross a creek, then begin to contour to the northeast. Ski along a faint, snow-covered road through interspersed stands of spruce trees and small clearings, all the while following the south and eastern perimeter of a large wetland meadow. Intersect a north/south road (shown on the USGS maps) on the eastern edge of the meadow. Cross this intersection and continue east to another north/south road (on the USGS maps), which is marked with blue diamonds. The Dallas Trail continues across the road to the east.

The trail now enters the forest and begins a 1.2-mile traverse across tributaries of Stough Draw. En route the trail crosses a large meadow on the northeast aspect of a ridge. Circled with aspen trees, this meadow drops down to ranch country and is a very scenic spot, with great views north and east toward Mount Sneffels. The trail crosses a flowing creek just before arriving at the ridge-top road above the West Fork of Dallas Creek (marked by a wooden Forest Service sign).

Once you reach the road, turn north and descend along the eastern edge of the ridge, along the crest, until you break out of the forest into a ridge-top clearing, surrounded by aspen trees and even more panoramic views of the Sneffels Range. Just before you enter the clearing, a sign shows where the trail descends into the large treeless basin of Dallas Creek. The terrain here is open, and it is easy to choose your own route down to the creek.

Once at Dallas Creek, cross it (at about 9,300 feet) and ski east into the a clearing on the eastern edge of the basin. Locating the trail into the woods on this side of the creek is a little tricky. Search around the northeastern corner of the clearing and look for a blue diamond. The trail contours around a small, wooded ridge to the east, where you descend through aspen trees into Box Factory Park, a magnificent lunch spot below massive alpine cirques and precipitous walls.

To exit the park, pass through a red gate in a barbwire fence by a Dallas Trail sign, and drop down to Dallas Creek. Cross the creek to a small clearing on the eastern side, then turn north and make a very short climb onto a tiny bench. On top of this bench is a "Dallas Trail #200" sign marking where the trail exits West Dallas Road to continue east. If you miss this turn, you will know it, as West Dallas Road heads steeply downhill to the north/northeast and eventually reaches shrublands.

Back on the West Dallas Trail, begin a short, steep climb. Cross what appears to be a road (actually an aqueduct) and continue climbing east over a small ridge. Drop down off the side of the ridge and rejoin, but do not follow, the aqueduct. Near a small creek drainage that runs north/south, leave the aqueduct and enter the forest via a gentle, indistinct trail. Here you begin the long 2.5-mile traverse eastward to Cocan Flats.

After 0.5 mile, you reach a sloping meadow. Cross the meadow, following a series of posts and aiming for a small trail marker where the trail re-enters the woods. Continue traversing across steep, forested slopes, crossing two deep drainages. From the bottom of the second gully, you'll see a treeless, shrub-covered hill to the north. Climb out of the creek, heading

West Dallas Creek Trailhead 7,640

Routes Connect to maps on page 292 & 293

48 A

Dallas

47 B

47 A

47 A

UNCOMPAHGRE NATIONAL FOREST

North Pole Hut 9,960

San Juan Hut System
Telluride to Ridgway

Scale 1:24,000   Contour Interval 40 Feet

SCALE IN MILES

0   1/2   1

MN 12°

Hut

Trailhead

Wilderness - - - - -

Trails, including US Forest Service trails may or may not be marked. USFS trails and roads are not maintained and their exact location may vary. This map is not a substitute for good route-finding skills. This map is an aid to help locate routes. These are suggested routes only. Hazards exist in the backcountry, including avalanches. Common sense and good judgement can reduce but not eliminate these hazards.

© 1996 Brian Litz

2.00 miles to North Pole Hut
5.50 miles to Last Dollar Hut

HAYDEN PEAK

MOUNT SNEFFELS WILDERNESS

Blue Lakes Hut
9,300'

7.00 miles to West Dallas Trailhead
3.20 miles to Blue Lakes Hut

MOUNT SNEFFELS
TELLURIDE

SAMS
GRAYHEAD

MESA

CREEK

46B

46A

Last Dollar Hut
10,980'

4.90 miles to North Pole Hut
2.60 miles to Last Dollar Hut

2.65 miles to Last Dollar Hut
1.80 miles to Deep Creek Mesa

Deep Creek Mesa Trailhead
9,040'

northeast. Cross over a buried fence, then follow a road upward and east to a saddle south of the shrub-covered hill.

Descend across the creek, then turn upstream (south/southeast), following an indistinct road across a low, forested pass and down along a creek into Cocan Flats, which also offers great views of Mount Sneffels. Ski across the flats on a southeasterly course, intercept the road into East Dallas Creek and begin the descent to the hut. This road is easy to follow, but it does cross a few steep, normally inactive avalanche-prone slopes — so be careful!

Coast down the road to a point roughly 80 feet above East Dallas Creek, where a small road forks south onto to a tiny bench below an old logged-over area. Turn onto the road and follow it a few hundred feet to the Blue Lakes Hut, which is on the left, overlooking the creek.

48   BLUE LAKES HUT

Blue Lakes Hut lies below Mount Sneffels on a small bench above East Dallas Creek. One of the simplest of the San Juan huts to reach, Blue Lakes Hut is a good beginner destination. Nice skiing is available close to the hut, the surrounding hillsides are great for telemarking, and Cocan Flats and the East Fork of Dallas Creek make fine touring areas.

Skiing from Blue Lakes Hut to the North Pole Hut or the Ridgway Hut requires greater experience and much more stamina than is required to reach this hut from the trailhead.

Although Blue Lakes Hut is one of the smaller structures in this system, it can accommodate up to eight skiers. Make reservations through the San Juan Hut System (see Appendix A).

Mark Kelley skiing to Blue Lakes Hut.

TOUR 48A   EAST DALLAS CREEK TRAILHEAD

Difficulty:	Novice/Intermediate
Time:	4 to 6 hours
Distance:	5.2 miles
Elevations:	Trailhead 8,200', Hut 9,380', +1,180'
Avalanche Note:	Some avalanche terrain encountered; easily avoided
Maps:	USGS 7.5': Mount Sneffels, 1987
	National Forest: Uncompahgre
	Trails Illustrated: Map #141 (Silverton/ Ouray/Telluride/Lake City)
	See map pages 269 and 292-293

To reach the trailhead, drive on CO 62 to East Dallas Creek Road (CR 7). This turnoff is marked by a national forest access sign 4.9 miles west of the US 550 intersection in Ridgway. Turn south onto this dirt road and follow national forest signs approximately 4 miles to the end of the plowed road. Watch carefully for these signs because it is easy to turn onto private ranch roads.

From the trailhead, ski south along the forest access road up the East Fork of Dallas Creek valley. Be sure to remain on the main road above the creek until you contour to the south/southwest into a large, willowy meadow. Ski due south up the slowly narrowing valley through increasingly forested terrain until the road begins to climb around a hairpin turn, heading back to the north. Once past this turn, keep an eye open for a left turn onto a small knoblike bench. Ski several hundred feet to the small Blue Lakes Hut, which is in the open on the left.

TOUR 48B BLUE LAKES HUT TO RIDGWAY HUT

Difficulty:	Advanced
Time:	5 to 7 hours
Distance:	5 to 5.5 miles
Elevations:	BL Hut 9,380', R Hut 10,200', +2,040'/-1,200'
Avalanche Note:	Route crosses avalanche slopes; prone to skier-triggered avalanches during high-hazard periods
Maps:	USGS 7.5': Mount Sneffels, 1987
	National Forest: Uncompahgre
	Trails Illustrated: Map #141 (Silverton/ Ouray/Telluride/Lake City)
	See map pages 269 and 292-293

This is another challenging stretch of trail in the San Juan Hut System. While it is only 5 to 5.5 miles long, the trail is not marked, and the ascent over the ridge between the huts gains and loses considerable elevation.

Descending to the Ridgway Hut requires advanced downhill ski techniques and good route-finding skills, as the thick forest around the hut has few obvious landmarks. In addition, there are several old logging roads that are not shown on the USGS topo map. Navigating to the hut can be confusing if you wander off the route.

Skiing this route in reverse (east to west), from the Ridgway Hut to the Blue Lakes Hut, can be even more difficult, as the descent west consists of even steeper, more demanding tree skiing. With no powder snow, this descent will test the best. Skiers attempting this tour without a guide must be skilled at wilderness navigation, route-finding, and tree skiing.

Leave the Blue Lakes Hut and return to the main road, then drop down along the road into the East Fork of Dallas Creek drainage. Rather than following the road north along this large drainage, drop down to the creek and cross to the east side. The best spot for this stream crossing varies throughout the winter, depending on snow conditions. Once across the creek, begin a traversing climb to the northeast across steep, forested slopes. After reaching a ridge crest, a gain of about 250 feet in elevation, drop down to Wilson Creek.

At Wilson Creek, turn upstream and ascend through the valley, paying attention to potential avalanche paths to the south. Ski up the narrowing valley for approximately 0.7 mile to around 9,800 feet. Following the path of least resistance, head northeast, up and away from the creek. Gain over 1,000 feet and reach a small knob on the western edge of the ridge. Ski east onto the main ridge and contour around the northeast side of a higher forested knob, then follow the ridge for 0.2 mile to a tiny, nondescript pass at 11,000 feet, located at the base of a steeper, section of the ridge. The top of the pass affords a spectacular panorama of the Sneffels Range.

The descent off the ridge to the northeast is superb, featuring incredible telemark opportunities through widely spaced trees. Skiing between the ridge and the Ridgway Hut requires astute route finding, so keep one eye on your map and compass. It is critical to begin the descent at the right spot. Be sure you drop off the ridge on the far, southeast end, just below the point where the ridge begins to climb steeply upward toward treeline and Elevation Point 11,786'. (Climbing this ridge to treeline is a superb day trip; see Tour 49A).

Descend approximately 700 feet and search for a logging road traversing east out of the drainage. This road is easy to miss, and the exact spot to descend may be further obscured by a confusion of old ski tracks. Double pole east along the road into more gentle terrain and thinned trees. Break into a small, flat clearing surrounded by immature evergreens. The Ridgway Hut is due north of this clearing.

49   RIDGWAY HUT

The Ridgway Hut, which sleeps eight, was the second hut erected in the San Juan Hut System, and it is one of the most popular. The route to the hut follows one of the most beautiful and scenic trails in the state, touring past rustic wooden fences and tall aspen trees (many covered with bear claw marks), up into the forest below Mount Ridgway.

Backcountry skiing around the Ridgway Hut is like tree skiing at a downhill area — minus the lifts and crowds. The skiing here is best suited to strong intermediate and expert skiers. You must have at least intermediate downhill skills to fully enjoy the skiing above the hut as well as a solid understanding of backcountry safety and avalanche procedures. Be cautious of several large avalanche gullies south of the hut.

The telemark skiing above the hut is absolutely incredible. Either climb directly south from the hut, or head south and then west to the top of the ridge to tackle superb — and safe — telemark runs of 1,400 vertical feet. In addition to experiencing great telemark skiing, those willing to climb to the ridge will also be treated to intimate views of Blaine Basin and the north faces of Mount Sneffels and Cirque Mountain.

Evening at the Ridgway Hut, the San Juan Hut System.

Extreme skiing is available in the gullies and chutes above the hut near treeline. These routes are not covered in this book due to their capricious nature. Call the San Juan Hut System for information on these thrilling routes, fees for guides, and to reserve the hut (see Appendix A). Keep in mind that you will encounter serious wilderness skiing around this hut, so come prepared with the proper safety equipment.

TOUR 49A   GIRL SCOUT CAMP ROAD TRAILHEAD

Difficulty:	Intermediate/Advanced
Time:	5 to 7 hours
Distance:	7 to 7.5 miles
Elevations:	Trailhead 8,720', Hut 10,200', +1,980'/-450'
Avalanche Note:	Some avalanche terrain encountered; easily avoided
Maps:	USGS 7.5': Mount Sneffels, 1987
	National Forest: Uncompahgre
	Trails Illustrated: Map #141 (Silverton/ Ouray/Telluride/Lake City)
	See map pages 269 and 292-293

This is an interesting trail. Its upper half follows distinct trails and roads, none of which appear on the most recent revision of the USGS 7.5-minute topo map. Well-traveled and scenic, this is a recommended trip for skiers with limited time to spend in the San Juan Hut System.

Not only is this trail physically demanding, but skiers also need to pay close attention to the map and the landscape in order to keep from making a wrong turn. When leaving the hut, less proficient skiers would be wise to use skins on their skis to slow the descent to Beaver Creek, for the trail drops down a forested ridge via a steep, twisting road.

To reach the trailhead, drive on CO 62 to CR 5, also called the Girl Scout Camp Road. This turnoff is on the western edge of Ridgway, 0.8 mile west of US 550. Turn south onto CR 5, contour sharply right after 0.2 mile, then drive to a fork in the road and a barbwire fence, a total of 5.5 miles from CO 62. The left fork goes to the Elk Meadows Development, which is private property. The right fork crosses a cattleguard and is marked by a "Leaving Ridgway Fire Protection" sign. This is the public access route, which crosses private property for several miles. Either park off the road to the right after crossing the cattleguard, or park along the road just before the fork in the road. Local conditions (mud and snow) may dictate where you park.

Leave the cars and ski along the road in an ascending traverse across the north aspect of Elevation Point 9,204'. Contour around this point, then ascend south across a very wide, treeless drainage. Gain the south edge of a bluff that overlooks the vast Beaver Creek drainage, where you'll have an unobstructed panorama of the Sneffels Range, and then ski down the bluff to the southeast on a long, traversing road.

Tour south along this gentle road toward the forest. Soon the trail is hemmed by trees and occasional fences. Continue along the road, passing green metal signs reading "Beaver Creek Wildlife Preserve — No Hunting." Follow the road across Coal Creek, then double pole east past a yellow metal gate that marks the national forest boundary. Turn south into a large, forested gully and begin a moderate climb for 0.3 mile to a tiny clearing below aspen trees. From this clearing, which is marked by several small pieces of orange flagging, the most obvious trail heads due east into the trees. This route is the trail to the Burn Hut (Tour 50A) and is usually buzzing with snowmobilers. Do not take this trail.

Turn sharply west and follow a narrow trail, marked with blue diamonds, over a small ridge. Descend off the ridge via a steep drop along a barbwire fence, cross a creek, then ascend onto a wide ridge that is topped by a large, secluded meadow in the middle of an aspen forest. (The section of the trail from this meadow to the hut follows roads and trails that are not on the USGS topo map.)

Cross to the west side of the meadow, then continue west down a short, steep drop, crossing another creek. Climb out of this small drainage, ski down a subtle ridge and cross a wide, shallow basin covered with aspen trees. Follow this trail west through the aspens, then slightly north, until the trail reaches a tiny creek. The trail immediately intersects the road that descends left (south) to Beaver Creek. This intersection, marked with orange flagging tied to a small evergreen tree, is easy to miss.

Turn south onto this road and climb slightly before dropping into the Beaver Creek drainage. Follow the road on a northwesterly course up onto a forested ridge, cross another creek to the west, then begin the last steep ascent. This climb heads directly south up a thickly forested ridge via a sharply switchbacking road. After gaining roughly 600 feet in elevation, the road traverses off the west side of the ridge to a creek. Cross the creek and follow the trail along a gentle traverse west through immature trees until you reach the Ridgway Hut.

RECOMMENDED DAY TOURS. Skiers can explore above the hut to the south as far as treeline and spend hours, if not days, telemark skiing. While there are no exact routes, skiers comfortable with off-trail backcountry skiing will be able to wander all over, exploring the glades of the upper Beaver Creek drainage.

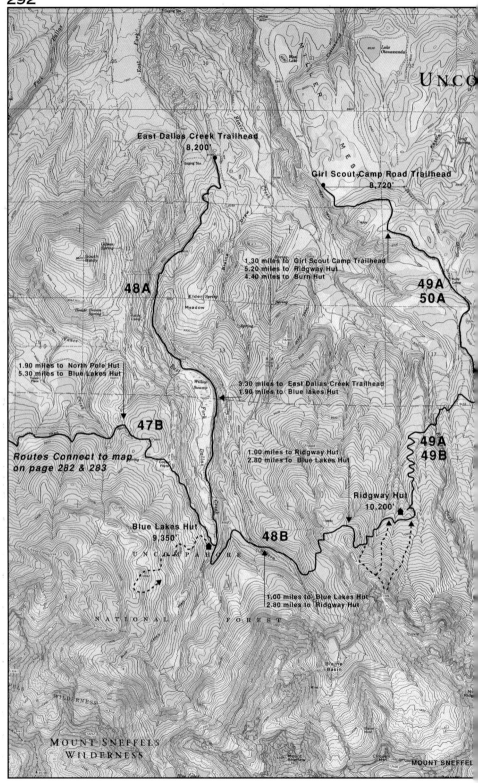

East Dallas Creek Trailhead
8,200'

Girl Scout Camp Road Trailhead
8,720'

UNCO

48A

**49A
50A**

1.30 miles to Girl Scout Camp Trailhead
5.20 miles to Ridgway Hut
4.40 miles to Burn Hut

1.90 miles to North Pole Hut
5.30 miles to Blue Lakes Hut

3.30 miles to East Dallas Creek Trailhead
1.90 miles to Blue lakes Hut

47B

*Routes Connect to map
on page 282 & 283*

**49A
49B**

1.00 miles to Ridgway Hut
2.80 miles to Blue Lakes Hut

Ridgway Hut
10,200'

Blue Lakes Hut
9,350'

48B

1.00 miles to Blue Lakes Hut
2.80 miles to Ridgway Hut

NATIONAL   FOREST

MOUNT SNEFFELS
WILDERNESS

MOUNT SNEFFEL

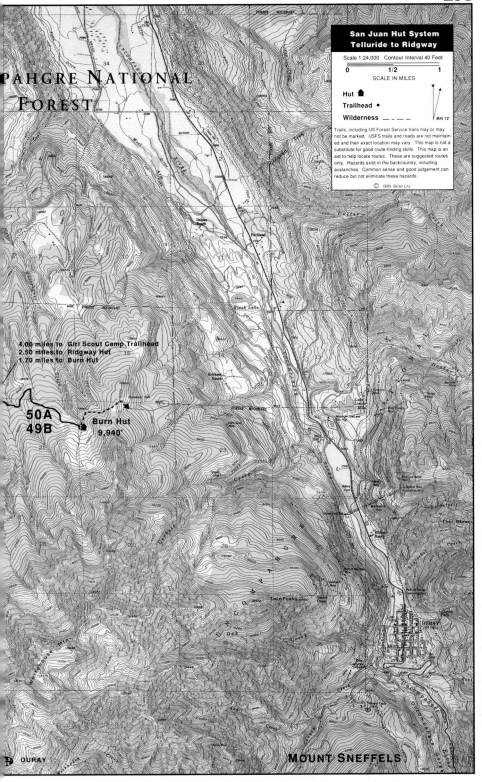

San Juan Hut System
Telluride to Ridgway

Scale 1:24,000   Contour Interval 40 Feet

0   1/2   1
SCALE IN MILES

Hut
Trailhead   •
Wilderness   _ _ _ _

MN 12°

Trails, including US Forest Service trails may or may not be marked. USFS trails and roads are not maintained and their exact location may vary. This map is not a substitute for good route-finding skills. This map is an aid to help locate routes. These are suggested routes only. Hazards exist in the backcountry, including avalanches. Common sense and good judgement can reduce but not eliminate these hazards.

PAHGRE NATIONAL
FOREST

4.00 miles to Girl Scout Camp Trailhead
2.50 miles to Ridgway Hut
1.70 miles to Burn Hut

50A
49B

Burn Hut
9,940'

OURAY

MOUNT SNEFFELS

TOUR 49B   RIDGWAY HUT TO BURN HUT

Difficulty:	Intermediate/Advanced
Time:	3 to 5 hours
Distance:	4.2 miles
Elevations:	R Hut 10,200', B Hut 9,940', +900'/-1160'
Avalanche Note:	Some avalanche terrain encountered; easily avoided
Maps:	USGS 7.5': Mount Sneffels, 1987; Ouray, 1983
	National Forest: Uncompahgre
	Trails Illustrated: Map #141 (Silverton/ Ouray/Telluride/Lake City)
	See map pages 269 and 292-293

The Burn Hut Trail and the Ridgway Hut Trail overlap for the first 4 miles, until they reach a small clearing at 9,400 feet. From that spot, the trails split into a Y. The trail between the Ridgway and Burn huts follows the upper arms of the Y, dropping from one hut to the meadow, then climbing back to the other. The information summary above gives the trail data for skiers traveling west to east from the Ridgway Hut to the Burn Hut. Obviously it can be, and often is, skied from east to west.

Because this tour covers terrain that is discussed under other trail descriptions, refer to the two Girl Scout Camp Road Trailhead tours (Tour 49A and Tour 50A) for specific directions to each hut from the clearing where the trail splits.

50   BURN HUT

The "new" Burn Hut is a fine destination for beginning and intermediate skiers, mixed groups, and aspiring backcountry skiers who may not be ready to cope with serious avalanche hazards and complicated route finding. The route to the hut is somewhat long for a novice-level tour, but overall it is very moderate. The trail follows a low-gradient road, which is challenging but not overwhelming.

The old Burn Hut was moved slightly, to a better location, and was replaced with a nicer, yet still simple structure. The hut is now down the hill to the east from where the old one was, just across Coal Creek in a stately stand of aspen. Now all of the high peaks to the south are visible, framed through the pale limbs of the trees. For all intents and purposes this move does not affect the nature of the approach. The final mile of the tour is still the steepest. The cabin, which sleeps eight, is surrounded by meadows, forests, and rolling hills that are ideal for all levels of skiers to explore. For reservations call the San Juan Hut System (see Appendix A).

TOUR 50A   GIRL SCOUT CAMP ROAD TRAILHEAD

Difficulty:	Novice/Intermediate
Time:	4 to 7 hours
Distance:	5.7 miles
Elevations:	Trailhead 8,720', Hut 9,880', +1,420'/-230'
Avalanche Note:	Some avalanche terrain encountered; easily avoided
Maps:	USGS 7.5': Mount Sneffels, 1987; Ouray, 1982
	National Forest: Uncompahgre
	Trails Illustrated: Map #141 (Silverton/ Ouray/Telluride/Lake City)
	See map pages 269 and 292-293

This trail shares the trailhead and the first several miles with the Girl Scout Camp Road/Ridgway Hut tour. Refer to Tour 49A for directions to the small clearing at 9,400 feet. From the small clearing, follow the road east through a stand of spruce trees and begin the 1.3-mile climb to the hut. Travel up the road 0.3 mile on a moderately steep climb until you break into a small meadow along a creek drainage. Proceed past a gray, fenced-in water-gauging station and continue up through a switchback onto a ridge.

Continue climbing through the forest until you enter a large meadow ("the burn"). Continue east into and across the meadow. Head slightly east and southeast, veering just to the right of the road. Aim for a thick stand of aspens across the creek. The Burn Hut sits on right in the center of these aspens and is obscured by the trees.

RECOMMENDED DAY TRIP: One quick trip proceeds along the road that is just to the north of the hut, climbing to the northeast up and over a ridge. The views only get better the further you go. Once over the ridge, the trail just barely enters a clearing before exiting to the south into the woods again. Look around a bit if you don't immediately find the trail into the woods.

Once you have found the trail, follow it east across a creek drainage and another clearing. From here, follow the creek upstream east/southeast for a few hundred feet until you crest a small saddle, where the treeless Moonshine Park rolls down to the east. There is superb skiing here. Far below is Ouray and, to the east, the ragged summits and needles of the Cimmaron Group of the San Juan Mountains. This is the only spot in the San Juan Hut System where this view can be seen. It is truly incredible!

A backcountry skier's signature.

SAN JUAN HUT SYSTEM — BIKE (TELLURIDE TO MOAB)

The journey from Telluride to Moab, Utah, is as much an exploration into the geology and ecology of the American West as it is a mountain biking adventure. Islands of alpine peaks float in a sea of piñon/juniper forests and sandstone mesas. The lonesome and seemingly desolate lands found in western Colorado and southeastern Utah are home to a great wealth of plants, animals, and people as colorful as the polychromatic countryside.

From Telluride, a Victorian mining town cradled high in a picturesque canyon in the San Juan Mountains, Last Dollar Road climbs up and over the western corner of the Sneffels Range. The road then strikes off to the north and west across the fascinating Uncompahgre Plateau. Formed 10 to 40 million years ago, the San Juans tell a story of volcanic mountain building and glacial sculpting, while the Uncompahgre Plateau exhibits massive uplift caused by internal disturbances of the earth's crust.

The broad expanse of the Colorado Plateau sweeps west across southern Utah. Formed from ancient dunes, tidal flats, and riverbeds compressed over eons into a complex layer cake of sedimentary rocks, Utah's high desert contains some of North America's most compelling and beautiful topography. Deeply etched by water and wind, this environment is a moisture-starved labyrinth of deadend arroyos, impassable gorges, and delicate rock towers.

Mountain biking through this country is not easy, but it is very rewarding. Sweet, aromatic sagebrush, crimson sunsets, and an overwhelming sense of solitude creates an experience that will leave you with a feeling of accomplishment and satisfaction. The 207-mile tour is described from Telluride to Moab, which is the most desirable direction of travel, since Moab is several thousand feet lower than Telluride. Because the trip is a one-way journey, shuttles must be arranged for the end of your tour.

The route requires more stamina than technical riding skill, as nearly the entire tour travels over well-maintained forest roads. Riding to the Last Dollar Hut and to the La Sal Hut represent the most difficult days, with steep and consistent ascents providing the primary challenges. The majority of the trip, however, is mostly through rolling countryside amid thick evergreen forests interspersed with panoramic vistas.

Mike Turrin and Joe Ryan and the staff of the San Juan Hut System will work with your group to custom-tailor a trip to your requirements. Your trip can be guided, food and menu planning can be arranged, or you can simply rent the huts for your own self-contained mountain bike expedition.

The huts are open from June 1 through October 1, with pleasant touring all summer long. Daytime temperatures in August and into September can soar. Early summer and autumn, with warm days and brisk evenings, are perhaps the best times to cover the route. Remember that western skies are notorious for turning inky black with violent thunderstorms throughout the summer. Carry rain clothes and be prepared to sit out short storms. Early- and late-season riders may also experience light snow at higher elevations, so plan accordingly. Whenever you go, be sure to carry several water bottles.

Each shelter is equipped with propane lights and a cook stove, a wood-burning stove for heat, cookware and utensils, a water supply, an outdoor toilet, and even sleeping bags, pads and bunks. During the summer months, riders are encouraged to sleep under the stars — to experience the expansive heavens that have inspired so many western artists, Native American story-tellers, and singing coyotes.

A few rules to remember when using the huts: conserve water, place water jugs on top of wood/food boxes (to foil mice!), shut off propane, re-hang sleeping bags, burn paper, hang trash out of reach of animals (hut system staff will pack the trash out), sweep and clean, put out fire in wood stove, fasten and lock all doors and windows.

The Telluride-to-Moab mountain bike tour is becoming very popular so plan your trip early! Make reservations through the San Juan Hut System (see Appendix A).

Riding along Last Dollar Road outside of Telluride.

300

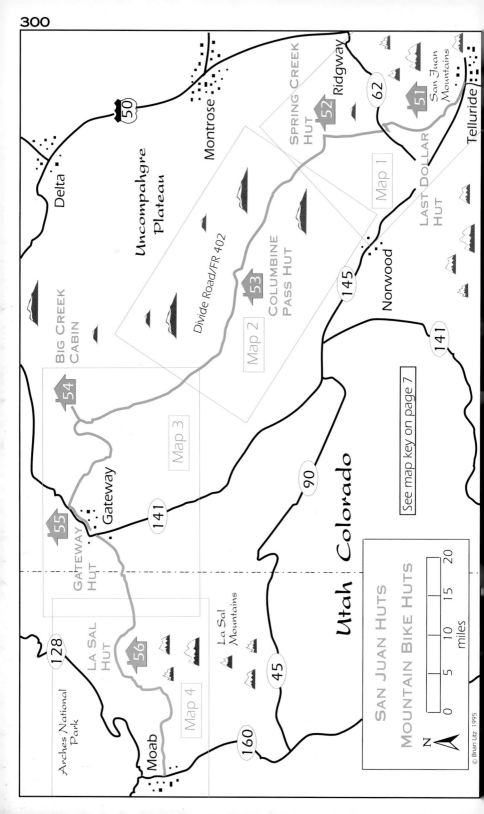

A rest stop provides opportunities to enjoy high-country views.

51 LAST DOLLAR HUT

The Last Dollar Hut, which sleeps eight, is the highest-elevation hut on the Telluride-to-Moab route. The road to the hut is steep and scenic. The first day of riding is relatively short with respect to mileage, but it is at a high elevation with continual climbing during the final portion of the ride. Last Dollar Road is one of the most scenic and most photographed back roads in Colorado. For reservations call the San Juan Hut System (see Appendix A).

TOUR 51A TELLURIDE TO
DAY 1 LAST DOLLAR HUT

Difficulty:	Intermediate	
Time:	3 to 6 hours	
Distance:	14.9 miles	
Elevations:	Trailhead 8,800', Hut 10,980',+2,700'/-550'	
Maps:	National Forest: Uncompahgre	
	See map pages 300 and 303	

This tour overlooks the La Sal Mountains and the state of Utah to the west, the Wilson Peaks to the south, and the Silverton West Group of the San Juan Mountains to the east. Whether your trip is planned during the summer when the wildflowers are in bloom or in the autumn when the mountains are awash in golden aspen, you will enjoy the finest mountain scenery that Colorado and Utah have to offer.

The tour begins at the San Juan Hut System Office in Telluride. Head west out of town to Society Turn, where CO 145 turns south to Ophir, Lizard Head Pass, and Dolores. From here turn north onto the airport road (FR 638) at mile 4.1. Leave the pavement at a stop sign and go right at mile 6.2 on a dirt road. The airport runway and hangars will be in view. Descend 400 feet into the Deep Creek valley and cross the creek via a bridge at mile 8.4 (do not take a left here!).

Continue up this road until you see a sign for Willow Creek at mile 11.1. Pass an Uncompahgre National Forest sign at mile 12. Ride past an old homestead, fallen-down cabins, and some beaver ponds, then cross the creek and begin ascending switchbacks at mile 13.1. Pass the Whipple Mountain Trail (sign No. 419) at mile 14.4 and continue to Last Dollar Pass at mile 14.7.

The hut is 0.25 mile and 300 vertical feet up the ridge to the east/northeast. Pedal directly up the steep and rocky path to a point where it becomes too steep to ride. Walk your bike to the hut, which can be seen when you are roughly 70 feet away.

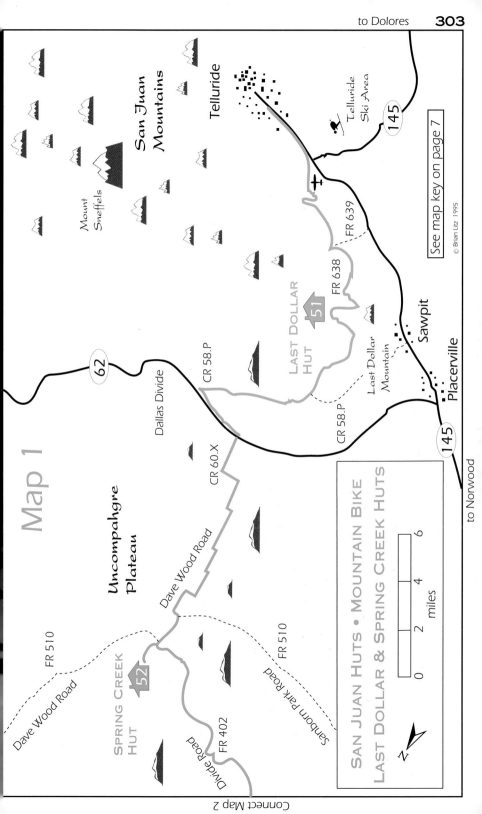

to Dolores

San Juan Mountains

Telluride

Telluride Ski Area

145

See map key on page 7

© Brian Litz 1995

Mount Sneffels

FR 639

FR 638

LAST DOLLAR HUT **51**

62

Sawpit

Placerville

CR 58.P.

Dallas Divide

Last Dollar Mountain

CR 58.P.

145

Uncompahgre Plateau

CR 60.X

to Norwood

Dave Wood Road

SAN JUAN HUTS • MOUNTAIN BIKE
LAST DOLLAR & SPRING CREEK HUTS

FR 510

FR 510

Sanborn Park Road

0   2   4   6
miles

N

SPRING CREEK HUT **52**

Dave Wood Road

FR 402

Divide Road

Connect Map 2

52 SPRING CREEK HUT

The second leg of the journey to Moab begins with a massive loss in altitude as you leave the Last Dollar Hut and descend to Dallas Divide. From Dallas Divide the route climbs onto the Uncompahgre Plateau and begins a traverse that lasts for two-and-a-half days across this impressive geologic feature. The roads in this area are secondary dirt roads characterized by technically easy riding.

TOUR 52A LAST DOLLAR HUT
DAY 2 TO SPRING CREEK HUT

Difficulty:	Intermediate
Time:	4 to 6 hours
Distance:	26.3 miles
Elevations:	LD Hut 10,980', SC Hut 9,200', +1,600'/-3,000'
Maps:	National Forest: Uncompahgre
	See map pages 300 and 303

Pick up the route from near the front door of Last Dollar Hut and descend on foot to the north (this is not the route taken to the hut!). To control erosion, walk your bike for 250 feet to a point where the trail is wide enough to drive a truck. From here, return back down to the summit of Last Dollar Pass (FR 638) at mile 0.25.

Descend the north side of the pass to Alder Creek at mile 4.2. Climb out of Alder Creek up onto Hastings Mesa to CR 58P. Near here you will pass Sawpit Road intersecting from the left at mile 5.8; this road is marked by old corrals and livestock-loading chutes and is to be avoided.

Continue on CR 58P (Last Dollar Road), passing San Juan Vista on your right. You will eventually reach an intersection with CO 62 (paved) at mile 11.0. Turn west for a rapid ride down CO 62 to CR 60X (passing CR 62X on the right). Leaving CO 62 near an abandoned ski cabin at mile 13.6, turn north onto CR 60X and ascend into Buck Canyon.

Climb 400 feet up out of Buck Canyon and enter Howard Flats at mile 14.6. This was the site of an old Ute Indian horse-racing track. From here the route stair-steps through a series of 90-degree turns. Continue north to mile 15.7, where the road turns west at a small intersection. Go west (CR Z.60) until the main road turns north (CR 59.Z). Stay on the main road as it again makes a turn west on the Montrose/San Miguel county line. Turn north (CR JJ58) at mile 19.1. Stay on CR JJ.58 until you turn west onto CR 11, and then make a final 90-degree turn onto Dave Wood Road at mile 20.9. Ride under power lines, descend to a broad valley and cross Horsefly Creek at mile 23.4.

At a marked intersection with the Sanborn Park Road on the left (west) at mile 23.9, turn right onto FR 510 and begin the second 400-foot ascent of the day. Pass Johnson Spring on the right at mile 25.4 (potable water flows from a black hose), then turn left onto FR 402 at mile 25.6. The Dave Wood Road and FR 402 (Divide Road) intersect near a sign for Columbine Pass.

Follow FR 402 until you reach a firewood area and turn right onto a small secondary road with a cattleguard at mile 25.8. Cross the first cattleguard, then two additional cattleguards. After passing the last cattleguard, ride to the third water-bar ditch running out to the left. Near the ditch is a large Douglas fir stump marking the spot where a path leads from the road to the hut. Spring Creek Hut is 150 feet away in the woods at mile 26.3.

Pedaling through aspen en route to the Spring Creek Hut.

53 COLUMBINE PASS HUT

The route connecting Spring Creek Hut and Columbine Pass Hut follows good secondary roads over gently rolling terrain. It is nontechnical, and mountain bikers of all abilities will be able to enjoy this stretch of riding. Keep an eye open for vehicles traveling over these roads. Potable water is available at Columbine Campground.

TOUR 53A   SPRING CREEK HUT
DAY 3   TO COLUMBINE PASS HUT

Difficulty:	Intermediate	🚲
Time:	5 to 7 hours	
Distance:	34.3 miles	
Elevations:	SC Hut 9,200', CP Hut 9,205', +1,800'/-1,800'	
Maps:	National Forest: Uncompahgre	
	See map pages 300, 303, and 307	

Leave Spring Creek Hut and retrace the route to FR 402 (Divide Road). Leave the firewood cutting area, and at mile 1.1 head right (north) along FR 402 toward Columbine Pass. Pass the Spring Creek Trailhead on the right at mile 8. Go past the intersection at FR 540 (this intersection is also marked by a sign for Old Highway 90), and turn left here at mile 15.3. Continue west along FR 402 toward Columbine Pass, bypassing Old Highway 90, which is now on the left.

Pedal past Transfer Road East on the right at mile 16. At a cattleguard, head left toward Antone Spring, bypassing the second Transfer Road (FR 508) on the right at mile 17.1. Ride past Houser Flats (FR 603) on the left at mile 20.1 and past Tabeguache Overlook at mile 31.2, also on the left.

When you reach Columbine Pass at mile 32, go right on FR 503. Columbine Campground is at mile 32.7 (stop here if you need water). Ride past the now-defunct Columbine Ranger Station to the intersection of FR 402 and FR 503 at mile 32.9. Head west following FR 402 toward Windy Point, the second left turn, at mile 34.2. Turn and ride approximately 200 yards to the Columbine Pass Hut.

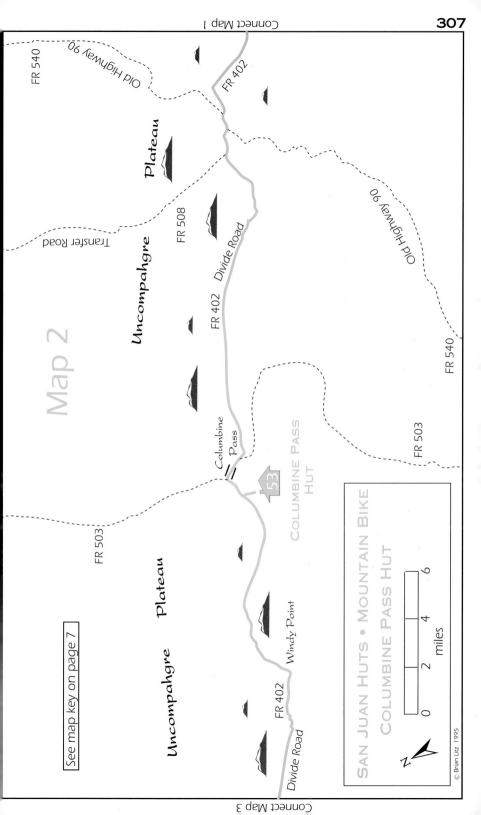

Map 2

See map key on page 7

FR 540

Old Highway 90

FR 402

Plateau

Transfer Road

FR 508

Divide Road

FR 402

Uncompahgre

Old Highway 90

FR 540

Columbine Pass

FR 503

FR 503

Plateau

Uncompahgre

Windy Point

FR 402

Divide Road

53

COLUMBINE PASS HUT

SAN JUAN HUTS • MOUNTAIN BIKE

COLUMBINE PASS HUT

0   2   4   6
miles

N

© Brian Litz 1995

54 BIG CREEK CABIN

This is a spectacular leg of the journey to Moab. The road clings to the western edge of the Uncompahgre Plateau, rolling over undulating terrain. To the west, riders can see the incredible vistas of the La Sal Mountains and the high desert of southeastern Utah.

TOUR 54A COLUMBINE HUT
DAY 4 TO BIG CREEK CABIN

Difficulty:	Novice/Intermediate
Time:	5 to 7 hours
Distance:	37.2 miles
Elevations:	CP Hut 9,205', BC Cabin 8,300', +1,600'/-2,200'
Maps:	National Forest: Uncompahgre
	See map pages 300, 307, and 310

Begin the day by retracing the route back to FR 402 (Divide Road) and ride toward Windy Point. Bypass Windy Point at mile 9.5, stopping to enjoy the great views of the La Sal Mountains to the west. Leave Montrose County and enter Mesa County at mile 14. Continue past Club Cow Camp on the left at mile 15.4 and past a Monument Hill sign on the right at mile 17. Pass Campbell Point on the right at mile 20.6 and Cold Springs Ranger Station on the right at mile 29.3. Begin to descend at mile 31.8 and then start climbing when the road veers to the right at mile 33.1.

You'll arrive at Divide Forks Campground at mile 33.5. There is potable water at the campground, so stop here if you need to refill your water bottles. At the intersection of FR 402 and FR 404, turn to the right at mile 33.8 and head toward Grand Junction.

Descend along this road to a cattleguard and a sign for Telephone Trail at mile 36.9. Turn left here and leave the main road to follow a two-track road along a zig-zag pole fence. Continue following the fence (which soon turns into a wire fence) as it corners 90 degrees to the left. Ride for another 400 feet and climb over a small hill to the cabin. Big Creek Cabin is a log building on the edge of a meadow. It is situated in a group of aspen trees on the opposite side of the fence. Cross the barbwire fence carefully and walk to the cabin.

Bernice Notenboom and Mike Turrin outside
Big Creek Cabin, Uncompahgre Plateau

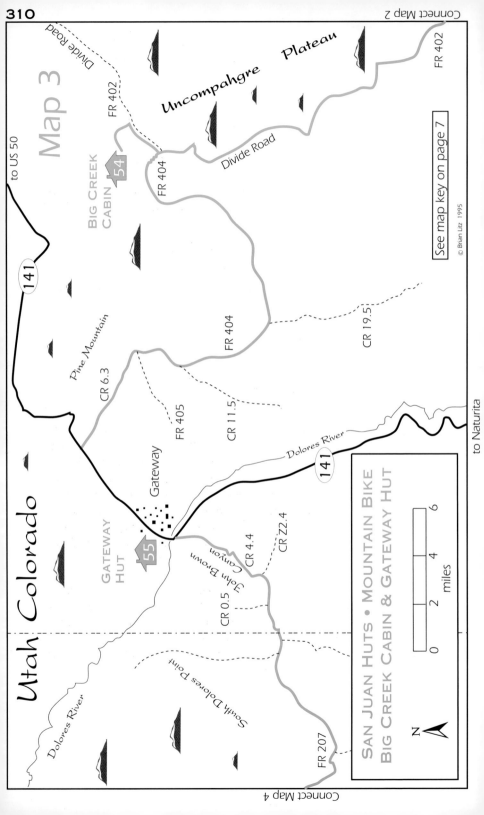

55 GATEWAY HUT

Riding to Gateway Hut involves some serious fun, exciting descents, and knuckle-cramping braking as you drop 4,400 feet from the cool forests of the Uncompahgre Plateau into the Dolores River valley. This is an exciting day with minimal climbing and maximum downhill road action. Tune your brakes!

TOUR 55A: BIG CREEK CABIN
DAY 5 TO GATEWAY HUT

Difficulty:	Novice/Intermediate
Time:	4 to 7 hours
Distance:	30.4 miles
Elevations:	BC Cabin 8,300', G Hut 4,600', +2,100'/-4,900'
Maps:	National Forest: Uncompahgre
	See map pages 300 and 310

Return to the FR 402/FR 404 intersection and turn right (northwest) onto FR 404 (Uranium Road) at mile 3.5. Ride past Rim Trail at mile 6.5, and at mile 8.1 begin the first major descent of the day (2,000 feet!) down to Indian Creek. A gate and cattleguard mark the bottom of the descent at mile 14.3.

At a sign marking the turnoff to the town of Gateway at mile 14.6, turn right onto CR 6.3/FR 405 toward Pine Mountain Road. Begin an arduous climb at mile 16.8. At mile 19.6, you will come to a four-way intersection. Turn right here (remaining on CR 6.3/FR 405). Proceed straight through the intersection with CR 10.8/FR 405 at mile 23.2 and continue your descent along CR 6.3 toward Gateway.

Cross a cattleguard at mile 23.4 and then enter a flash-flood zone at mile 26.8. You will intersect CO 141 (paved) at a stop sign at mile 28.6. Turn left (west) and head toward the town of Gateway. Continue on through the town of Gateway. The road to the hut is just before the bridge over the Dolores River. Take this dirt road right, to the north, and follow for 0.25 mile to the hut under the cottonwood trees beside the Dolores River.

56   LA SAL HUT

The ascent from Gateway Hut to the La Sal Hut is far and away the most difficult leg of the Telluride-to-Moab tour. With more than 3,600 feet of elevation gain, this is not a ride for the faint of lung.

TOUR 56A   GATEWAY HUT
DAY 6   TO LA SAL HUT

Difficulty:	Advanced	🚲
Time:	6 to 10 hours	
Distance:	25.5 miles	
Elevations:	G Hut 4,600', LS Hut 8,200', +4,400'/ -700'	
Maps:	National Forest: Manti-La Sal	
	See map pages 300, 310 and 313	

Gateway Hut is located deep in the Dolores River valley, and summertime temperatures can easily soar over 100 degrees. Because of this, proper planning is essential to having a successful day. Leave as early as possible to take advantage of the cooler morning temperatures, take a break during the hottest part of the afternoon and drink lots of water.

Return to CO 141, cross the Dolores River and follow the road as it bends to the left. At the turnoff for John Brown Canyon, turn right into the canyon at mile 3.3. Proceed past a mining equipment yard to the end of the pavement. You will begin ascending at mile 4.3 and see a sign that reads: "Warning — Entering Uranium Mining Area" at mile 9.9. Turn right at the intersection at mile 10.

At mile 11.7 you will reach another intersection with a gate to the right. Turn left! Cross the Utah state line at mile 12.4. Cross a cattleguard at mile 14.2, turn left at an intersection and then cross two more cattleguards at mile 16 and 17.7. When you reach the La Sal Mountain State Forest sign at mile 18.4, continue in the direction of the mountains. Do not turn left!

Ride past the Taylor Ranch (red gate and cattleguard) at mile 18.7 and proceed past a turnoff on the left at a sign reading "5 Bar A, Sally's Hollow, Kirk's Basin" at mile 20.3. Do not turn left! Descend across a stream. You will pass a "Leaving State Land" sign, some old corrals, a cattleguard and a sign for the Taylor Livestock Company. Continue climbing.

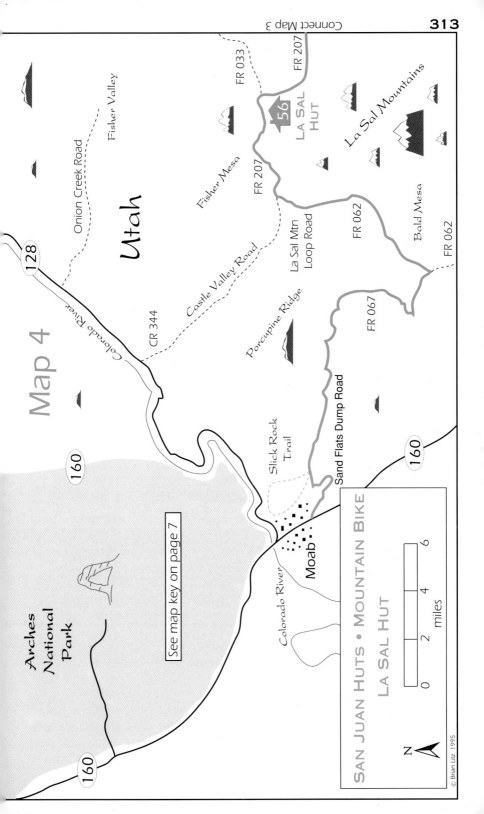

FR 033

FR 207

LA SAL HUT

56

La Sal Mountains

FR 062

Bald Mesa

FR 062

Fisher Valley

Onion Creek Road

Utah

Fisher Mesa

FR 207

La Sal Mtn Loop Road

Castle Valley Road

CR 344

Colorado River

128

FR 067

Porcupine Ridge

Map 4

160

Arches National Park

See map key on page 7

Slick Rock Trail

Sand Flats Dump Road

160

Colorado River

Moab

SAN JUAN HUTS • MOUNTAIN BIKE

LA SAL HUT

N

0 2 4 6
miles

© Brian Litz 1995

At mile 22.7, pass a road on the left at a sign reading "Don's Lake, Beaver Basin, Sally's Hollow, Gateway, and Hidden Lake." Stay right, ride under power lines and begin to descend at mile 23.5. Pass the Manti-La Sal National Forest sign, a cattleguard and a gravel site at mile 25. Pass a red stake and a six-foot-wide, clear-cut corridor (running up the hillside into the forest) that mark the boundary between private land and national forest land.

You will arrive at a **T** intersection at mile 25.4, marked with a sign reading "Moab/North Beaver Mesa." From this intersection, retrace your route south about 500 feet toward the large ponderosa pines. On the west side of the road is a small grassy pull-off with an old fire ring. From the southwest corner of the clearing, a four-wheel-drive road enters a dense oak thicket. Follow this road approximately 400 feet to a clearing and the tan-colored yurt.

The La Sal Hut is well hidden and can be difficult to locate if you do not find the proper trail. The oak forest here is also full of game trails that resemble foot paths.

TOUR 56B   LA SAL HUT
DAY 7   TO MOAB, UTAH

Difficulty:	Intermediate/Advanced	
Time:	5 to 7 hours	
Distance:	38.4 miles	
Elevations:	LS Hut 8,200', Moab 4,200', +1,700'/-5,500'	
Maps:	National Forest: Manti-La Sal	
	See map pages 300 and 313	

The leg of the trip from La Sal Hut to Moab is a fitting finale to this 207-mile journey. From the high forests of the La Sal Mountains, the route overlooks western Colorado and eastern Utah. Good secondary roads allow you to concentrate on the scenery rather than on boulders during the incredible 5,000-foot-plus descent to the surrealistic canyonlands of Utah.

From the La Sal Hut, return to the road, proceed back to the **T** intersection and turn west toward Moab. At mile 2.1 begin a 2,000-plus-foot descent. When you reach gravel piles on the right, follow a small dirt road on the north into the woods to the cliffs at Fisher Valley Overlook at mile 2.4.

Pavement begins at mile 4.4, ends at mile 5.1 and begins again at mile 5.4. Cross a cattleguard and a stream at mile 6.5, then exit the Manti-La Sal National Forest at mile 7.5. At the head of Castle Valley you'll see a sign reading "Moab, La Sal Mountain Loop Road" and "Oowah Lake, Warner Campground, Moab." Turn left onto the La Sal Mountain Loop Road at mile

8 and begin ascending. There is a spectacular view of Castleton Tower at mile 9.2.

Pass Manti-La Sal National Forest and Harpole Mesa signs at mile 9.9 and begin switchbacking at mile 10.5. Pass a sign reading "Miner's Basin/Pinhook Battleground." Stay on the pavement, which ends at mile 13.5. Pass communications towers on the left and ride under power lines at mile 16.6, where the descent begins.

When you reach FR 67 (Sand Flats Road) on the right at mile 17, turn right and ride through a T intersection under power lines at mile 17.6. Leave Manti-La Sal National Forest at a cattleguard at mile 20.5 and proceed through a right turn near a blue-roofed house, which is across a shallow, rock canyon. Remain on the main road, paralleling the canyon on the left and re-enter the national forest.

Descend a steep switchback and cross a cattleguard at mile 22.5. Leave the national forest again at mile 23.9. Enter a canyon via a shelf road at mile 24.2. You will reach pavement at mile 34.2, pass the Slickrock Trail at mile 34.6. You've done it! Moab!

Bernice Notenboom enjoys an autumn day near La Sal Hut in Utah.

Setting sun viewed from the Last Dollar Hut,
San Juan Hut System

NEW HUTS: Reservations & Information

The huts and hut systems listed here are such recent additions to Colorado's backcountry landscape that we were unable to "field-check" them in time for this printing. For more information on these new structures, please contact the appropriate parties using the following information:

1. 10th MOUNTAIN DIVISION HUTS

The 10th Mountain Division has added four new huts. To the north of Vail in the Gore Range is the popular Eiseman Hut. North of Vail and southeast of Vance's Cabin is the privately owned Belvedere Hut, whose trailhead is near Leadville at the foot of Fremont Pass. Near Aspen are the Benedict Huts. These two huts keep each other company on the southern end of the 10th's system and are named for the hut system's founder and his wife — Fritz's Cabin and Fabi's Cabin. Each hut is booked separately. For more information, contact the 10th Mountain Division Hut Association (Appendix A).

2. ELWOOD PASS CABIN

Elwood Pass lies deep in the southern San Juan Mountains between Wolf Creek Pass to the north and west and the South San Juan Wilderness/Cumbres Pass area to the south. This cabin is an old Forest Service structure that has been renovated for public use.

Rio Grande NF - Conejos Peak Ranger District   719-274-8971
P.O. Box 420
La Jara, CO 81140

3. GROUSE CREEK YURT

The Southwest Nordic Center has added the new Grouse Creek Yurt to the north of three existing huts, opening up a new area to backcountry skiers. For more information, contact the Southwest Nordic Center (Appendix A).

4. HIDDEN TREASURE YURT

The Hidden Treasure Yurt is located south of the towns of Edwards and Eagle in close proximity to the 10th Mountain Division's Polar Star Inn. Access is via the same trails as the inn.

Hidden Treasure Adventures   970-926-4822
P.O. Box 441   800-444-2813
Edwards, CO 81632-0441

5. HIGH LONESOME HUT

The High Lonesome Hut is a new hut within a new hut system north of the Winter Park/Fraser area in Grand County.

High Lonesome Huts   970-726-4099
P.O. Box 145
Fraser, CO 80442
E-mail: lonesome-hut@lonesome-hut.com Website: http://lonesome-hut.com

6. NOKHU CABIN (LAKE AGNES CABIN)

The Lake Agnes Cabin has been closed by the Colorado State Forest due to deteriorating structural integrity. Never Summer Nordic Yurts has been granted a permit to construct and operate a new cabin slightly to the north of the Lake Agnes site. The name of the new cabin will be the Nokhu Cabin. For more information, see Appendix A.

7. NEVER SUMMER NORDIC YURTS

Never Summer Nordic Yurts has opened two new yurts high in the drainage near Montgomery Pass. They sit roughly halfway between the Grass Creek Yurt and the Ruby Jewel Yurt to the north. For more information, see Appendix A.

8. PHOENIX RIDGE YURTS

High above the historic mining town of Creede stand the Phoenix Ridge Yurts, a two-yurt "compound" that whispers of an upscale backcountry destination resort. The Meadow Yurt and the Phoenix Ridge Yurt sit close to each other. They can be reached via an easy cross-country trail, or a longer, rougher backcountry route, and serve as a base camp for extended tours.

Phoenix Ridge Yurts - Vertical Reality, LLC   800-984-6275
P.O. Box 434
Creede, CO 81130

9. SAN JUAN SNOWTREKS

Between Wolf Creek Pass and Creede is a vast wilderness that sees few winter visitors. San Juan Snowtreks has two existing structures — a cabin and a yurt — in this area. The ultimate goal is to create a series of huts that will connect to the summit of Wolf Creek Pass.

San Juan Snowtreks   505-892-2926
539 Paige Loop   505-672-3042
Los Alamos, NM 87544

10. SPRUCE HOLE YURT

Cumbres Nordic Adventures operates the Spruce Hole Yurt near La Manga Pass in southern Colorado. La Manga Pass is the northern summit of Cumbres Pass, which connects the San Luis Valley to the northern New Mexico town of Chama.

Cumbres Nordic Adventures   888-660-9878
P.O. Box 73
Chama, NM 87520
Website: www.yurtsogood.com

11. SUMMIT COUNTY HUTS

Summit County Huts and the National Forest Service have refurbished the old Section House, and a nearby cabin, atop Boreas Pass. This is a beautiful hut, and living museum, with great views and ski-touring. For more information, contact the Summit Huts Association or the 10th Mountain Division Hut Association (Appendix A).

12. WOLF CREEK BACKCOUNTRY

Wolf Creek Backcountry is a new yurt system operating to the east and south of Wolf Creek Pass and the Wolf Creek Pass ski area. Currently consisting of one yurt, the system is slated for future expansion.

Wolf Creek Backcountry   970-731-2486
P.O. Box 143
Pagosa Springs, CO 81147

APPENDIX A
Reservations & Information

NORTHERN HUTS

Never Summer Nordic Yurts & Nokhu Cabin (formerly Lake Agnes Cabin)
P.O. Box 1983   970-482-9411
Fort Collins, CO 80633

Colorado Mountain Club (Brainard Lake Cabin & Guinn Mountain Hut)
Chautauqua Park   303-449-1135
900 Baseline Road
Boulder, CO 80302

Eldora Nordic Center (Tennessee Mountain Cabin)   303-440-8700
P.O. Box 430
Nederland, CO 80466

US Forest Service (Gwen Andrews Hut & First Creek Cabin)
Sulphur Ranger District   970-887-4100
P.O. Box 10
Granby, CO 80446

CENTRAL HUTS

Summit Huts Association   970-453-8583
P.O. Box 2830
Breckenridge, CO 80424
E-mail: sumhuts@colorado.net Website: www.huts.org
For reservations, contact 10th Mountain Division Huts   970-925-5775

10th Mountain Division Hut Association   970-925-5775
1280 Ute Avenue
Aspen, CO 81611
Website: www.huts.org

Double Diamond Bed & Breakfast   970-927-3404
P.O. Box 2
Meredith, CO 81642
(This bed and breakfast provides overnight accommodations
for 10th Mountain Division Hut visitors)

Alfred A. Braun Memorial Hut System*
P.O. Box 7937
Aspen, CO 81612
Website: www.huts.org
For reservations, contact 10th Mountain Division Huts   970-925-5775
* For information on gondola rides to the summit of Aspen Mountain, call
970-925-1220 or 1-800-525-6200.

Adventures to the Edge (Cement Creek Yurt)   970-349-5219
P.O. Box 91
Crested Butte, CO 81224

CENTRAL HUTS continued

Crested Butte Nordic Center (Gothic Cabin)   970-349-1707
P.O. Box 1269
620 2nd Street
Crested Butte, CO 81224

Elkton Cabins (Elkton Cabin, Miner's Delight, Silver Jewel) 970-349-1815
P.O. Box 1269
Crested Butte, CO 81224
E-Mail: elkton@rmi.net

Continental Divide Hut System, LLC (Lost Wonder Hut)   303-670-1082
c/o Colman
28310 Pine Drive
Evergreen, CO 80439
Website: www.lostwonder.com

Sunlight Mountain Resort Nordic Center   800-445-7931
10901 Road 117   970-945-7491
Glenwood Springs, CO 81601
Website: www.sunlightmtn.com

SOUTHERN HUTS

Southwest Nordic Center   505-758-4761
P.O. Box 3212
Taos, NM 87571

Hinsdale Haute Route   970-944-2269
P.O. Box 771
925 Ocean View Drive
Lake City, CO 81235

Saint Paul Lodge   970-387-5367
P.O. Box 463   970-387-5494
Silverton, CO 81433

Scotch Creek Yurt   970-967-2402
Rico Snowcountry Tours
P.O. Box 4
Rico, CO 81332

San Juan Hut System   970-728-6935
P.O. Box 1663
Telluride, CO 81435
E-mail: info@sanjuanhuts.com Website: www.sanjuanhuts.com

APPENDIX B
Road & Weather Conditions

National Weather Service   303-494-4221
Colorado Road Conditions   303-639-1234

APPENDIX C
County Sheriffs & National Forests

In case of immediate, life-threatening emergencies always call 911. Dialing 911 will connect you with the nearest emergency response network. Be prepared to provide as much information as possible concerning the type of emergency, your location (huts, roads, creek names), etc. The sheriff department phone numbers listed below are non-emergency numbers that connect you with their dispatchers, 24 hours a day. Use these numbers for problems such as stolen cars or to report lost skiers who have returned to safety on their own. Note: Conejos County (Southwest Nordic Center) is not on the 911 system at this time; call the number below for all types of emergencies.

Never Summer Nordic Yurts & Nokhu Cabin (formerly Lake Agnes Cabin)
Jackson County Sheriff	970-723-4242
Colorado State Forest	970-723-8366

Brainard Lake, Guinn Mountain & Tennessee Mountain
Boulder County Sheriff	303-441-4444
Arapaho & Roosevelt NF - Boulder Ranger District	970-444-6600

First Creek Cabin & Gwen Andrews Cabin
Grand County Sheriff	970-725-3343
Arapaho & Roosevelt NF - Sulphur Ranger District	970-887-4100

Summit Huts Association
Summit County Sheriff	970-453-6222
Arapaho & Roosevelt NF - Dillon Ranger District	970-468-5400

10th Mountain Division Hut Association
Eagle County Sheriff (Vail/Eagle area)	970-328-6611
Lake County Sheriff (Leadville)	719-539-2596
Pitkin County Sheriff	970-920-5310
Pike & San Isabel NF - Leadville Ranger District	719-486-0749
White River NF - Holy Cross Ranger District	970-945-2521
White River NF - Aspen Ranger District	970-925-3445

Alfred A. Braun Memorial Hut Association
Pitkin County Sheriff (Aspen)	970-920-5310
Gunnison County Sheriff (CB)	970-641-8000
White River NF - Aspen Ranger District	970-925-3445

Friends Hut, Elkton Cabins, Gothic Cabin, and Cement Creek Yurt
Gunnison County Sheriff (CB)	970-641-8000
Grand Mesa, Uncompahgre & Gunnison NFs - Taylor River Ranger District	970-874-7691

Lost Wonder Hut
Chaffee County Sheriff	719-539-2596
Pike & San Isabel NF - Salida Ranger District	719-539-3591

Sunlight Backcountry Cabin
Garfield County Sheriff	970-945-9151
White River NF - Sopris Ranger District	970-963-2266

Southwest Nordic Center
Conejos County Sheriff	719-376-5921
Rio Grande NF - Conejos Peak Ranger District	719-274-8971

Hinsdale Haute Route
    Hinsdale County Sheriff   970-944-2291
    Grand Mesa, Uncompahgre & Gunnison NFs - Taylor River Ranger District
                                                    970-874-7691
    Rio Grande NF - Divide Ranger District   719-852-5941

Saint Paul Lodge
    San Juan County Sheriff   970-387-5531
    Ouray County Sheriff   970-325-7272
    San Juan NF - Columbine Ranger District   970-247-4874

Scotch Creek Yurt
    Dolores County Sheriff   970-677-2257
    San Juan NF - Dolores Ranger District   970-882-7296

San Juan Hut System
    San Miguel County Sheriff   970-728-3081
    Ouray County Sheriff   970-325-7272
    Montrose County Sheriff   970-249-6606
    Mesa County Sheriff   970-242-6707
    Grand County Sheriff, Utah   435-259-8115
                                                435-259-5541
    Grand Mesa, Uncompahgre & Gunnison NFs - Ouray Ranger District
                                                       970-240-5300
    Manti-La Sal NF - Moab/Monticello Ranger District, Utah   435-259-7155

For general information about national forests:
    US Forest Service   303-275-5350
    Rocky Mountain Regional Office
    Box 25127
    Lakewood, CO 80225

APPENDIX D

For information on guide services, please call the reservation number
for the particular hut system that you are interested in visiting.

APPENDIX E
Avalanche Training & Information

American Avalanche Institute
P.O. Box 308
Wilson, WY 83014
307-733-3315
E-mail: aai@wyoming.com

**American Association of
Avalanche Professionals**
P.O. Box 1032
Bozeman, MT 59771
406-587-3830

Silverton Avalanche School
San Juan Search & Rescue
P.O. Box 178
Silverton, CO 81433
970-387-5531

Avalanche information continued on page 324

APPENDIX E continued

AVALANCHE INFORMATION PHONE NUMBERS

Colorado Avalanche Information Center:

Denver/Boulder Area (CAIC statewide forecast)	303-499-9650
Fort Collins (CAIC statewide forecast)	970-482-0457
Colorado Springs (CAIC statewide forecast)	719-520-0020
Summit/Eagle County (CAIC regional forecast)	970-668-0600
Durango (CAIC regional forecast)	970-247-8187

United States Forest Service Backcountry Avalanche Information:

Minturn (Vail/Eagle County regional forecast)	970-827-5687
Aspen (Aspen/Carbondale/Crested Butte regional forecast)	970-920-1664

Utah Avalanche Information:

Grand County, Utah	435-259-7669

Most skiing and backcountry equipment shops can provide skiers with information on groups and clubs offering avalanche training. Additionally, many city and county recreation departments offer weekend and evening training courses.

APPENDIX F
Recommended Equipment Checklist

SKI CLOTHING

Long underwear (wool, silk, polypro, etc.)
Insulating pant layer (wool, pile, Polarplus, or nylon)
Medium weight shirt
Heavy pile or wool jacket
Mountain parka or wind & snow shell
Light weight gloves (for warm days)
Heavy gloves or mittens
Sunglasses and goggles
Baseball cap
Wool cap or balaclava
Neck gaiter or scarf
Hut slippers
Down vest or coat
Wind & snow shell pants
Leg gaiters or Super Gaiters (for extreme cold)
Spare sunglasses

SKI EQUIPMENT
*Indicates group equipment

Skis, boots & poles
Climbing skins
Wax kit*
Backpack (medium to large capacity: 3,000 to 6,000 cu. in.)
Day pack or fanny pack (for day trips)
Sleeping bag (+10 to -25 degree range)
Sunscreen & lip balm
Stove & pot
Maps & guidebooks
Bivouac sack or tarp* (for hasty shelters)
Snow kit for avalanche analysis*
Spare batteries
Shovel
Avalanche transceivers
Avalanche probes*
Ensolite pad to sit on
Headlamp or flashlight
Mirror
Moisturizing lotion
Water bottle & thermos
First-aid kit*
Compass
Altimeter*

SKI REPAIR KIT/EMERGENCY KIT

High-energy snacks & drinks
Duct tape (always!)
Long-burning candles
Lighter & waterproof matches
Razor blades
Ski tips
Steel wool
Knife or Leatherman
Spare bindings, baskets, and cables
Note pad and pens

Space blanket
Stove parts
Webbing
Hot packs
Screws
Alpine cord
Glue sticks
Sewing materials
Wire
Safety pins

BIKE CLOTHING

Tights or long underwear
Pile tights or sweat pants
Wind pants & wind shell
Rain jacket or poncho
Shell gloves for rain and wind
Light, insulative cap
Medium-weight sweater or shirt
    (wool, polypro, Capilene)
Biking gloves and/or light gloves
    for hiking

Heavy sweater, jacket, or vest
Down vest or heavy sweater
    (optional)
Biking/hiking shorts
Bathing suit
Baseball cap or wide-brimmed hat
Biking/hiking socks & sock
    liners

BIKE EQUIPMENT

Mountain bike
Biking and/or hiking shoes
Helmet
Bike packs
Day pack or fanny pack
Flashlight or head lamp

Water bottles (at least two)
Sunscreen & lip balm
Moisturizing lotion
Sunglasses
First-aid kit

BIKING REPAIR KIT AND TOOLS
***Indicates group tools; some tools may vary depending on
your particular bike components, but these are the most standard.**

Phillips screwdriver
Crescent wrench
Headset tools: 32mm, 36mm*
Hub wrenches: 13mm, 15mm*
Bottom bracket tools*
Extra tire*
Extra rear derailleur cable*
Chain lube*
Large, adjustable open-ended wrench*
Box-ended wrench: 17mm*
Note pad and pens

Extra tube
Chain oil (small bottle)
Tire patch kit
Extra brake cables
Spoke nipples
Duct tape (always!)
Tire pump
Allen keys: 2.5, 4, 5, 6mm
Tire irons
Spoke wrench

APPENDIX G
Bibliography

Avalanche, Weather & Environmental Information

Armstrong, Betsy R. and Knox Williams. *The Avalanche Book*. Rev. ed. Golden: Fulcrum Publishing Company, 1992.

Chronic, John. *Roadside Geology of Colorado*. Missoula: Mountain Press Publishing Company, 1980.

Chronic, John and Halka. *Prairie, Peak & Plateau: A Guide to the Geology of Colorado*. (Bulletin 32). Denver: Colorado Geological Survey, 1972.

Daffern, Tony. *Avalanche Safety for Climbers and Skiers*. Seattle: Cloud Cap Press, 1983.

Fredston, Jill A. and Doug Fesler. *Snow Sense: A Guide to Evaluating Snow Avalanche Hazard*. 4th ed. Anchorage: Alaska Mountain Safety Center, Inc., 1995.

Halfpenny, James C. and Roy Douglas Ozanne. *Winter: An Ecological Handbook*. Boulder: Johnson Books, 1989.

Keen, Richard. *Skywatch: The Western Weather Guide*. Golden: Fulcrum Publishing, 1987.

LaChapelle, Edward R. *The ABCs of Avalanche Safety*. 2nd ed. Seattle: The Mountaineers, 1985.

Mutel, Cornelia Fleischer and John Emerick. *Grassland to Glacier*. Boulder: Johnson Books, 1984.

Skiing Information, Instruction and Training

Barnett, Steve. *Crosscountry Downhill*. 3rd ed. Chester: Globe Pequot Press, 1987.

Bein, Vic. *Mountain Skiing*. Seattle: The Mountaineers, 1982

Cliff, Peter. *Ski Mountaineering*. Seattle: Pacific Search Press, 1987.

Gillette, Edward and John Dostal. *Cross Country Skiing*. 3rd ed. Seattle: The Mountaineers, 1988.

Kals, W.S. *Land Navigation Handbook: The Sierra Club Guide to Map and Compass*. San Francisco: Sierra Club Books, 1983.

Lindholm, Claudia, Donna Orr and Richard Sukey. *The NOLS Cookery: Experience the Art of Outdoor Cooking*. Lander: The National Outdoor Leadership School, 1988.

Masia, Seth. *Ski Maintenance and Repair*. Chicago: Contemporary Books, Inc., 1987.

Parker, Paul and Steve McDonald. *Freeheel Skiing: The Secrets of Telemark and Parallel Skiing in All Conditions*. 2nd ed. Seattle: The Mountaineers, 1995.

Peters, Ed, ed. *Mountaineering: The Freedom of the Hills*. 5th ed. Seattle: The Mountaineers, 1992.

Sharkey, Brian J. *Training For Crosscountry Ski Racing*. Champaign: Human Kinetics Publishers, Inc., 1984.

Sheahan, Casey. *Crosscountry Skiing: A Complete Guide*. New York: Sports Illustrated: Winning Circle Books, 1988.

Tejada-Flores, Lito. *Backcountry Skiing: The Sierra Club Guide to Skiing Off the Beaten Tracks*. San Francisco: Sierra Club Books, 1981.

First Aid

Bexruchka, Stephen, M.D. *The Pocket Doctor*. Seattle: The Mountaineers, 1988.

Carline, Jan D., Ph.D., ed. *Mountaineering First Aid*. 3rd ed. Seattle: The Mountaineers, 1985.

Gill, Paul G., Jr. *Pocket Guide to Wilderness First Aid*. New York: Simon & Schuster, 1991.

History

Bates, Margaret. *A Quick History of Lake City, Colorado*. Colorado Springs: Little London Press, 1973.

Blair, Edward and E. Richard Churchill. *Everybody Came to Leadville*. Colorado Springs: Little London Press, 1977.

Dusenbery, Harris. *Ski the High Trail: World War II Ski Troopers in the High Colorado Rockies*. Portland: Binford & Mort Publishing, 1991.

Eberhart, Perry. *Guide to the Colorado Ghost Towns and Mining Camps*. 4th ed. Athens: Swallow Press, 1981.

Gilliland, Mary Ellen. *Breckenridge*. Silverthorne: Alpenrose Press, 1988.

Gilliland, Mary Ellen. *Summit: A Gold Rush History*. Silverthorne: Alpenrose Press, 1980.

Griffiths, Thomas M. *San Juan Country*. Boulder: Pruett Publishing, 1988.

Hall, Denis B. *Mountains, Minerals, Miners & Moguls*. Crested Butte: Denis B. Hall, 1990.

Hughes, J. Donald. *American Indians in Colorado*. 2nd ed. Boulder: Pruett Publishing, 1987.

Ubbelohde, Carl, Maxine Benson and Duane A. Smith. *A Colorado History*. 6th ed. Boulder: Pruett, 1988.

Vandenbusche, Duane. *The Gunnison Country*. Gunnison: B & B Printers, 1980.

Weber, Rose. *A Quick History of Telluride*. Colorado Springs: Little London Press, 1974.

Wolle, Muriel Sibell. *Stampede to Timberline: Ghost Towns and Mining Camps of Colorado*. Boulder: Muriel Sibell Wolle.

Miscellaneous Colorado Guides
Caughey, Bruce and Dean Winstanley. *The Colorado Guide.* 3rd ed. Golden: Fulcrum Publishing, 1994.
Litz, Brian and Kurt Lankford. *Skiing Colorado's Backcountry: Northern Mountain Trails and Tours.* Golden: Fulcrum Publishing, 1989.

APPENDIX H
Map Sources

Colorado Atlas & Gazetter
DeLorme Mapping
P.O. Box 298
Freeport, ME 04032
207-865-4171

Trails Illustrated
P.O. Box 3610
Evergreen, CO 80439
303-670-3457
800-962-1643

United States Geological Survey
Denver Federal Center
P.O. Box 25286
Lakewood, CO 80225
303-236-7477

USGS Topographical Maps
National Cartographic Center
507 National Center
Reston, VA 22092
703-648-6045

Most USGS topographic maps and Trail Illustrated maps can be purchased through outdoor, ski, and mountaineering shops. US Forest Service maps can also be purchased through retail sporting goods stores as well as from their respective offices (see Appendix C for phone numbers).

One last word: Everyday more and more people are visiting the backcountry — on foot and on machine. It is important for skiers to exercise their collective voices in an effort to maintain the quality and integrity of the Colorado backcountry. Please write your state and federal representatives and the U.S. Forest Service to voice your support for human-powered sports. Additionally, you can contact and join the Backcountry Skiers Alliance (BSA) — a Colorado skiers advocacy group dedicated to resolving conflicts between motorized and non-motorized groups and to preserving the overall quality of the nordic experience. BSA is a non-profit, membership organization. For more information on BSA, write or call:

Backcountry Skiers Alliance
P.O. Box 134
Boulder, CO 80306
303-444-3722

And finally, if you notice any inconsistencies between this book and the real world, please contact us with your observations and suggestions by writing Westcliffe Publishers, P.O. Box 1261, Englewood, Colorado 80150, or e-mailing us at: editor@westcliffepublishers.com.

INDEX

Note: Citations followed by the letter "p" denote photos; citations followed by the letter "m" denote maps.

BRIAN LITZ

Since his first hut trip to the Tagert and Markley huts with the Denver Junior Group of the Colorado Mountain Club in 1976, Brian Litz has been a confirmed hut addict. His mountain travels began with family ski trips and have continued for more than 28 years.

Litz is an avid downhill and cross-country skier, mountaineer, rock climber, and bicyclist whose insatiable appetite for exploration and adventure has lead him throughout the western United States, Mexico, Canada, Australia, and New Zealand.

A graduate of the University of Colorado School of Business, Litz is managing editor of *Back Country* magazine. He is also a freelance writer and photographer and is a member of the North American Ski Journalists Association. As trainer and facilitator with the Colorado Outward Bound School, he works in the Mountain and Professional Development programs with private, public, and non-profit organizations. A Colorado resident for 34 of his 38 years, Litz lives in Boulder.